THE RISE AND FALL OF THE AMERICAN SYSTEM: NATIONALISM AND THE DEVELOPMENT OF THE AMERICAN ECONOMY, 1790–1837

FINANCIAL HISTORY

Series Editor: Robert E. Wright

Titles in this Series

1 Slave Agriculture and Financial Markets in Antebellum America: The Bank of the United States in Mississippi, 1831–1852
Richard Holcombe Kilbourne, Jr

2 The Political Economy of Sentiment: Paper Credit and the Scottish Enlightenment in Early Republic Boston, 1780–1820
Jose R. Torre

3 Baring Brothers and the Birth of Modern Finance
Peter E. Austin

4 Gambling on the American Dream: Atlantic City and the Casino Era
James R. Karmel

5 Government Debts and Financial Markets in Europe
Fausto Piola Caselli (ed.)

6 Virginia and the Panic of 1819: The First Great Depression and the Commonwealth
Clyde A. Haulman

7 Towards Modern Public Finance: The American War with Mexico, 1846–1848
James W. Cummings

8 The Revenue Imperative: The Union's Financial Policies during the American Civil War
Jane Flaherty

9 Guilty Money: The City of London in Victorian and Edwardian Culture, 1815–1914
Ranald C. Michie

10 Financial Markets and the Banking Sector: Roles and Responsibilities in a Global World
Elisabeth Paulet (ed.)

11 Argentina's Parallel Currency: The Economy of the Poor
Georgina M. Gómez

FORTHCOMING TITLES

Convergence and Divergence of National Financial Systems: Evidence from the Gold Standards, 1871–1971
Patrice Baubeau and Anders Ögren (eds)

www.pickeringchatto.com/financialhistory

THE RISE AND FALL OF THE AMERICAN SYSTEM: NATIONALISM AND THE DEVELOPMENT OF THE AMERICAN ECONOMY, 1790–1837

BY
Songho Ha

LONDON
PICKERING & CHATTO
2009

Published by Pickering & Chatto (Publishers) Limited
21 Bloomsbury Way, London WC1A 2TH

2252 Ridge Road, Brookfield, Vermont 05036-9704, USA

www.pickeringchatto.com

All rights reserved.
No part of this publication may be reproduced,
stored in a retrieval system, or transmitted in any form or by any means,
electronic, mechanical, photocopying, recording, or otherwise
without prior permission of the publisher.

© Pickering & Chatto (Publishers) Ltd 2009
© Songho Ha 2009

BRITISH LIBRARY CATALOGUING IN PUBLICATION DATA

Ha, Songho.
The rise and fall of the American System: nationalism and the development of the American economy, 1790–1837. – (Financial history) 1. United States – Economic policy – To 1933. 2. United States – Commercial policy – History – 19th century. 3. United States – Politics and government – 1815–1861. 4. United States – Politics and government – 1789–1815.
I. Title II. Series
338.9'73'009034-dc22

ISBN-13: 9781851969999
e: 9781851966943

This publication is printed on acid-free paper that conforms to the American National Standard for the Permanence of Paper for Printed Library Materials.

Typeset by Pickering & Chatto (Publishers) Limited
Printed in Great Britain by the MPG Books Group, Bodmin and King's Lynn

CONTENTS

Acknowledgements	ix
List of Tables and Figures	xi
Introduction: What Was the American System?	1
1. Emergence of the American System, 1790–1815	15
2. The Growth of the American System and Its Challenges, 1815–24	45
3. Reform Mentalities and the Implementation of the American System, 1825–9	79
4. Decline of the American System, 1829–37	107
Conclusion: The American System and American Society and Economy, 1790–1837	129
Notes	135
Works Cited	169
Index	179

For my mother Kang Sookhee,
late father Ha Youngmin
and late grandmother Kim Moim

ACKNOWLEDGEMENTS

It is with deep gratitude that I acknowledge the contributions of many people to the completion of this book. The late Richard E. Ellis, my dissertation advisor, imparted his passion for early American history in me and first proposed the American System as a dissertation topic many years ago. His insights bear imprints on every page of this book. I am deeply saddened that he did not see its completion. Tamara P. Thornton and Erik Seeman read the manuscript at the dissertation stage, providing penetrating insights and asking very challenging questions. Georg and Wilma Iggers also read earlier versions of the dissertation and gave me useful comments. John L. Larson of Purdue University read the original dissertation and has since offered me many invaluable insights on this topic. John Van Atta, Caedmon Liburd and Melinda Nicholson read the proofs of this book, corrected me on a number of points, and greatly improved the prose. I have also benefited from conversations with and comments by the following scholars: Daniel Walker Howe, John L. Brooke, Daniel Feller, Michael A. Morrison, Daniel Preston and Monica Najar. The comments of my two outside reviewers for Pickering & Chatto were also extremely useful.

Two people have been particularly important in the completion of this project: Thomas H. Cox and Robert E. Wright. Tom has read this manuscript many times since the dissertation stage, corrected numerous mistakes and commented on every sentence. This book would have taken much longer without his help. Bob Wright also offered many useful comments on the manuscript at the dissertation stage and helped to secure publication through the Financial History Series of Pickering & Chatto, of which he is the Series Editor. Daire Carr, editor at Pickering & Chatto has expertly and patiently guided me through the many stages of the publication process. My book project editor, Paul Lee, has also done an excellent job on the manuscript. Of course, I am responsible for any remaining errors.

Without the help of librarians and curators at libraries and archives, historians would be powerless. Charles D'Aniello of Lockwood Library at the University at Buffalo and Robin Hansen, Kevin Keating, Brian L. Hawkins and Dawn Berg at the Consortium Library of the University of Alaska Anchorage acquired copious research materials for my work. The reference librarians at the Library Company of Philadelphia and the Library of Congress were most helpful.

James Liszka, Dean of the College of Arts and Sciences, and Elizabeth Dennison, Chair of UAA History Department granted me a course release in Fall 2008 to expedite my writing. My colleagues at the History Department of UAA and my former colleagues at the University of New Brunswick Saint John, Canada and the University of Northern Colorado encouraged me in my research and writing. All their collegial support is appreciated. The students in the course *Early National Period 1800–1850* that I taught in the Spring 2009 semester provided a good soundboard for most of the arguments that I employ in this book.

Various agencies and grants supported my study and research. In previous years I received a Fulbright Fellowship, a Yang Baek/Chair Scholarship from the Korean-American Scholarship Foundation, a Mark Diamond Research Grant from the Graduate Studies Association of the University at Buffalo and a grant from the Lockwood Research Fund from the History Department of the University at Buffalo. The Provost's Office, the Dean's Office of the College of Arts and Sciences and the Center for Advancing Faculty Excellence (CAFE) of the University of Alaska Anchorage provided several travel and research grants. UAA's Complex System Group provided a grant to hire a student research assistant. My assistant Orion Allen worked tirelessly for this book, creating tables, finding citations, checking styles and more. I am very grateful for his important contribution.

My family has always been the source of inspiration and moral support. They all rooted for me in my long journey studying American history. When I first started a graduate programme, my grandmother and both parents were still alive. Many years later I can only remember and miss my late grandmother and father, but am most grateful that I can show this book to my mother. This token of my appreciation for their generosity and sacrifice is dedicated to them with the deepest respect and love.

LIST OF FIGURES AND TABLES

Table I.1. Comparative Voting Records on Protective Tariff and National Bank	9
Table 1.1. Average *ad valorem* Tariff Rates, 1789–1812	20
Table 1.2. Amount of National Debt, 1801–08	24
Table 1.3. Number of the Branches of the 1BUS	29
Table 1.4. Number of State Banks and Business Volume, 1809–18	31
Table 1.5. Land Sales, 1796–1820	38
Table 1.6. The Amounts Owed by Purchasers to the Federal Government, in dollars, from 1800–19	39
Table 2.1. Roll Call Analysis on the Tariff Act of 1816	49
Table 2.2. Percentage of Specie to Notes for First BUS and State Banks (1 January 1811)	50
Table 2.3. Notes Issued by BUS and State Banks, in Dollars, 1811–29	51
Table 2.4. Comparison of Domestic Bank Note Exchange Rates, 1816–29	51
Table 2.5. Vote Analysis on the 1816 Bank Bill	53
Table 2.6. Slave Population in Southern States, 1800–60, in thousands	58
Table 2.7. Vote Analysis on the Land Act of 1820	63
Table 2.8. Roll Call Analysis on the Tariff Bill of 1820	67
Table 2.9. Representatives under Each Apportionment	67
Table 2.10. Votes on the Bonus Bill and Survey Bill by Region	72
Table 2.11. Roll Call Analysis on the Tariff Act of 1824	75
Table 3.1. Vote Analysis on the Graduation Bill	92
Table 3.2. Federal Government Expenditures for Internal Improvements	96
Table 3.3. Subscriptions to Internal Improvement Projects by the Federal Government	97
Table 3.4. Notes and Deposits of the Second Bank of the United State	98
Table 3.5. Notes and Deposits of State Banks and the Second Bank of the United States (1 January 1820)	98
Table 3.6. Notes and Deposits of State Banks and the Second Bank of the United States (end of 1829)	99
Table 3.7. Discounts and Loans of the Second Bank of the United States	99

Table 3.8. Percentage of Specie to Notes and Specie to Deposits from the 2BUS and State Banks	101
Table 3.9. Roll Call Analysis on the Tariff Act of 1828	104
Table 4.1. Vote Analysis of the Indian Removal Bill in 1828	111
Table 4.2. General Population in Southern States from 1800 to 1860, in thousands	113
Table 4.3. Northwestern State Admission into the Union	114
Table 4.4. Population in Northwestern States from 1800 to 1860, in thousands	114
Table 4.5. Northwestern Population Growth within the United States	115
Table 4.6. Federal Expenditure for Internal Improvements under John Q. Adams and Andrew Jackson	118
Table 4.7. Congressional Votes on the Distribution Bill of 1833	120
Table 4.8. Public Land Sales, 1820–41	126
Figure 1.1. Land Sales, 1796–1820	38
Figure 1.2. Balance of Debts from Land Sales, 1800–19	39
Figure 2.1. Slave Population Growth, 1800–60	58
Figure 4.1. General Population Growth in the South, 1800–60	113
Figure 4.2. Federal Expenditure for Internal Improvements under Adams and Jackson	118
Figure 4.3. Public Land Sales, 1820–41	126

'I suppose that the sacrifice of the Indians and the interest of internal improvement and domestic industry will strengthen, rather than weaken, the popularity of the present Administration. I have cherished the principle and the system of internal improvement, under a conviction that is was for this nation the only path to increasing comforts and well-being, to honor, to glory, and finally to the general improvement of mankind. This system has had its fluctuations from the time of establishment of the present Constitution of the United States. During the Administration of Mr. Monroe it was constantly acquiring strength in Congress and in the public opinion. It was then favored by Calhoun and Lowndes, both of whom had hopes of rising upon it, and with them the State of South Carolina was devoted to it. The combination in Congress became by their means so strong that it overpowered the resistance of Mr. Monroe and produced the Act of Congress of April, 1824. The slaveholders of the South have since discovered that it will operate against their interests. Calhoun has turned his back upon it, and Jackson, who to promote his election and obtain Western votes truckled to it for a time, has now taken his decided stand against it. My devotion to it has sharpened all the fangs of envy and malice against it, multitudes oppose it only because its success would contribute to my reputation. The cause will no doubt survive me, and, if the Union is destined to continue, will no doubt ultimately triumph. At present it is desperate.'

25 June 1830, *Memoirs of John Quincy Adams,* ed. C. F. Adams, 12 vols (1874–7; Freeport, NY: Books For Libraries Press, 1969, original publication), vol. 8, p. 233.

INTRODUCTION: WHAT WAS THE AMERICAN SYSTEM?

One of the enduring questions in the study of early American history is how to characterize antebellum American society. Charles Sellers, Jr in his landmark study *The Market Revolution: Jacksonian America, 1815–1846* lamented the eclipse of democracy before market forces in the antebellum United States.[1] On the other hand, Sean Wilentz's *The Rise of American Democracy: Jefferson to Lincoln* argued that the United States actually became more democratic over the course of the nineteenth century.[2] Daniel Walker Howe in his 2008 Pulitzer Prize winning book *What Hath God Wrought: The Transformation of America, 1815–1848* explores the role of the communication and transportation revolutions in the development of antebellum American politics, society and economy.[3] Howe argued that two rival political visions competed in America between 1815 and 1848. The first programme was based on the hope of people who 'felt largely satisfied with their society the way it was, slavery and all, especially with the autonomy it provided to so many individual white men and their local communities'.[4] These individuals wanted to see their familiar image of America spread across space. On the other hand, other Americans looked forward to diversifying American economy and reforming American society: 'They envisioned qualitative, not just quantitative, progress for America.'[5] Howe masterfully discusses the dreams and achievements of the second group of people, paying keen attention both to social and cultural as well as political and economic transformation of American history accompanied by the communication and transportation revolutions.[6]

This study builds on Howe's research and details the American System, the most significant political programme of the early 1800s that sought the economic and moral improvement of American society. I argue that the American System lay at the centre of political and social transformation in the early republic. Its emergence as an intellectual notion among reform-minded Americans since the start of the presidency of George Washington, its sophistication during the Jeffersonian era, its implementation under the presidencies of James Monroe and John Quincy Adams, and its failure in the wake of the levelling tendencies of the

Jacksonian period and the economic chaos of the Panic of 1837, bore important repercussions for the antebellum political, economic and social life of the United States. Proponents of the American System envisioned a country that was politically united, internationally free of European conflicts, economically diversified and culturally advanced. To realize this vision, political leaders like Henry Clay of Kentucky and John Quincy Adams of Massachusetts implemented protective tariffs, executed internal improvements of roads and canals, opened a national bank and sold federal land to raise revenue. Not content with merely economic reforms, they sought to improve the intellectual and social quality of American life by creating observatories, building libraries, investing in steam technology and organizing a national university. As such, the American System represented to its framers nothing less than an attempt to create an economically unified and culturally refined nation.

The American System and Nationalism

The American System refers to a programme for the economic and cultural development of the United States espoused by such important politicians as Henry Clay (1777–1852; US Congressman, US Senator, Secretary of State, Presidential candidate) of Kentucky and John Quincy Adams (1767–1848; Secretary of State, President, US Congressman) of Massachusetts.

It was first and foremost a political expression of American nationalism. The term 'American System' also signified a political proposal to promote American nationalism against European domination through economic independence. The history of the term, and the context in which Clay used it, indicates that he clearly perceived it as a political phrase demanding the separation of the States from the political and economic influence of Europe.

Alexander Hamilton first used the term 'American System' in his *Federalist* number 11, which he wrote to defend the Constitution from a commercial perspective.[7] In this now classic defence of the Constitution, Hamilton stated, '[l]et the thirteen States bound together in a strict and indissoluble Union, concur in erecting one great American system, superior to the control of all transatlantic force or influence, and able to dictate the terms of the connection between the old and the new world!'[8]

Jefferson, once the archenemy of Hamilton, also used the term in a similar way. On 26 June 1817, he wrote a letter to the American Society for the Encouragement of Domestic Manufactures in New York, advocating the promotion of domestic manufactures. He stated in the letter, 'I hope that twenty years more will place the *American hemisphere under a system of its own*, essentially peaceable and industrious, and not needing to extract its *comforts* out of the external fires raging in the old world.'[9]

Henry Clay also used the term 'American System' in the same political sense. In his speech on 10 May 1820 before the House of Representatives, Clay urged the United States to recognize the former Spanish colonies in South America as independent states before European countries could do so. He said that '[l]et us break these commercial and political fetters [of Europe]; let us no longer watch the nod of any European politician; let us become real and true Americans, and place ourselves at the head of the American System.'[10] When President James Monroe defiantly declared in his annual message of 2 December 1823 that 'we should consider any attempt on their [European countries'] part to extend their system to any portion of this hemisphere as dangerous to our peace and security',[11] Clay wholeheartedly supported the President's position. When Clay met Monroe's State Secretary John Quincy Adams later that same evening, he told Secretary Adams that the part relating to foreign affairs was the best part of the annual message.[12] So from Hamilton during the winter of 1787 to Clay in 1823, the term 'American System' was used to depict an American political and commercial system that was separate from Europe.

When Clay used the term again in his speech on the tariff bill of 1824, he was also comparing his American System to a European one. He stated,

> [a]re we doomed to behold our industry languish and decay yet more and more [because of a restrictive European market]? But there is a remedy, and that remedy consists in modifying our foreign policy, and in adopting a genuine American system. We must naturalize them by the only means which the wisdom of nations has yet discovered to be effectual - by adequate protection against the otherwise overwhelming influence of foreigners.[13]

In other words, Clay promoted the American System as a system of economic policies for the political as well as commercial independence of the United States from Europe.

The American System and Protective Tariffs

When Henry Clay first christened the 'American System' in 1824 he referred only to a high tariff policy for an 'adequate protection of American industry' with the purpose of the creation of a domestic market.[14] Later, however, contemporary politicians and historians used the term to also include the Second Bank of the United States (2BUS), a federal programme of internal improvements such as roads and canals and, occasionally, a scheme to distribute federal land sales to individual states.[15]

Clay presented his notion of the American System in two major speeches in Congress on the tariff acts of 1824 and 1832.[16] Both speeches were widely circulated as pamphlets entitled *Speech in Support of an American System for the Protection of American Industry* and *Speech of Henry Clay in Defense of the Amer-*

ican System, against the British Colonial System. In both, Clay hammered home the expediency and constitutionality of protective tariffs.

Other contemporary defenders of the American System likewise focused on the issue of tariffs. In 1828, economist Daniel Raymond published a pamphlet entitled *The American System* in which he used the term to refer to protective tariffs.[17] *Niles' Weekly Register*, the main organ for supporters of domestic manufactures, published a long article entitled 'Southern Excitement' on Southern opposition to protective tariffs. Later the article was printed as a separate pamphlet under the title *Southern Excitement, against the American System*. The article copied newspaper articles, resolutions, and letters from Southern states against protective tariffs.[18]

Enemies also conceived of the American System mainly as a measure for protective tariffs. On 21 February 1827, William B. Giles, a senior Virginia politician, gave a long speech in the Virginia House of Delegates in response to one of Clay's speeches on protective tariffs.[19] Clay's and Giles's speeches were later published jointly as *Mr. Clay's Speech upon the Tariff, or, The 'American System', so called...* On 2 July 1827, Dr Thomas Cooper, the President of South Carolina College, gave an important speech at the meeting against the idea of the American System at the Columbia town hall.[20] He criticized that the American System was a system in which 'we of the south hold our plantations under this system, as the serfs and operatives of the north, subject to the orders, and laboring for the benefit of the master minds of Massachusetts, the lords of the spinning jenny, and peers of the power loom!'[21] On 23 March 1830, Philip P. Barbour of Virginia, probably the most effective anti-tariff orator in Congress, argued in the House of Representatives against federal funding for a proposed road between Buffalo and New Orleans. He stated during the debate 'I would reduce so much of the taxes as to have no surplus, even though it affected the protecting policy, commonly called the American system.'[22]

The American System and Internal Improvements

As opposed to nineteenth-century politicians, twentieth- and twenty-first century historians used the term 'American System' in a broader sense to include a variety of governmental policies. For example, Samuel Flagg Bemis, Glyndon G. Van Deusen, Daniel Feller and Robert V. Remini discussed the American System more broadly to include a nationally sponsored programme of internal improvements such as the construction of roads and canals.[23] Contemporary opponents of the American System contributed significantly to the expansion of the scope of the concept for future generations of scholars, by attacking both protective tariffs and internal improvements simultaneously. For example, the South Carolina legislature passed resolutions on 16 December 1825 that read:

1. *Resolved*, That Congress does not possess the power, under the constitution, to adopt a general system of internal improvement as a national measure ...

5. *Resolved*, That it is an unconstitutional exercise of power, on the part of Congress, to pay duties to protect domestic manufactures. [24]

The Virginia legislature passed similar resolutions on 4 March 1826, and the Georgia legislature followed suit on 24 December 1827.[25]

Political elites who disapproved of the American System often argued that internal improvements were merely the excuse for the continued maintenance of high protective tariffs. For instance, Giles argued that 'a high tariff was found indispensably necessary in the first place, to raise ample funds for splendid, internal improvements'.[26] Philip P. Barbour likewise stated that

> [a]nother objection to this system [of internal improvements] is, that it has a direct and almost irresistible tendency to perpetuate upon us a revenue, having no reference to the ordinary demands upon the Government, but one which will always afford a large excess for the execution of these projects.[27]

President Andrew Jackson also used this logic in his famous Maysville Veto message, rejecting a congressional plan to subscribe $1.5 million in a company that proposed the construction of a sixty-mile road connecting Maysville and Lexington in Kentucky.[28] Giles, Barbour and Jackson thus saw internal improvements as an excuse to continue the hated protective tariff. They calculated that opposing internal improvements would have the added benefit of undermining the financial justification for protective tariffs.

The American System and National Banks

In addition to internal improvements, historians also included the 2BUS under the broad rubric of the American System. In 1965, historian George Dangerfield stated that the American System consisted of 'three pillars', which meant protective tariffs, internal improvements and a national bank.[29] Thirty years later Maurice G. Baxter and David P. Currie also added the National Bank to their notions of the American System.[30]

It is hardly surprising that later generations of academics would lump a national bank and governmental support for internal improvements into the concept of the American System. All three policies rested on a broad construction of the US Constitution. After all, the issue of a national bank had generated the first important argument for a broader interpretation of federal power in the 1790s. On 14 December 1790, Alexander Hamilton submitted a report to the House of Representative suggesting that Congress incorporate a national bank, which later resulted in the incorporation of the First Bank of the United States (1BUS).[31] The Senate and House passed the incorporation bill on 20 January 1791 and 8 February 1791 respectively.[32] When the bill reached his office, President George Washington remained uncertain of the proposed bank's constitutionality and so asked his Secretary of State Thomas Jefferson and Attorney General Edmund Randolph for their opinions.[33] Both pointed out that the Tenth Amendment to United States Constitution stated that '[t]he powers not delegated to the United States by the constitution, not prohibited by it to the States, are reserved to the States respectively, or to the people', and that the Constitution did not expressly allow Congress to charter a bank. Therefore, the incorporation scheme was unconstitutional.[34]

When Washington put the same question to Hamilton, however, the Treasury Secretary responded in a letter, dated 23 February 1791, which defended the constitutionality of the Bank by the doctrine of 'implied powers'. According to Hamilton, the Constitution granted the federal government not only enumerated but also implied powers, which included the authority to incorporate a national bank. Hamilton explained that '[i]t is conceded, that implied powers are to be considered as delegated equally with express ones.' In this context the power of incorporation was implied as an auxiliary power. He said, '[t]he power to erect corporations, is not to be considered as an independent and substantive power, but as an incidental and auxiliary one; and was, therefore, more properly left to implication, than expressly granted.' By what criterion could the power of incorporation be implied? It depended on whether the power was 'necessary and proper' for the execution of specific powers enumerated in the Constitution. Hamilton defined the phrase 'necessary' loosely to mean 'no more than *needful, requisite, incidental, useful,* or *conductive to*'. For Hamilton the criterion of whether a specific power was constitutional or not was 'the *end* to which the measure relates as a *mean*. If the end be clearly comprehended within any of the specified powers, & if the measure have an obvious relation to that end, and is not forbidden by any particular provision of the constitution – it may be deemed to come within the compass of national authority'. In this context, he argued that the bank was related 'to the power of collecting taxes; to that of borrowing money; to that of regulating trade between the states; and to those of raising, supporting & maintaining fleets and armies'. For example, Hamilton argued, the bank was related to the collection of taxes, '*indirectly*, by increasing the quantity of circulating medium & quickening circulation, which facilitates the means of paying – *directly*, by creating a *convenient species* of *medium* in which they are to be paid'. Therefore the bank was constitutional.[35] Hamilton's logic became one of the most important theoretical bases for broad construction of the United States Constitution. His doctrine of 'implied powers', reaffirmed by Chief Justice John Marshall in *McCulloch* v. *Maryland*,[36] directly influenced the arguments that constitutionality upheld protective tariffs and internal improvements as well as national banks.

When Clay defended the constitutionality of the General Survey Bill of 1824, which authorized federal surveys for internal improvements, he also argued for a broad construction of the United States Constitution, albeit with a different logic. He argued that federal power should be broadly interpreted to accommodate the reality that the country had geographically grown since the creation of the Constitution.[37] Clay was suggesting that the Constitution was an organic document, the interpretation of which should correspond to the changing conditions of the country.

In his pamphlet *The American System,* published in 1828, Daniel Raymond argued for an expansive range of the federal government's powers with another rationale: the federal government could exercise all powers not specifically prohibited by the Constitution. As the Constitution did not prohibit Congress from passing laws for protective tariffs, Raymond concluded, the Congress could pass such laws.[38] Whether drawing on a broad construction of the Constitution or the necessity to adapt the supreme law of the land to changing social conditions, the proponents of the American System argued that the federal government possessed the authority to actively engage in the economy through a variety of means.

In addition to contributing to the constitutional defence of protective tariffs and internal improvements, the 1BUS also helped the development of domestic manufactures and internal improvements in a more practical sense. For instance, the 1BUS functioned as a commercial bank, a bank for the benefit of commerce, and provided financial services to the federal government. Such duties included purchasing promissory notes, inland drafts and foreign bills of exchange through discount (paying the face value minus interest until the time of maturity).

The 2BUS, incorporated in 1816, carried out these same duties on a larger scale. For example, the 2BUS's statement on 1 August 1828 shows that the Bank had assets of bills discounted on personal security by $29,316,745.45, on funded debt by $142,212.73, and on bank stock by $1,350,380.56. The amount of discounted domestic bills of exchange stood at $6,013,890.15 and foreign bills of exchange at $340,185.23.[39] After 1825, the Bank became active in the foreign exchange business.[40] By having their bills discounted, merchants did not have to wait until the maturity of their bills to get payment for their goods. These merchants then had cash to pay suppliers such as farmers. The bank was particularly useful for Western and Southern agricultural interests in other ways. It extended loans for farmers to make long-term investments like purchasing lands and slaves.[41] Bank business in these sections increased when public land sales increased. The receipts from federal government's land sales reached more than $2 million in 1818, 1819 and 1830–3. The Second Bank's business expanded greatly during these same periods because of increased volumes of business in the West and South.[42] One indication of the bank's active role in business was the large quantity of notes issued in these regions as the bank extended its credit.[43] Western and Southern branches issued more banknotes than those branches in New England and the Middle

Atlantic states.[44] In the most extreme case of September 1818, just before the Panic of 1819 hit the country, the Western and Southern branches issued almost four times the amount of notes as were issued in the Northeast.[45]

Preliminary evidence also suggests that both BUSs contributed to the success of domestic manufactures. As early as 1786, Philadelphians argued that 'houses and ships were built, and improvements in manufactures of all kinds were carried on, by money borrowed occasionally at the bank [of North America]'. The bank had extended loans to 'ship and house carpenters, blacksmiths, nailers, painters, sail and mast makers, brickmakers, and masons'.[46] In the early nineteenth century, the private banking house of Stephen Girard in Philadelphia made between 10 and 15 per cent of its loans to artisans and mechanics.[47] It is unlikely that the 1BUS and 2BUS, which competed fiercely with other commercial banks for businesses, would have rejected manufacturers when other banks were lending to them. We also have indirect testimony on the 1BUS's involvement in business with manufacturers. While defending the renewal of the 1BUS's charter, which was due to expire in 1811, Senator William H. Crawford of Georgia stated in the Senate on 11 February 1811 that '[s]ome of the delegation of the mechanics [of Philadelphia] ... had been dealers with that bank [of the United States] for twelve years.'[48] The availability of the credits from national banks must also have contributed to the success of domestic manufactures and internal improvements in general, because credits to merchants from banks were re-loaned to manufacturers.[49]

Sectional differences over the issue of national banks also paralleled those over protective tariffs and internal improvements. Northwestern and eastern political leaders tended to support protective tariffs, internal improvements and national banking while Southerners opposed them. For example, when Congress voted to recharter the 2BUS and create a protective tariff act in 1832, New England, Mid-Atlantic and Northwestern Congressmen either supported the measures or split their votes. On the other hand, South Atlantic and Southwestern representatives voted against the bank bill while supporting the tariff bill. But Southwestern support for the tariff bill of 1832 was a notable exception to a general rule. A more typical Southern response was the vote on the Protective Tariff Act of 1824, when South Atlantic delegates voted against the bill by a vote of one to fifty, and their Southwestern colleagues voted two to fourteen against the bill.[50] The reason the Southern opposition to a protective tariff bill in 1832 was so muted was that John Quincy Adams, who had returned to Congress as a Massachusetts representative after losing the presidential election in 1828, used his newly found position as Chairman of the Committee on Manufactures to slash duties on the cheap woollens which Southern slaves wore from 45 per cent to 5 per cent.[51] But even this conciliatory gesture did not stop the delegations of Georgia, South Carolina and Louisiana casting more votes against the Protective Tariff Bill of 1832 than for the bill.

Table I.1. Comparative Voting Records on Protective Tariff and National Bank.

	Bank Bill of 1832		Tariff Bill of 1832	
	Yeas	Nays	Yeas	Nays
New England	24	12	17	17
Connecticut	6	–	2	3
Maine	1	6	6	1
Massachusetts	12	–	4	8
New Hampshire	–	6	5	–
Rhode Island	2	–	–	2
Vermont	3	–	–	3
Mid–Atlantic	48	21	52	18
Delaware	1	–	–	1
Maryland	5	3	8	–
New Jersey	6	–	3	3
New York	12	17	27	2
Pennsylvania	24	1	14	12
Northwest	18	10	27	3
Illinois	–	–	1	–
Indiana	1	2	3	–
Kentucky	6	5	9	3
Missouri	1	–	1	–
Ohio	10	3	13	–
South Atlantic	12	32	23	24
Georgia	–	7	1	6
North Carolina	4	8	8	4
South Carolina	2	6	3	6
Virginia	6	11	11	8
Southwest	5	11	13	3
Tennessee	2	7	9	–
Alabama	–	3	2	1
Louisiana	3	–	1	2
Mississippi	–	1	1	–
Total	107	86	132	65

Source: *House Journal*, 22nd Cong., 1st sess. (3 July 1832), p. 1074; ibid. (28 June 1832), pp. 1023–4.

The American System and Public Land Policies

Over the past thirty years, historians have further expanded the concept of the American System, to include specific land policies which were opposed to drastically cutting public land prices or granting free lands, and which culminated in the Distribution Bill of 1832, a plan to distribute the revenue from public land sales to states based on their population. Major L. Wilson, Merrill D. Peterson, Daniel Feller, Michael F. Holt, John R. Van Atta and Pamela L. Baker have undertaken such studies.[52] But these works show notable differences of opinion over the precise ways in which land policies fit into the American System. Wilson and Peterson have argued that the American System's supporters saw Western land mainly as a source of revenue to help finance internal improvement projects rather than as a space to be speedily settled by new immigrants. They have also claimed that proponents of the American System did not press the settlement of the West too hard, for fear that rapid expansion would divert capital and labour from eastern manufactures and internal improvements. Thus advocates of the American System wanted to develop the east before turning their attention westward.[53]

On the other hand, Van Atta has argued that the idea of the American System, especially as conceived by Henry Clay, saw western settlement as equally significant as protecting domestic manufactures. Van Atta asserted that Clay opposed Missouri Senator Thomas Hart Benton's proposal of 'graduation', a substantial reduction of public land prices to effect a speedy western settlement, partly because the Kentucky Senator wanted to attract 'men of average means' to the West, but not 'lower-class easterners and impoverished immigrants'.[54]

Historical records show that proponents of the American System opposed rapid western expansion. They felt that western development ought not to come at the expense of draining revenue or population away from the East, and wanted to generate and use the revenue from land sales to finance internal improvements, just as they wanted to use tariff revenue for this purpose. In his first annual message of 6 December 1825, President John Quincy Adams stated that '[u]nder the system of sales ... the lands will continue as they have become an abundant source of revenue'. Thus when national debt was paid off, 'the swelling tide of wealth with which they replenish the common Treasury may be made to reflow in unfailing streams of improvement from the Atlantic to the Pacific Ocean'.[55] In a report on land sales submitted to the Senate in 1832, Clay stated that 'a majority of the committee believe it better, as an alternative for the scheme of cession [of public lands] to the new States, and, as being most likely to give general satisfaction, that the residue [from sales of public lands] be divided among the twenty-four States according to their federal representative population'. Such funds should 'be applied to education, internal improvement, or colonization, or to the redemption of any existing debt contracted for internal improvements, as each State, judging for itself, shall deem most comfortable with its own interests and policy'.[56] Richard Rush, the Treasury Secretary under Adams, argued that land prices should not be lowered excessively, lest cheap land accelerate western migration.[57] Clay also argued that the rapid growth of western states demonstrated that 'whilst the spirit of free emigration should not be checked or counteracted, it stands in no need of any fresh stimulus'.[58] Hezekiah Niles, the editor of *Niles' Weekly Register* and a strong supporter of the American System, also opposed excessive immigration westward. In the 5 February 1820 issue of his journal, Niles commented, '[i]t is also the dictates of a sound policy we apprehend, to present a check to the greater spread of our population for sometime to come, by refusing to open new offices in new territories ... and any further scattering of our people must tend to weaken the effective force of the nation without benefiting individuals'.[59]

As the above record indicates, American System supporters were conservatives as far as land policy was concerned. The leaders of land reforms during the first three decades of the nineteenth century were often representatives of Western interests. It was William H. Harrison of Ohio, Senator Thomas H. Williams of Mississippi and Senator Thomas Hart Benton of Missouri, rather than Richard Rush or Adams, who promoted and consistently demanded cheap Western lands.[60] Unlike protective tariffs, internal improvements or the national bank, American System enthusiasts were very cautious on the issue of the public lands, trying to appropriate Western demands for cheap land for their own purposes. Thus the only systematic articulation by the proponents of the American System on the land issue was Clay's report to the Senate in 1832.[61] The timing is also important. Clay's major speeches on protective tariffs were made in 1824 and 1832. His major speech on internal improvements, in which he defended the General Survey Bill, occurred in 1824. He defended the incorporation of the 2BUS in 1816, and consistently supported the bank afterwards. However, his major speech on land issues did not come until 1832, as a preparation for his run for president.[62] After seeing Andrew Jackson prevail in the presidential election of 1828, by no small measure because of his popularity in the Western states, Clay understood that he had to offer westerners something they wanted – cheap land – if he was to gain their support in future elections. He did not plan to divert from traditional land policies of the American government until his political ambition made it absolutely necessary. Even his land bill, the Distribution Bill of 1832, was predicated on the overall premise of the priority of revenue concerns over land issues. In sum, the promoters of the American System were not eager to tackle land issues unless forced to do so by political necessity.

The American System and Home Market

The ultimate goal of the American System was the creation of a domestic market. In his 1824 speech, Clay argued that the objective of instituting a protective tariff was to create a national home market. According to Clay, the American economy had been dependent upon 'an extraordinary war in Europe' and a 'foreign market' which no longer existed.[63] He was referring to the economic prosperity the United States enjoyed due to the strong demand for American produce and shipping from European countries locked in the French Revolution and Napoleonic Wars. Since this foreign market had substantially diminished after the end of European conflicts, argued Clay, the United States should learn to rely on its own domestic market.[64]

This study analyses issues such as protective tariffs, internal improvements, national banks and public lands as integral components of the American System rather than separate and disconnected issues. Protective tariffs and revenue-oriented land policy were preconditions for federally sponsored internal improvements, just as a stable national currency controlled by a national bank was also a precondition for the development of domestic manufactures and a home market.

The American System and Cultural Improvement

As shown above, the political and economic aspects of the American System have so far received excellent scholarly attention. Daniel Walker Howe's intellectual biography of Henry Clay 'Henry Clay, Ideologue of the Center' in *The Political Culture of the American Whigs* (1979) opened a new avenue in the study of the American System by exploring its cultural aspect. Howe argued that '[t]he American System was predicated on the basis of a harmony of interests.'[65] According to Howe, Henry Clay believed that the policies of the American System could harmoniously promote a common interest of the diverse sections of the United States.

Howe's study led other scholars to combine cultural and social history with political and economic narratives. For examples, in tariff issues, Lawrence A. Peskin studied the intellectual origin of American protectionism in his book *Manufacturing Revolution: The Intellectual Origins of Early American Industry* (2003). In internal improvements, Carol Sheriff's book *The Artificial River: The Erie Canal and the Paradox of Progress 1817–1862* (1996) postulates how middle-class Americans saw the Erie Canal as a symbol of progress, a way to improve backcountry society according to their notion of progress.[66] Andrew M. Schocket's book *Founding Corporate Power in Early National Philadelphia* (2007) discusses the cultural history of corporations, including banks in the early national Philadelphia, exploring the relationship between economic development and democracy.[67] Van Atta's articles, which I have already discussed above, analyse the cultural dimension of the issue of public lands. My study looks further into the importance of cultural aspects of the political and economic issues of the American System.

I argue that the proponents of the American System believed in the idea of improvement (or progress in more modern usage), in addition to the belief in the harmony of sectional interests in the union. Up to a certain measure, this is not a new thesis. The great biographer of John Quincy Adams, Samuel Flagg Bemis, pointed out that '[in] the back of Adams's mind, taking shape in his conscience, lurked a final improvement – moral improvement.'[68] Howe concurred: '[t]he American System was a highly organized articulation of Whig political culture. The leading values of the culture, such as order, harmony, purposefulness and improvement, found expression in the form an economic program.'[69] It is true Clay and particularly Adams strongly advocated the idea of improvement. In his first annual message, on 6 December 1825, he proposed the improvement of roads and canals. He stated that 'Roads and canals, by multiplying and facilitating the communications and intercourse between distant regions and multitudes of men are among the most important means of improvement.' At the same time, he also included 'moral, political, intellectual improvement' in the category of internal improvement, and stated 'moral, political, intellectual improvement are duties assigned by the Author of Our Existence to social no less to individual man.'[70] Thus he proposed the establishment of a national university in Washington DC, an astronomical observatory, the construction of a ship for the exploration of the whole Northwest coast and the creation of a new Department of the Interior.[71]

My study explores the history of the idea of cultural improvement in more detail along with political and economic developments of American society in the early republic. More specifically, I will accomplish three things in my book. First, I will discuss the history of the American System from its rise to its demise between 1790 and 1837. Second, I will discuss how various economic policies of the American System were connected to form an integrated system. Third, I will explore the cultural dimension of the American System in more detail. I will argue that the American System reflected the religious and philosophical basis of the Reform Movements, the Second Great Awakening. My study shows the importance of the concept of improvement to Clay, which has been less studied so far. In addition, I analyse the aggressive side of the idea of improvement as expressed in the American System. Recently, historian John L. Brooke stated in an article that 'The failure of Federalist nation-building in 1800 led to both the revival of early modern composite governance by Jeffersonians and Jacksonians and the deployment of benevolence as a vehicle of cultural nation-building by defeated Federalists.'[72] Although I do not think that benevolence was a concept owned solely by the Federalist, I agree that benevolence was a vehicle of cultural nation-building, and I argue that the American System was part of this movement toward cultural nationalism. Finally, I suggest some of the consequences of the failure of the American System for contemporary American society, politics and economy.

1 EMERGENCE OF THE AMERICAN SYSTEM, 1790–1815

The idea of the American System emerged from the start of George Washington's administration. Both Federalist and Republican administrations wanted to promote domestic manufactures through protective tariffs, advocated construction of roads and canals, and started and supported the 1BUS. They also tried to refine American culture by establishing cultural institutions, including a university. But the presence of a large amount of national debt and tumultuous international relations with European countries prevented political leaders' attempts to implement their ambitious programs.

George Washington and the Origin of the American System

From George Washington's first presidential term, an embryonic form of the American System existed in American political discourse. In his first annual message to Congress, Washington suggested 'the expediency of giving effectual encouragement ... to the exertions of skill and genius in producing them [inventions] at home, and of facilitating the intercourse between the distant parts of our country'. He also solicited Congressional patronage to promote 'science and literature' and advised legislators to consider 'aids to seminaries of learning already established or creation of a national university'.[1] Washington repeated and elaborated on his vision of a more refined nation by calling for the protection of domestic manufactures, construction of internal improvements and support of science and culture throughout his tenure as President.

In his Farewell Address to the American people, on 17 September 1796, Washington advocated the creation of a domestic market in which the north, south, east and west sections would exchange their products. He stated that the North 'in an unrestrained intercourse with the South ... finds in the productions of the latter great additional resources of maritime and commercial enterprise and precious materials of manufacturing industry'. The South, argued Washington, 'sees its agriculture grow and its commerce expand' through intercourse with the North. The East, in trading with the West, finds 'a valuable vent for the commodities which it brings from abroad or manufactures at home'. The West likewise receives from the East 'supplies requisite to its growth and comfort', and 'must ... owe the *secure* enjoyment of indispensible *outlets* for its own productions'.[2] Washington concluded by arguing that all sections of the Union shared a common interest in supporting the national union. As such, 'Here [in the common interest] every portion of our country finds the most commanding motives for carefully guarding and preserving the union of the whole.'[3] In particular, Washington felt that 'all the parts combined' find 'greater strength, greater resource ... greater security from external danger, a less frequent interruption of their peace by foreign nations'.[4] To facilitate the creation of such a domestic market, particularly for East–West commerce, Washington expected a 'progressive improvement of interior communications by land and water'.[5]

Washington's vision of what would eventually become the American System rested upon a positive conception of federal power. He also stated in his farewell address that 'your union ought to be considered as a main prop of your liberty, and that the love of the one ought to endear to you the preservation of the other'.[6] It is important to note that Washington did not foresee any conflict between federal power and the liberty of ordinary Americans. This positive view of a strong central government would later prove an essential component of the American System. Washington continued to lay out his plans for a powerful and free nation by urging his fellow citizens to establish 'institutions for the general diffusion of knowledge', because 'it is essential that public opinion should be enlightened'.[7]

In his eighth and last annual message to Congress on 7 December 1796, Washington stated that '[t]he object [of the encouragement of manufactures] is of too much consequence not to insure a continuance of their [Congresses'] efforts in every way which shall appear eligible.'[8] He also exhorted Congress to consider establishing a national university and also a military academy, because 'a flourishing state of the arts and sciences contributes to national prosperity and reputation'. To help jumpstart such a project, Washington offered twenty acres of public land in the District of Columbia and his fifty shares of Potomac Company stock.[9] Washington's speech provided two very important reasons for the national government to establish educational institutions: the need for a larger fund for such an institution and a need to train groups of future leaders who would share common perspectives. He stated that although there were already many excellent local universities, 'the funds upon which they rest are too narrow to command the ablest professors in the different departments of liberal knowledge'. A national university, however, would contribute to 'the assimilation of the principles, opinions, and manners of our countrymen by the common education of a portion of our youth from every quarter'.[10] He stated '[t]he more homogeneous our citizens can be made ... the greater will be our prospect of permanent union.'[11]

It is clear that Washington understood the establishment of cultural institutions such as a national university under the auspices of the federal government as essential to the long-term preservation of the union. In a sense, it was very natural for George Washington to be nationalistic. Although he started his political and military career as a member of the colonial Virginia legislature and an officer of the colonial Virginia militia, Washington came to national prominence as Commander in Chief of the Continental Army, President of the Constitutional Convention of 1787 and, most importantly, the first President of the United States.[12] His long experience on the national scene expanded the breadth of his political vision, which was not always the case with some of his colleagues.

John Adams and Cultural Improvements

Washington's successor, John Adams, also advocated the cultural development of the United States. In his inaugural address, Adams included in his long list of duties as President 'a love of science and letters and a wish to patronize every rational effort to encourage schools, colleges, universities and religion among all classes of the people'.[13] The international problems between France and the United States, however, consumed most of Adams's time and energy. In addition, the inability of the federal government to raise sufficient revenue kept Adams from actively pursuing a plan of internal improvements. To be certain, on 24 April 1800, President John Adams signed a bill which authorized him to remove various Executive Departments to Washington DC, the permanent capital of the United States. The legislation appropriated $5,000 'for the purchase of such books as may be necessary for the use of Congress ... and for fitting up a suitable apartment for containing them'. Yet, the creation of the Library of Congress represented Adams's only real contribution to encouraging education on the national level.[14]

Alexander Hamilton's *Report on Manufactures*, a Precursor of the American System

Alexander Hamilton, George Washington's protégé and the first United States Treasury Secretary, shared his mentor's nationalistic outlook. Born on the island of Nevis in the West Indies, Hamilton did not set foot on the North American mainland until 1772 to enrol in King's College in the colony of New York. Thus, Hamilton was not attached to any single state by birth. Instead, he developed an important political and personal relationship with Washington, serving as the General's aide-de-camp during the American Revolution. Hamilton continued to support his former commander as a New York delegate to the Constitutional

Convention in 1787. Hamilton helped to draft the Constitution and promote it through publication of the *Federalist Papers* in no small part to create a national government in which to fulfil his unbounded political ambition.[15] It was therefore no coincidence that Hamilton titled a series of political and economic essays he wrote in 1781 and 1782, 'The Continentalist', in which he demanded more power for the federal government over state interests.[16]

Hamilton presented a rudimentary blueprint for a system of national improvements in his famous report on manufactures, delivered to the House of Representatives on 5 December 1791. In his report, Hamilton advocated the encouragement and protection of domestic manufactures.[17] In classical Hamiltonian style, the report comprehensively discussed the various justifications for protecting domestic manufactures, the arguments against such protectionism, a constitutional rationale for federal tariffs, the positive long-term effects of protective tariffs for raising revenue, a survey of the currently established domestic manufactures and the means of promoting domestic manufactures.[18]

Hamilton's report rested on the basic assumption that the success of domestic manufactures was necessary for the independence of the United States, especially for the independent supplying of military necessities. At the start of the report, Hamilton wrote that '[t]he Secretary of the Treasury ... has applied his attention ... to the subject of Manufactures, and particularly to the means of promoting such as will tend to render the United States independent of foreign nations, for military and other essential supplies.'[19] Hamilton's desire for protectionism accordingly hinged on nationalist sentiment, a motive which future politicians would likewise invoke to promote protective tariffs.

Another important argument for protection pioneered by Hamilton was that of a home market for 'creating ... a new, and securing, in all, a more certain and steady demand for the surplus produce of the soil'. He argued that foreign (European) demand for American agricultural produce was 'too uncertain' and that there was a strong reason to 'desire a substitute for it in an extensive domestic market'.[20] Hamilton argued that such a 'home market' was logical given the economic compatibility of America's various regions. Southern agricultural produce and raw materials could provide ample fodder for North and Middle State factories.[21] In his report, Hamilton defended the constitutionality of protection by citing the defence and general welfare clauses in the Constitution.[22] He also argued that protection in the long run would increase, rather than decrease federal tax dollars.[23] Hamilton's report carried all the important elements of later protectionism, including its rationale, underlying assumption, constitutional and financial justification.

Hamilton's economic policies would in later years become topics of intense academic debate. Most notably, historian John Nelson argued in his 1987 book, *Liberty and Property*, that Hamilton's concern for manufacturing was not genuine. According to Nelson, Hamilton's famous *Report on Manufactures* was no more than a publicity piece for the SEUM (Society for Establishing Useful Manufactures), with which he was heavily involved. Hamilton supposedly promoted the SEUM in the autumn of 1791 as a way to boost a depressed security market, because the SEUM was subscribed in governmental or bank stocks.[24] Stock market stabilization was therefore the 'ultimate arbiter' of Hamilton's activities as Treasury Secretary.[25] In this sense, argued Nelson, Hamilton's celebrated report on manufactures was no more than an advertising writer's jingle written as 'a purely aesthetic endeavor'.[26] After all, Hamilton had opposed protective tariffs because tariff duties made up nine-tenths of the federal government's revenue.[27]

Yet, in presenting this line of argument, Nelson confuses Hamilton the visionary with Hamilton the policy maker. Hamilton's failure to insist on protective tariffs stemmed not from a lack of interest in domestic manufactures but from the need to practically resolve the most pressing financial problem facing the young nation: the repayment of America's revolutionary war debts. As Hamilton had pointed out in his earlier essay *The Continentalist No. V*, published in April 1782, 'moderate duties are more productive [of revenue] than high ones' because high tariffs tend to prohibit import itself (hence the term 'protective tariff'), leading to reduced tariff revenue. As Treasury Secretary, he needed every dollar of tariff revenue to pay the operating costs of the new federal government and pay down the national debt. Hamilton thus genuinely tried to promote domestic manufactures through SEUM even under the financial restraints imposed by the revolutionary debts. His involvement with SEUM accordingly confirms his honest desire to promote domestic manufactures. In addition, the publication of Hamilton's report on manufactures, which combined a powerful and sophisticated narrative advocating domestic manufactures and detailed information on the various kinds of industries struggling to survive in early America belied considerably more than merely a 'publicist's jingle'.

Timid Protectionism in Tariff Acts from 1789 to 1812

Although he failed to understand Hamilton on the issue of protectionism, Nelson correctly pointed out that tariff rates during the Federalist era did not reach a protective level at all. In fact, all of the tariff acts between 1789 and 1812 sought repeatedly to raise revenue rather than protect domestic manufactures. To be certain, the specific phrasing of these tariff acts indicates that protection was a concern of the United States Congress. For example, the preamble of the Tariff Act of 1789 stated that the objectives of the act were 'the discharge of the debts of the United States, and the encouragement and protection of manufactures'.[28] After the War for Independence, American manufacturers and artisans suffered from outpourings of cheap British manufactured goods into the American market.[29] Not surprisingly, manufacturers and mechanics from Baltimore, New York, Philadelphia and Boston petitioned Congress, demanding encouragement for and protection of American manufactured goods, creating a political constituency that was hard to put off.[30]

Nevertheless, the Tariff Act of 1789 remained essentially a revenue act in both conception and implementation. The Tariff Act levied specific duties on thirty-six items and *ad valorem* duties[31] on other goods. Seventeen articles were exempted from duties.[32] The average *ad valorem* rate was a mere 5 per cent.[33] Usually a 20 or 25 per cent *ad valorem* rate was considered as the minimum level for the purpose of protection.[34] In fact, federal tariffs did not even reflect a protectivist sentiment until 1816. There were twenty-five acts regarding tariffs between 1792 and 1812.[35] All aimed at raising revenue. The average tariff rates increased gradually from 5 per cent in the Tariff Act of 1789 to 30 per cent in the tariff act of 1812. But these increases were forced to meet specific financial needs rather than to protect domestic manufactures. For example, the Tariff Act of 26 March 1804 increased the average *ad valorem* rate from 12 ½ to 15 per cent.[36] The purpose of the increased tariff rates was to finance the war against the Barbary powers of the Mediterranean Sea, who had plundered American merchant ships. So the fund from the increased rate was dubbed the 'Mediterranean Fund' and put into a separate account.[37] The Congress doubled duties on all products in the tariff act of 1 July 1812 from the average *ad valorem* rate of 15 to 30 per cent to finance the War of 1812, which was declared on 18 June 1812.[38] In addition, the additional duty was to continue only for one year after the conclusion of a peace treaty.

The federal government's revenue-oriented tariff policies during this period represented a rational choice on the part of American government. It was a definite advantage for the United States to maintain a free trade policy with low rather than high tariff walls. The French Revolution and Napoleonic Wars, which raged in Europe from 1792 to 1815, left the United States as the pri-

Table 1.1. Average *ad valorem* Tariff Rates, 1789–1812.

Year	Tariff Rate
1789	5%
1790	5%
1791	5%
1792	7%
1794	10%
1797	10%
1800	12%
1804	15%
1812	30%

Source: H. C. Adams, *Taxation in the United States, 1789–1816* (New York, Johns Hopkins University, 1884), p. 36.

mary supplier and transporter of agricultural goods to European countries and their West Indian colonies. Between 1792 and 1807, the value of American exports – mainly wheat, flour, rice, tobacco and cotton – rose from $21 million to $108 million.[39]

Not only did the value of American exports increase, but the terms of trade (relative prices of export to import) for US goods improved as well. The terms of trade declined between 1790 and 1794 but afterwards remained above 100, reaching 162.6 in 1799, not dropping below 100 until 1808.[40] The re-export trade, which connected belligerent European powers to their Caribbean colonies through the use of American ports as stopover points, also dramatically increased during this period. Overall, profits from the re-export trade grew from $1 million in 1792 to $60 million in 1807.[41] European powers such as Holland and Spain, after being drawn into the Napoleonic Wars, suffered from enormous shipping losses. Consequently the net earnings of the United States shipping industry rose from $7.4 million in 1792 to $42.1 million in 1807.[42] During this same period, the American shipping industry increased in tonnage as well, from 127,000 tons in 1789 to 848,000 tons in 1807.[43]

Jeffersonians and Protectionism

When Thomas Jefferson became President in 1801, he did not try to change the revenue-oriented tariff policies of the United States government. Despite the underlying revenue focus of the tariff policies, however, he showed a certain amount of interest in the protection principle. It is true that Jefferson had once berated manufactures in his famous *Notes on the State of Virginia*, in which he stated:

> for the general operations of manufacture, let our workshops remain in Europe. It is better to carry provisions and materials to workmen there, than bring them to the provisions and materials, and with them their manners and principles. The loss by the transportation of commodities across the Atlantic will be made up in happiness and permanence of government. The mobs of great cities add just so much to the support of pure government, as sores do to the strength of the human body.[44]

But once in power, Jefferson did not hesitate to express his desire to see the development of domestic manufactures. In his first annual message of 8 December 1801, Jefferson called '[a]griculture, manufactures, commerce, and navigation' the 'four pillars of our prosperity' and suggested that '[p]rotection ... may sometimes be seasonably interposed'.[45] In his second annual message of 5 December 1802, Jefferson listed 'protect[ing] the manufactures adapted to our circumstances' as one of the 'landmarks' of his administration.[46] His successor and friend James Madison agreed. In his first inaugural address of 4 March 1809, Madison stated that one of the principles he would bring with him to office would be the promotion of 'by authorized means[,] improvements friendly to agriculture, to manufactures, and to external as well as internal commerce'.[47]

Pressure from manufacturers, artisans and mechanics for protective tariffs prompted Jefferson to take an interest in the subject. Most of the petitions Jefferson read argued repeatedly that tariffs were essential to protect 'infant' domestic manufactures until they matured sufficiently to be able to compete with foreign goods. For instance, on 4 February 1803, gun manufacturers in the borough of Lancaster, Pennsylvania demanded that the House reverse its resolution exempting foreign arms from import duties. They argued that 'by giving a loose to the facility of importing arms, the Government of the United States will crush this manufacture in its infant establishment ... A few years' more protection from Government, and this manufacture, in this country ... will be too firmly established to be destroyed by the importation of foreign arms'.[48] Philadelphia artisans, in their memorial to the Senate and House on 9 December 1803, concurred that 'an infant manufacture must have *some* protection, to enable it to contend with an old establishment'.[49]

Industrialists who raised arguments of economic independence were soon joined by those who claimed that nothing less than the cause of American independence hung on the issue of protective tariffs. In a memorial to the House on 30 March 1802, iron manufacturers from Morris, Sussex and Bergen, New Jersey argued that manufactories were 'a permanent source of wealth and independence to this country, and a profitable employment to themselves'.[50] The aforementioned Pennsylvania gunsmiths agreed that manufactures were 'essential to national safety, national independence, and national reputation'.[51]

Proponents of protective tariffs often interwove economic and nationalistic rationales in their arguments. On 22 January 1811, residents of Fayette county, Kentucky petitioned Congress to change the direction of the national economy from international to domestic trade after the Napoleonic Wars ended. The memorialists argued that '[a]n eternal war in Europe is not to be expected ... that one party must give way when its resources are exhausted, or it is humbled by the victories of its enemy.' Then 'we shall be compelled to look to other resources, to preserve the wealth which we have acquired'. The petitioners rhetorically asked '[b]ut how can it be preserved, if we do not change our system, and Congress does not give another direction to the industry of the country? Where shall we find a market for the productions of our soil?'[52] Eventually the argument for a home market emerged to become the most important rationale for protectionism after the end of the War of 1812.

Employing various arguments, petitions poured into Congress from iron, copper and cotton manufacturers throughout the War of 1812.[53] This outpouring of petitions stemmed partly from the fact that by 1815 American domestic manufactures had increased exponentially.[54] For instance, in 1808 there were only fifteen cotton mills in the United States. At the end of 1809, the number increased to 102. During this same period, capacity increased from 8,000 to 31,000 spindles.[55] Historian Victor S. Clark estimated that between 1800 and 1823, 557 manufacturing firms were incorporated with a combined authorized capital of over $72 million. Over half of those companies were incorporated and about half of their total capital was authorized between 1812 and 1815.[56] However, such industrial growth did not yet lead to the legislation of protective tariff laws until 1816.

Jeffersonians and Internal Improvements

It was in the area of internal improvement that the spirit of the American System was more successful before 1815. When the Republican Party came to power in 1801, the 'triumvirate' of President Thomas Jefferson, Secretary of State James Madison and Secretary of Treasury Albert Gallatin already enjoyed solid records of promoting internal improvement projects. As early as 1784, Jefferson emphasized to Washington the necessity of navigation on the Potomac and Ohio Rivers. The union of the Ohio and Potomac Rivers, Jefferson stated, would be 'among the strongest links of connection between the eastern and western sides of our confederacy'. 'It will', Jefferson continued, 'moreover, add to the commerce of Virginia, in particular, all the upper parts of the Ohio and its waters'. Also, referring to a plan to construct a canal between the Elizabeth River and the Sound River, Jefferson stated that it was 'much better that these should be done at public [rather] than private expense'.[57] This letter exchanged between future presidents foreshadowed the three most important ideas relating to internal improvements that would gain currency during the Jefferson administrations: 1) that such projects would strengthen the political union of the country; 2) that internal improvements were necessary to improve domestic commerce (or markets), and 3) that these projects were best accomplished through national, rather than state or private support.

It was James Madison who, with Washington's support, had engineered the passage of two bills in the Virginia Assembly in 1784 to clear the Potomac and James Rivers. He personally drafted the bill that incorporated the James River Company, creating the first 'mixed' corporation initiated by private subscriptions with public support in the young United States.[58] Madison thus pioneered a mechanism for the input of public support into private internal improvement projects.

After emigrating from his native Switzerland, Albert Gallatin eventually settled in the western part of Pennsylvania, beyond the Alleghenies.[59] As a member of the Pennsylvania House of Representatives, he enthusiastically supported all internal improvement projects, including the creation of a turnpike from Philadelphia to Lancaster.[60] His firsthand experience of the difficulty of travelling to Philadelphia to attend the Pennsylvania Legislature probably contributed to his warm support for such projects. However, Jefferson's first inaugural address did not reflect any support for internal improvements.[61] One reason for such an omission doubtless stemmed from financial considerations. The national debt, which stood at $75 million at the start of Federalist administration in 1791, had increased, rather than decreased, to $83 million in 1801 at the start of Jefferson's administration.[62] Despite his previous warm support for internal improvements, Jefferson's desire to reduce national debts left him unable to initiate costly projects.

Table 1.2. Amount of National Debt, 1801–8.

Year	Debt (million $)	Year	Debt (million $)
1801	83	1805	82
1802	81	1806	76
1803	77	1807	69
1804	86	1808	65

Source: Davis Rich Dewey, *Financial History of the United States* (New York: Longmans, 1903), p. 125.

Despite financial concerns, however, Republicans embarked on some internal improvement projects soon after they came to power. The first important Republican policy effort was the creation of the Cumberland, or National, Road. On 30 April 1802, Congress passed the Ohio Enabling Act. Section seven of the act authorized the President to use 2 per cent of the proceeds from the sale of Ohio land to build a road connecting the East with the Ohio territory.[63] The road started from Cumberland, Maryland and later reached Wheeling, Ohio by 1818.

To justify such a project Congress relied on the legal mechanism of a compact between the federal and state governments. In theory the federal government would agree to build a public road to link Western states to the East. In exchange, various state governments would exempt from taxation the purchasers of public lands within the state for a certain number of years. Each state had a different compact with the federal government. In the case of Ohio, the federal government granted 5 per cent of the proceeds to the state, out of which 2 per cent was to be used for a national road, in return for a five-year tax exemption.[64] Gallatin spearheaded the idea of a compact; although Congress revised his initial plan of granting 10 per cent of the land proceeds in return for ten-year tax exemptions.

Nationalism remained one of the motivations to construct the road. In his letter of 13 February 1802 to Representative William B. Giles of Virginia, chairman of a select committee to oversee the carving up of the Northwest Territory into individual states to be brought into the Union, Gallatin explained the political aspect of the project. He stated:

> such roads to be laid out under the authority of Congress, with the consent of the several States through which the same shall pass ... But a due attention to the particular geographical situation of that Territory and of the adjacent Western districts of the Atlantic States, will not fail to impress you strongly with the importance of that provision, in a political point of view, so far as it will contribute towards cementing the bonds of the Union between those parts of the United States whose local interests have been considered as most dissimilar.[65]

It is important to note that Gallatin adopted a very cautious nationalism in the letter. Seeking to avoid antagonizing state interests, Gallatin's proposal assumed the 'consent' of states through which the road should pass as a necessary precondition for the project. He did not assume that Congress had the authority to implement such a project without it.

Debates over the construction of the bill show that Gallatin's caution was more than warranted. Giles reported to Congress on 30 March 1802 a series of resolutions, which followed Gallatin's suggestions to the letter.[66] The next day, Roger Griswold of Connecticut (Federalist), representing New England interests, attacked the proposal as an attempt to use the proceeds from public land sales to benefit Virginia and Pennsylvania. On 19 December 1805, a Senate Committee led by Uriah Tracy of Connecticut (Federalist) recommended the construction of a road from Cumberland, on the northern bank of the Potomac River in Maryland to the Ohio River. Pennsylvania and Virginia opposed this proposed route, because they were Maryland's competitors in the struggle for trade with the West. Thus, when the bill came to the House for debates, Representative Michael Leib of Pennsylvania moved to indefinitely postpone the bill while Virginia's Christopher H. Clark suggested that three roads be built, starting from the states of Pennsylvania, Maryland and Virginia respectively. Clark's suggestion met with scorn from Western Congressmen who were eager to see the start of construction of a road regardless of where it began. George M. Bedinger of Kentucky, Jeremiah Morrow of Ohio and Roger Nelson of Maryland rose to strike the various motions of their eastern colleagues. They argued that their route was the shortest, conducive to both Western and national interests and the most convenient route for all parties involved, including the states of Pennsylvania and Virginia. Regional interests thus trumped political ideology in the debates over the Cumberland Road. When the construction bill passed the House on 24 March 1806, by a vote of sixty-six to fifty, only four of Pennsylvania's eighteen members and two of Virginia's twenty-two were among the majority.

Gallatin continued to reveal his interest in internal improvements through the publication of a well-received report on internal improvements of 1808. In this report, Gallatin tried to promote the construction of roads and canals to strengthen the bonds of political union, but in a way accommodating the interests of different states and sections.

One of the preconditions that allowed Gallatin to write the report was the auspicious state of national finance. Due to the sound financial policies of Jefferson's two terms in office and the prosperous international trade during the Napoleonic Wars, the United States saw a substantial decrease in the national debt. Gallatin wrote to Jefferson in 1809 that

> [t]he reduction of the public debt was certainly the principal object in bringing me into office, and our success in that respect has been due both to the joint and continued efforts of the several branches of government and to the prosperous situation of the country.[67]

The amount of national debt, which stood at $83 million in 1801, dropped to $65 million in 1806, even overcoming an $11 million debt incurred by the Louisiana Purchase in 1803. From early on Jefferson considered using the possible future treasury surpluses for internal improvement projects. As early as 4 March 1805, Jefferson stated in his second inaugural address

> that redemption [of national debt] once effected the revenue thereby liberated may, by a just repartition of it among the States and a corresponding amendment of the Constitution, be applied *in time of peace* to rivers, canals, roads, arts, manufactures, education, and other great objects within each State.[68]

Gallatin presented his report to the Senate on 6 April 1808.[69] In the report, Gallatin first argued that only the federal government could remove the two obstacles to internal improvement projects: lack of capital and low population densities in frontier regions.[70] But Gallatin ultimately argued that internal improvements were necessary politically, to strengthen the union of the country. He stated that '[g]ood roads and canals will shorten distances, facilitate commercial and personal intercourse and unite, by a still more intimate community of interests, the more remote quarters of the United States.' Therefore, Gallatin assessed '[n]o other single operation, within the power of Government, can more effectually tend to strengthen and perpetuate that Union which secures external independence, domestic peace, and internal liberty.'[71]

Gallatin suggested federal aid to create a national system of internal improvements for various projects: 1) construction of canals and a great turnpike along the eastern seacoast, at a cost of $7.8 million; 2) expenditures of $4.8 million to connect the East and West via canals, turnpikes, and roads; 3) a proposition to improve inland rivers in northern and northwestern directions by $4 million, and 4) another expenditure of $3.4 million to compensate states that would benefit less from the aforesaid improvements. He justified spending in the last category by pointing out that his proposals would benefit the Atlantic States, through which western and northwestern roads and canals would pass, more than other Eastern and Southern states. The last proposal demonstrates sensitivity on Gallatin's part to the delicate balance of sectional interests.[72]

According to Gallatin's proposals, the total cost of such an internal improvements programme would be $20 million, or $2 million per year. He calculated that the average revenue of the government would be $14 million, while peacetime expenditures would not exceed $8.5 million, leaving a surplus of $5.5 million. Thus the government, Gallatin argued, could safely spend $2 million a year for internal improvements.[73] Gallatin's proposed expenditure of $20 million was a huge amount of money. The magnitude of the proposed sum can be understood by comparing it with the total amount of the 2 per cent fund for the Cumberland Road. Between 1 July 1802 and 31 October 1808, the 2 per cent fund from the sale of land in Ohio produced only about $44,700.[74]

In this sense, Gallatin's report was a powerful expression of American nationalism. It laid out the blueprint for a *national system* on a gigantic scale for the political purpose of strengthening the nation. Perhaps most brazenly, the report suggested building a *system* to incorporate all state and local level transportation projects. However, Gallatin's nationalism remained a cautious one. He conceded that the federal government could not unilaterally decide on the construction of roads and canals, stating that

> [t]he manner in which the public moneys be applied to such objects remains to be considered. It is evident that the United States cannot, under the constitution, open any road or canal, without the consent of the State though which such road or canal must pass.[75]

In sum, Gallatin's vision for the United States was grand but the proposed methods to reach that goal were very guarded.

Despite Gallatin's carefully constructed approach to the issue of internal improvements, his suggestions were not implemented. There is no record in the *Annals of Congress* showing that Congress did more than receive the report. Ultimately the complicated international relations leading to the War of 1812 distracted Congress and the Madison administration. Gallatin himself had acknowledged in his report that his proposed spending could operate 'to its full extent only in times of peace and under prosperous circumstances'.[76] However, Republicans' constitutional concerns also plagued his plans to implement federally funded internal improvements projects. In his second inaugural address on 4 March 1805, President Jefferson expressed a wish to apply federal revenue to construct 'rivers, canals, roads, arts, manufactures, and education'. But he stressed the need for 'a corresponding amendment of the Constitution' for such purposes.[77] President Madison, like his predecessor, acknowledged the utility of internal improvement projects but also indicated his concerns over constitutional authority. In his first inaugural address on 4 March 1809, Madison expressed his desire 'to promote *by authorized means* improvements friendly to agriculture, to manufactures, and to external as well as internal commerce'.[78]

Jeffersonians and the 1BUS

Despite constitutional controversy, the 1BUS flourished initially during Jefferson's administration. Originally the Jeffersonian-Republicans had argued that the 1BUS was unconstitutional. While serving as Secretary of State, Jefferson wrote an opinion to President George Washington against the constitutionality of the bank. In his 'Opinion on the Constitutionality of the Bill for Establishing a National Bank', submitted 15 February 1791, Jefferson cautioned Washington against a broad construction of the Constitution, arguing that the foundation of the Constitution lay in the Tenth Amendment's promise that '[t]he powers not delegated to the United States by the constitution, nor prohibited by it to the States, are reserved to the States respectively, or to the people.' Jefferson continued that '[t]o take a single step beyond the boundaries thus specially drawn around the powers of Congress, is to take possession of a boundless field of power, no longer susceptible of any definition.'[79] The possible benefits of the bank, such as the easy remittance of federal money, were no more than a *convenience,* which did not qualify the bank as a *necessity* for the execution of any enumerated power of the federal government.[80] Thus, concluded Jefferson, the bank was unconstitutional. Madison, in a speech in the House on 2 February 1791, agreed that the power of incorporation was not an implied power but 'a distinct, and independent, and substantive prerogative, which, not being enumerated in the constitution, could never have been meant to be included in it, and, not being included, could never be rightfully exercised'.[81]

When the Jeffersonians came to power, however, they did not antagonize the 1BUS but rather helped the bank to expand. For example, on 23 March 1804, the Democratic-Republican dominated Congress passed a law allowing the bank to establish a branch in New Orleans at the urging of Albert Gallatin, the Secretary of Treasury.[82] At first the directors of the bank were reluctant to open a branch in New Orleans. To help the bank's directors overcome their reluctance, Gallatin engineered the passage of the act of 23 March 1804, authorizing the bank 'to establish offices of discount and deposit in any part of the territories or dependencies of the United States'.[83]

Personally, Jefferson abhorred the bank. In his letter to Gallatin on 13 December 1803, Jefferson wrote that '[t]his institution is one of the most deadly hostility existing, against the principles and form of our Constitution', but he was practical enough to forgo his hatred of the bank and heed Gallatin's suggestion.[84] On 24 February 1807, Congress passed a law to make the counterfeiting of the bank's notes a federal felony, punishable by imprisonment, hard labour and stiff fines.[85] The passage of the act added to the security of the bank's notes. In fact, under Jeffersonian administration the bank expanded its branches from five in 1800 to eight in 1805.

Table 1.3. Number of the Branches of the 1BUS.

Year	Branches
1792	4
1800	5
1802	7
1805	8

Source: B. Hammond, *Banks and Politics in America from the Revolution to the Civil War* (Princeton, NJ: Princeton University Press, 1957), p. 127.

However, the business success of the bank did not shield it from persistent attacks. Realizing that the Bank's charter was to expire in 1811, shareholders applied to the House and Senate separately for rechartering in 1811. Secretary Treasury Albert Gallatin emphasized the benefits of the bank for both public finance and the economy as a whole. In his report to the Senate on 3 March 1809, he stated that the benefits of the bank are '*Safekeeping of the public moneys ... Transmission of public moneys ... Collection of the revenue ...* and *Loans* [to government].'[86] In another report to the Senate on 5 February 1811, Gallatin also predicted that the termination of a bank with $13 million notes in circulation and $14 million worth of outstanding loans would give 'a serious shock to commercial, banking, and national credit'. Gallatin also argued that the bank was constitutional, because its charter had been 'acted upon, or acquiesced in, as if constitutional, by all the constitutional authorities of the nation' for a number of years and he thought the use of the bank 'necessary for the exercise of the legitimate powers of the General Government'.[87] Needless to say, the last point utilized a very Hamiltonian logic in its defence of the 1BUS.

The Bank's opponents struck back with three central arguments: 1) the bank was unconstitutional; 2) British subjects wielded considerable influence over the bank as stockholders, and 3) the bank represented an unsettling concentration of economic power. Almost every Representative and Senator who spoke out against the bank challenged its constitutionality.[88] In future years Gallatin, in a letter to Nicholas Biddle, the President of the 2BUS, recalled the constitutional arguments levelled against the bank:

> [i]n 1810 the weight of the Administration was in favour of a renewal, Mr. Madison having made his opinion known that he considered the question as settled by precedent, and myself an open and strenuous advocate. We had the powerful support of Mr. Crawford in the Senate, and no formidable opponent in either House but Mr. Clay, a majority of political friends in both Houses, and almost all the Federal votes on that question, with no other untoward circumstances but the *personal* opposition to Mr. Madison and myself of the Clintons, and Maryland Smiths, Leib, and Giles; the banking system had not yet penetrated through the country, extending its ramifications through every hamlet, and the opposition due to the jealousy or selfishness of rival institutions was confined to a few cities; yet the question was lost [due to the constitutional issue].[89]

The attack on the alleged British influence on the bank also dealt a serious blow to the attempts to recharter it. For example, William B. Giles of Virginia stated that '[m]y objection arises from the enormous British influence[,] which notoriously pervades this country; and, I believe, affects the proceedings of Government so seriously, that it can hardly be said to be independent.'[90] It was true that a large percentage of the stockholders were British subjects. According to Gallatin's report to the Senate on 2 March 1809, foreigners held 18,000 shares of the stocks of the bank, while American stockholders owned only 7,000 shares.[91] But foreign stockholders had no voting rights under the charter. Regardless, bank opponents still described the institution as a pawn to British interests. Representative Erastus Root of New York testified to the effectiveness of this attack. He later reminisced that:

> I attempted to repel the notion of a supposed British influence in this country through the English stockholders ... As the English stockholders could have no agency - not even remote - in the management of the affairs of the Bank, they could have none of that influence which the disposition of pecuniary favours may be supposed to give ... All this reasoning was of no avail with the Republicans of Otsego and Delaware. With them it was a Federal Bank, a British Bank, which would keep us under Federal and British influence. They were my constituents, for I was their Representative in Congress. I was unwilling to displease my constituents and therefore stepped aside when the vote was taken on rechartering the Bank.[92]

Those who attacked the economic power of the bank appealed not just to the constitutional sensibilities but also to the raw emotions of the American people. Representative Richard M. Johnson of Kentucky criticized the bank for as being a 'moneyed aristocracy' exercising 'monopolies'.[93] Thomas Newton Jr of Virginia called the bank 'the root of evil'.[94]

But state banking interests were also an important factor in determining the fate of the national bank. Before the first national bank opened in 1791, there were only three banks in the United States.[95] The number increased to 117 in 1811.

Table 1.4. Number of State Banks and Business Volume, 1809–18.

Date	Number of State Banks	Loans and Discounts	Total Bank Notes in Circulation
1809	92	$12,630,000	$3,800,000
1810	102	$14,690,000	$5,580,000
1811	117	$16,220,000	$5,680,000
1812	143	$17,940,000	$6,320,000
1813	147	$21,650,000	$7,230,000
1814	202	$36,740,000	$13,690,000
1815	212	$44,070,000	$19,910,000
1816	232	$40,460,000	$17,220,000
1817	262	$32,760,000	$13,310,000
1818	338	$48,240,000	$18,070,000

Source: R. H. Timberlake, *The Origins of Central Banking in the United States* (Cambridge, MA: Harvard University Press, 1978), p. 15.

Some of the state banks resented the restraining power of the national bank. In the course of business, the national bank almost always played the role of creditor to state banks as state banknotes flowed into the possession of the 1BUS. For instance, if a merchant paid federal taxes with state bank notes, the notes were eventually deposited in a treasury department account in the national bank. By occasionally presenting these notes to the state bank for specie payment, the national bank restrained state banks from extending credits excessively.[96]

Some state-chartered banks resented this role of the national bank. The Farmers and Mechanics' Bank of Philadelphia refused to sign a petition, circulated by other state banks, asking for the renewal of the national bank's charter.[97] Representing this viewpoint, Senator Michael Leib of Pennsylvania called the national bank's restraining power 'a check like that of a shark upon the little fish around him'.[98] From the opposite viewpoint, Senator William H. Crawford criticized state banking interests. He argued that states wanted to kill the national bank out of avarice and a love for power. Crawford argued that states wanted to 'put down' the Bank of the United States, because

> [t]hey have erected banks, in many of which they hold stock to a considerable amount, and they wish to compel the United States to use their banks as places of deposite [*sic*] for their public money, by which they expect to increase their dividends.[99]

There was some truth to Crawford's claim. From 1790 to 1860, states heavily invested in the stocks of banks they had chartered. Massachusetts alone had invested as much as $1 million in the local Union Bank charted in 1793 and the Boston Bank incorporated in 1803. This gave the state more than one-eighth of the total banking capital of Massachusetts.[100] The state of Pennsylvania similarly invested $1 million in Bank of Pennsylvania stock in 1794[101] and twenty years later Virginia subscribed one-fifth of the $1.5 million stock of the Bank of Virginia.[102] In fact, in some cases, states owned local banks outright. South Carolina founded the Bank of South Carolina in 1812 as a totally state-owned bank.[103] Dividends from state investments and taxes on the banks made up about 25 per cent of total state revenues in the 1820s and about 50 per cent in the early 1830s. In the later part of the 1830s, bank revenues supplied more than 50 per cent of total state incomes.[104] Henry Clay, the most effective enemy of the national bank in 1811, served as a director for both a state-chartered bank based in Frankfort, Kentucky, and the Bank of Kentucky.[105] His first argument against the national bank, launched in a Senate speech on 15 February 1811, centred on what he considered the bank's unconstitutionality. He argued that the power to charter companies was 'not specified in the grant [of power in the Constitution]' and was 'of a nature not transferable by mere implication'.[106]

The availability of state banking services added to the strength of constitutional arguments against the 1BUS. Bank opponents argued that state banks could replace the roles the national bank played in federal finance and the national economy, so the national bank was merely 'useful' rather than 'necessary' under the enumerated powers of the Constitution.[107] Clay, in his above-mentioned speech, stated that 'the operations of that department [of treasury] may be as well conducted without, as with the bank [of the United States]'. He pointed out that Treasury Secretary Gallatin's report of 7 January 1811 showed that the Treasury Department had deposited more than one-third of its treasury reserve, which stood at a little over $2 million, with local banks. State banks including the Manhattan Bank in New York and the Bank of Columbia in Washington DC, therefore held a substantial amount of federal funds.[108] This fact was not necessarily surprising, for in his report to the Senate on 30 January 1811 Gallatin admitted that '[s]tate banks may be used, and must, in case of a non-renewal of the charter, be used by the treasury ... and it is believed that the ordinary business will be transacted, through their medium ... without any insuperable difficulty.'[109]

Clay drew upon Gallatin's own arguments and actions to reveal that state banks were not merely more constitutional than a national bank but also more practical regulating the national economy. In response to Gallatin's claims that destroying the bank would destabilize the American economy, Clay argued that the sudden withdrawal of the national bank's notes and loans could be compensated for by increased state bank notes once federal deposits were placed at the care of state banks.[110] In short, constitutional arguments against the bank proved effective fodder for state banking interests to use in attacking their greatest foe. By relying on two mutually reinforcing lines of attack, critics of the bank were successful in defeating a House bill for the rechartering of the 1BUS by a vote of sixty-five to sixty-four in 1811. Although the Senate tied the vote seventeen to seventeen,[111] Vice President George Clinton used his tie-breaking vote to kill the measure, citing the unconstitutionality of the bank to vindicate his actions.[112]

Despite the sanguine expectations of those claiming that state banks could substitute for a national bank, state banks failed to meet the test during the War of 1812. The period between the death of the 1BUS in March 1811 and the incorporation of the 2BUS in April 1816 represented one of the most difficult times in American financial and economic history. From June 1812 to January 1815 the nation fought a protracted war against Britain during which the American government faced serious problems, including suspension of specie payment by state banks and difficulties in securing loans for the war effort. In August and September of 1814, all American banks outside New England refused to pay specie (gold or silver) in exchange for bank notes or deposits[113] Problems with bank notes lay at the heart of this crisis.[114] After the folding of the first national bank in 1811, a large number of state-chartered banks arose to fill the void. The opportunity to receive lucrative federal deposits and the disappearance of the restraining power of a national bank enticed states and moneyed people to enter the banking industry. The number of banks increased progressively from 117 in 1811 to 143 in 1812, 147 in 1813, 202 in 1814, 212 in 1815 and 232 in 1816.[115] State banks correspondingly increased their notes in circulation from $22.7 million in January 1811 to $68 million in January 1816.[116] They did not resume specie payment until early 1817, after incorporation of the 2BUS. In the meantime, the paper money of various state banks depreciated. For example, in June 1816 Baltimore notes were at a 20 per cent discount, Philadelphia notes at a 17 per cent discount and New York notes at a 12.5 per cent discount.[117]

A more immediate problem for the government was the difficulty of attracting loans. Secretary of the Treasury A. J. Dallas's *Report on the State of the Finances*, delivered to the Senate on 8 December 1815, clearly elucidated the government's pressing fiscal problems. $42,269,776 worth of loans, subscribed in 1813 and 1814, in 6 per cent stocks had been sold at roughly a 15 per cent discount, bringing only $35,987,762 into the Treasury. This difficult situation did not change substantially after the end of the war. An act of 3 March 1815 authorized a loan not to exceed $18,452,800. Until 19 April 1815, however, loan subscriptions were offered at no more than 89 per cent of the nominal price of the stocks, in some cases even sinking as low as 75 per cent of the price. The Treasury Department declined such embarrassing offers. Only with difficulty was the Treasury Department able to float loans at rates between 95 and 98 per cent of the face value. Eventually the Treasury was able to receive subscriptions of only $9,284,044.38.[118] Dallas explains the general economic and financial difficulty of the US during the war:

> [t]he plan of finance, which was predicated upon the theory of defraying the extraordinary expenses of the war by successive loans, had already become inoperative. The product of the revenues had ceased to furnish an amount equal to the expenditures of the former peace establishment, with an addition of the interest upon the debt contracted on account of the war. And the sudden suspension of specie payments at the principal banks established in different States, (however it may be excused, or justified, by the apparent necessity of the case,) had exposed the Government, as well as private citizens, to all the inconveniences of a variable currency, devoid, alike, of national authority and of national circulation. The Treasury could no longer transfer its funds from place to place; and it became, of course, impracticable to maintain the accustomed punctuality in the payment of the public engagements.[119]

The difficult financial experiences during the War of 1812 left American politicians to work towards creation of a national bank once peace was concluded.

Public Land Policies in the Era of Federalists and Jeffersonians

Traditionally, scholars of America's westward expansion have argued that the two biggest land policy concerns faced by the federal government during the early republic were those of 'revenue' and 'settlement'.[120] It was Alexander Hamilton who, in 1790, argued that the two leading objectives in federal land policies were 'one, the facility of advantageous sales, according to the probable course of purchasers; the other the accommodation of individuals now inhabiting the western country, or who may hereafter emigrate thither'.[121] As has been noted, proponents of the American System did not consider land policies a critical element in their grand plan for national development. They considered land policies mainly as a financial means to achieve the desired goal of internal improvement projects. Significantly, neither of the major proponents of the American System – Henry Clay or John Quincy Adams – authored any major letters, pamphlets or speeches on the land issue. Although Clay eventually linked the issue of land reform to the American System, he did not do so until 1832.[122]

In approaching public lands mainly as a source of revenue, supporters of the American System employed a traditional conception of land in vogue since the start of Washington's administration. On 4 August 1790, the Federalist dominated Congress passed an act making provisions for the payment of public debts. The last section of the act stipulated that all proceeds from Western land sales would be applied to the sinking or discharging of the national debt.[123] As long as public debt remained a large financial burden to the United States, the federal government could not afford to invest money from land sales in public improvement schemes. But with the substantial retirement of the national debt during the Jeffersonian era, political leaders began to reorient federal land policy by combining revenue interests with the Western settlement goal.

In 1796 Congress passed another land act, primarily to raise revenue. It was Albert Gallatin, a leading Republican member in the House, who provided the driving force behind this measure. This act revealed Gallatin's primary interest in raising revenue through federal land sales, with only a secondary intention to help Western settlement. This measure provided a blueprint for the future selling off of federal land, including the surveying and division of public land into rectangular sections and townships six miles square and the creation of an auction system for land sales.[124]

Gallatin's most important contribution to the Land Act of 1796 was his proposal to sell lands in large and small sized tracts.[125] In its final form, the act authorized sales of half of the surveyed townships in quarter sized allotments to large land companies, with the remainder to be sold at the size of sections to ordinary Americans. One township was six miles square, or thirty-six sections. One section represented 640 acres. Thus a quarter township was 5,760 acres wide. The smaller lots were to be sold at auction for a minimum price of $2 per acre for a minimum purchase of 640 acres. The purchaser was required to pay 5 per cent of the purchase price in cash, 50 per cent within thirty days after the initial purchase and the remainder of the balance within a year. Gallatin explained that it was necessary to divide land sales in order to allow smaller farmers to purchase smaller lots while still allowing large speculators larger plots.[126]

As a Representative from backcountry Pennsylvania and a leader of the political party representing mainly Southern and Western interests, it was natural for Gallatin to promote Western settlement through land sales to small farmers. At the same time, however, he calculated that wealthy land speculators could best afford to buy large tracts and thereby contribute the most to the United States Treasury in the short run. While defending his proposal to divide land sales into two categories, Gallatin argued that the most important object for the United States was to extinguish 'the curse of the country, the Public Debt'. He continued that the United States had the power to eliminate the national debt within ten years through Western land sales.[127] As the national debt in 1796 stood at about $83.7 million,[128] the federal government would have had to raise more than $8 million per year from land sales for ten years in order to achieve Gallatin's goal. The actual average sale amounts from 1796 to 1820 were $1,870,000 per year.[129] Although Gallatin was overly optimistic in 1796, it is a testimony to the high hopes he and other American politicians had for the financial potential of public lands. Even though Gallatin tried to strike a balance between the purposes of settlement and revenue, his fiscal concerns featured more prominently in the Land Bill of 1796. Even in the case of smaller tracts, farmers had to come up with at least $1,280 within a year (640 acre minimum at $2 per acre), which was much more than most farmers could afford.

Despite Gallatin's optimistic expectation, the land act of 1796 failed. The revenues from land sales were $4,836.13 in 1796, $83,540.60 in 1797, $11,963.11 in 1798 and $443.75 in 1800. The total was only $100,783.59 for a five-year period,[130] which was far short of Gallatin's original expectations – thus Congress had to pass a new land act to compensate for the financial shortfall.

The economic necessity for Congress to develop a new federal land policy dovetailed with the demands of Western farmers to sell smaller land tracts with credit. A petition from citizens of the Northwest Territory to Congress in 1799 stated that because of the enormous size of the lands for sale, 'few persons will ... be in Situation [sic] to purchase any of these Tracts on the terms they are to be sold [according to the Act of 1796]'. In addition, the petitioners demanded 'a longer time for the different payments'.[131] The result was the Land Act of 10 May 1800 that tried to raise substantial revenue while meeting Western demands.[132]

The Land Act of 1800 reduced tract sizes and extended credit at a minimum price of $2. The minimum amount of land that could be purchased was likewise reduced to a half section of 320 acres.[133] Credit on land purchases was extended from one year under the terms of the 1796 land act to four years. A farmer could now start a farm with a mere $160. The balance could be paid in instalments over two, three and four years after the sale. If the purchaser failed to complete the payment within one year after the last instalment was due, the land could be forfeited and sold again. The instalments carried 6 per cent simple interest from the time of sale. Early payments received a discount of 8 per cent. With this discount, the minimum price of the land in cash was $1.84 per acre. In addition, the act also established four Land Offices in the southern Ohio Territory at Cincinnati, Chillicothe, Marietta and Steubenville.

The debates in the House show that the act was primarily intended to raise revenue. The debates on the bill centred mainly on the size of the tracts and preemption rights. Preemption rights referred to the rights of illegal settlers (squatters) on public lands to receive at cheap prices the titles to the lands they lived on. Northeastern Federalists in the House tried to strike the section of the land bill authorizing the sale of 320 acre lots, while Western delegates defended the measure. Representatives from New England argued that hiring surveyors to divide public lands into smaller lots would prove too costly. Furthermore, selling small plots of land would only encourage squatters. On the other hand, defenders of the provision argued that the sale of 320 acre tracts would encourage selling land to actual settlers rather than large land companies which would increase competition over individual plots, help shore up land prices and provide more opportunities to recover survey costs through increased land sales. In addition, Western Congressman pointed out that the land act of 1796 had failed to generate substantial revenue. Northeastern Congressmen could not answer this last point and therefore the House ultimately kept the provision for selling smaller lots.[134] This suggests that, ultimately, Congress sought to increase revenue from land sales by breaking up the lands to attract smaller farmers.

In the same spirit the House overwhelmingly rejected the motion of William C. C. Claiborne, a Tennessee Congressman and loyal Democratic-Republican, to grant preemption rights to 'every head of a family who shall have made an actual settlement or improvement on any part of the lands aforesaid, and shall reside on the same'. Although willing to sell western lands at cheap rates to appease Western voters, Congress was eager to protect what it considered federal property. Even Gallatin made a speech against the motion. Only seventeen Representatives supported the motion in the vote.[135]

In a sense, the Act of 1800 was a success in terms of overall land sales. The amount of land sales increased dramatically over the next two decades.[136] The Act of 1796 raised only $100,783.59 for the five years between 1796 and 1800, averaging only about $20,000 per year. On the other hand, the average land sales after 1801 were $2,325,199 per year. Land sales went over the $1 million mark in 1801, 1805, 1806 and 1811, remaining consistent from 1813 to 1820. The peak of such land sales occurred in 1818 at $8,238,309.21.

The increase of revenue from land sales was welcome news to the Treasury Department and Congress. But it also created a serious problem: speculation. Farmers frequently purchased lands beyond their financial means. The credit system gave farmers the false hope that they would be able to pay the balance of their purchase price if they could scrape together enough money for the initial payment of 25 per cent.[137] After all, the next payment would not be due for another two years, plenty of time to gather profits from successful harvests. A memorial from the Indiana Territorial Legislature to Congress, dated 21 September 1814, revealed such overly optimistic beliefs on the part of many Western farmers. The memorial stated that many of the settlers had purchased federal lands by investing all of their money with the expectation that produce from such fertile soil would quickly allow them to repay any outstanding debts.[138] Not only farmers, but almost every prominent Western politician such as Henry Clay, Andrew Jackson, Senator Thomas Hart Benton of Missouri, Senator John Walker of Alabama and Senator Ninian Edwards of Illinois also speculated in land.[139] Eventually land speculation based on credit became a serious practical problem for the federal government. As the following tables demonstrate, massive speculation created a mushrooming balance of debts from land sales.

Table 1.5. Land Sale, 1796–1820.

Year	Acres	Dollars	Average Price/Acre
1796	–	4,836.13	–
1797	–	83,540.60	–
1798	–	11,963.11	–
1799	–	0.00	–
1800	67,750.93	133,501.86	1.97
1801	497,939.36	1,031,893.26	2.07
1802	271,080.77	532,160.74	1.96
1803	174,156.04	349,292.18	2.01
1804	398,155.99	817,270.50	2.05
1805	581,971.91	1,186,562.09	2.04
1806	506,018.67	1,053,792.34	2.08
1807	320,945.79	659,709.17	2.06
1808	209,167.34	490,080.35	2.34
1809	275,004.09	605,970.20	2.20
1810	285,795.55	607,867.77	2.13
1811	575,067.18	1,216,447.28	2.12
1812	386,077.36	829,404.10	2.15
1813	505,647.82	1,066,372.33	2.11
1814	1,176,141.67	2,462,914.88	2.09
1815	1,306,368.33	2,713,414.36	2.08
1816	1,742,523.63	3,692,738.39	2.12
1817	1,886,163.96	4,478,820.40	2.37
1818	3,491,014.79	13,122,836.41	3.76
1819	2,968,390.80	8,238,309.21	2.78
1820	491,916.46	1,348,119.84	2.74

Sources: The data from 1796 to 1799 are from *American State Papers: Finance* 2:919. The data from 1800 to 1820 are from *Senate Document*, No. 246, 27th Cong., 3rd sess., p. 6. The figures for the year 1820 are land sales until 30 June 1820.

Figure 1.1. Land Sales from 1796 to 1820.

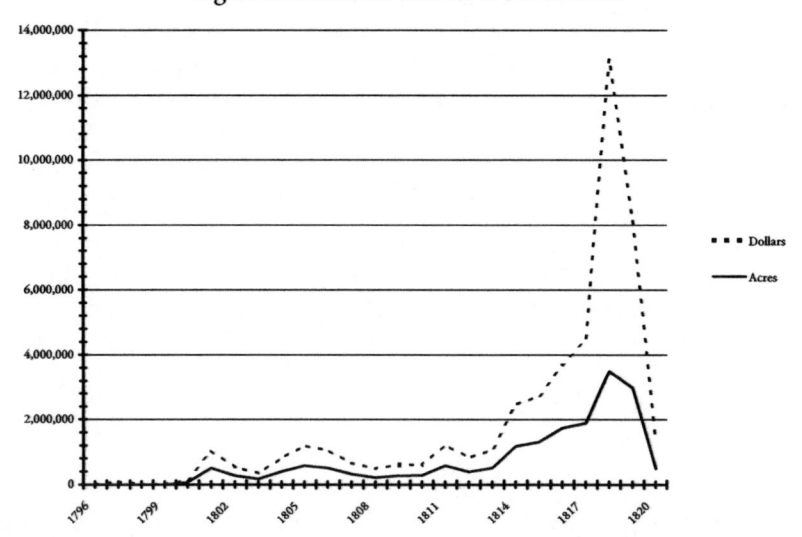

Table 1.6. The Amounts Owed by Purchasers to the Federal Government, in dollars, 1800–19.

Year	Northwest of the Ohio River	Alabama and Mississippi	Total
1800–01	586,426.02	–	586,426.02
1802	1,045,578.21	–	1,045,578.21
1803	1,092,390.17	–	1,092,390.17
1804	1,434,212.50	–	1,434,212.50
1805	2,094,305.85	–	2,094,305.85
1806	2,245,557.58	–	2,245,557.58
1807	2,153,306.42	111,913.50	2,265,219.92
1808	2,041,673.01	138,752.85	2,180,425.86
1809	1,912,703.86	273,482.85	2,186,186.71
1810	1,646,642.04	390,195.33	2,036,837.37
1811	1,496,371.67	474,541.23	1,970,912.90
1812	1,599,106.33	653,068.18	2,252,174.51
1813	1,483,861.10	630,274.63	2,114,135.73
1814	2,134,989.56	589,008.74	2,723,998.30
1815	3,163,936.55	531,732.79	3,695,669.34
1816	4,334,648.09	1,270,097.73	5,604,745.82
1817	5,627,797.02	2,526,410.36	8,154,207.38
1818	7,290,489.55	5,170,988.66	12,461,478.21
1819	9,868,295.48	12,132,362.16	22,000,657.64

Source: *American State Papers: Public Lands* 3:420.

Figure 1.2. Balance of Debts from Land Sales, 1800–19.

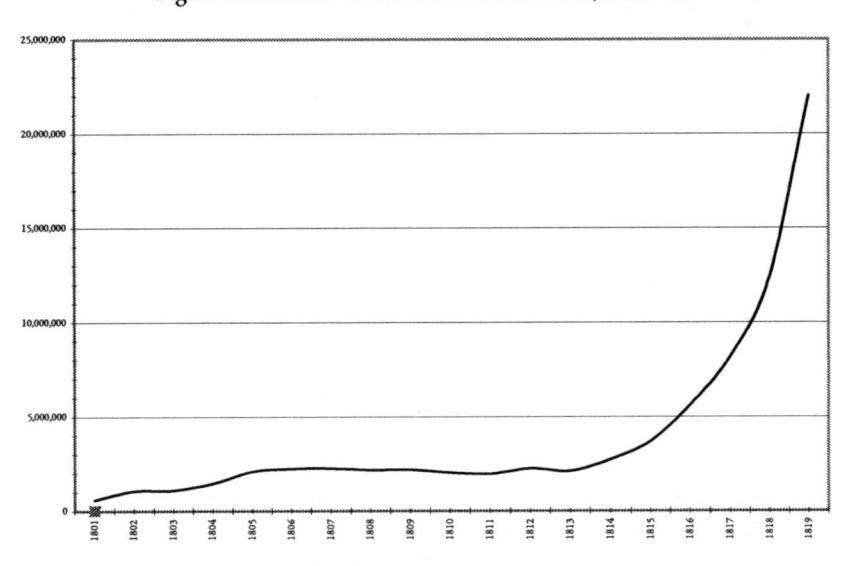

In 1820, the balance of debts reached $22 million. Congress failed to address this issue until the Land Act of 1820 because easy credit resulted in a substantial increase of land sales and hence more revenue into the federal treasury – thus fulfilling the basic objective of federal land policy. Instead of repairing the main cause for the rapid increase of debt, namely the credit system, Congress simply tried to modify the land system created under the Land Act of 1800. One such piecemeal attempt to reform the federal land system was the Land Act of 1804.

Like previous measures, the pressure to revamp the land system came from the West. Western petitions demanded grants of pre-emption rights and land sales of even smaller tracts at further reduced prices. Significantly, such petitions did not demand a repeal of the credit system but rather praised the Land Act of 1800 for containing such a system. The signers of a petition presented to Congress, on 20 February 1801, thanked the Congress for 'making an Act supplementary to the former Act, for settling the Publick [sic] Lands in this Territory, in which among other Advantages to Settlers is, dividing the Townships ... into half sections, and giving time for the payment of a part of the Money'.[140] Westerners were apparently quite satisfied with a credit system which made it easy for them to purchase larger tracts of land than possible under a cash-only system.

On 22 November 1803, the House organized a committee headed by Joseph Nicholson of Maryland (Republican) to consider such petitions.[141] On 1 December 1803, Nicholson's committee sent a series of enquiries to Treasury Secretary Albert Gallatin to get his opinion on the subject.[142] The questions were the following:

> Will the sales of the lands be retarded or accelerated; and how will the revenue be affected?
>
> 1st. By selling the lands in smaller tracts
>
> 2dly. By charging no interest on the amount of sales until after the purchaser has made default in payment.
>
> 3dly. By selling for cash, instead of giving the credit now authorized by law.
>
> 4thly. By reducing the price of the lands.
>
> 5thly. By making grants of small tracts to actual settlers and improvers.

As the leading question itself demonstrates, the Committee was primarily concerned with the effects of the proposals on land sales and revenue. But it is interesting to note that the third question, on the cash-only sales, was not part of the demands levelled by Western interests. This indicates that at least one, and possibly several, members of the Committee were looking into the possibility of abolishing the credit system.

Gallatin agreed with these reformers and responded by proposing the abolition of the credit system. He noted that the debts which landowners owed to the United States government would create difficulties for debt collection. But Gallatin's primary concern regarding land debts was political in nature. He argued that the 'daily increase' in federal land debts 'may ultimately create an interest hostile to the general welfare of the Union'.[143] He thus proposed to limit credit to forty days after land sales. As the abolition of credit would make it difficult for poor people to afford large payments, Gallatin proposed to moderately lower the minimum price of lands while similarly reducing the size of lands for sale.

Gallatin cautioned against a sharp reduction of minimum land prices, as such a measure would promote migration 'beyond its natural and necessary progress' and could throw Western lands into the hands of a few unscrupulous land speculators.[144] A modest reduction of land prices, however, would satisfy the demand for land by ordinary Americans 'without promoting migrations or speculations on a large scale'.[145] Gallatin also proposed to sell lands in half (320 acres) and quarter sections (160 acres), instead of sections (640 acres) and half sections (320 acres) as under the Land Act of 1800. He also suggested reducing land prices to $1.25 and $1.50 per acre for half and quarter sections of lands respectively. Gallatin hoped that the moderate changes he proposed would generate increased revenue. He stated that 'it would be easier to sell three hundred thousand acres at a dollar and a third, than two hundred thousand acres at two dollars an acre'.

Because of his interest in using land sales as a source of revenue, Gallatin was opposed to granting pre-emption rights to squatters. He stated that his recommendations would allow large portions of the actual settlers to become purchasers. But the right of pre-emption, Gallatin remarked, 'exclusively of the abuses to which it is liable, appears irreconcilable with the idea of drawing revenue from the sale of land'.[146]

Gallatin's proposed changes to the land system were guided by his primary goal, to raise federal revenue. He therefore opposed pre-emption, but was willing to lower land prices to satisfy the demands of actual and perspective settlers. Gallatin was therefore willing to stimulate western settlement as long as land reform did not undermine the revenue potential of land sales.[147]

Nicholson's Committee reported a series of resolutions to the House on 23 January 1804, incorporating all of Gallatin's ideas.[148] But in its final form the Land Act of 1804 differed from the Committee's resolutions in one important aspect – it carried over the credit system from the Land Act of 1800. To be sure, the act contained significant improvements over its predecessor. It allowed all public lands to be sold in units as small as 160 acres, half of the minimum tract allowed in the Land Act of 1800. Now a farmer could start his or her farm with just $80. The act also exempted the interest accrued on instalments. With such a provision, public land prices fell from $1.84 per acre to $1.64 in cash. Overall, the bill closely followed Gallatin's objectives: a modest reduction of minimum land prices, and sales of smaller land parcels. But compared to the continuation of the credit system, these changes were insignificant.

Why did Congress ignore Gallatin's advice to abolish the credit system? Many Western settlers and speculators opposed the end of the credit system. Debt increases from land sales frustrated the Secretary of the Treasury and some members of the House of Representatives, but ambitious farmers and speculators did not share such a perspective. As long as they were able to acquire large parcels of land with credit, they remained unconcerned about the long-term implications of so much debt. Westerners hoped that their debts could be somehow paid off or forgiven over time. But farmers were not entirely to blame for their predicament. Congress still saw Western land mainly as a source of revenue. On 22 March 1806, John Randolph, from the Ways and Means Committee, commented that 'the public lands form a great and increasing source of revenue'.[149] This was the attitude that dominated in Congress until 1820 and lingered for years afterward.[150]

This attitude can be corroborated by noting that the government reduced minimum land prices only slightly in the Land Act of 1804. The minimum cash price for land dropped from $1.84 in the Land Act of 1800 to $1.64, a discount of only $0.20 per acre. The minimum price remained at that level until the Land Act of 1820. This was a very high price compared to the minimum land prices set by individual states, like Kentucky, Massachusetts, Connecticut or Virginia. For example, between 1783 and 1821, Massachusetts sold nearly 5 million acres of lands at about $0.17 an acre.[151] In 1809, Jeremiah Morrow, the Chairman of the House Committee on Public Lands, stated that '[i]t is believed that the price of the lands of the United States is considerably higher than that at which the States have sold their vacant lands'.[152]

Jeffersonians and Cultural Improvements

Unlike land policies, the Jeffersonians failed to develop a comprehensive policy for promoting cultural improvements. Originally, Jefferson and Madison articulated a desire to culturally improve the nation. Jefferson in his second inaugural address stated: 'that redemption [of national debt] once effected the revenue thereby liberated may ... be applied ... to rivers, canals, roads, arts, manufactures, education, and other great objects'.[153] In his sixth annual message on 2 December 1806, he again urged 'application [of expected surplus revenue] to the great purposes of the public education, roads, rivers, canals, and such other objects of public improvement as it may be thought proper to add to the constitutional enumeration of Federal powers'. He boldly stated, 'By these operations new channels of communications will be opened between the States, the lines of separation will disappear, their interests will be identified, and their union cemented by new and indissoluble ties.'[154] He explained:

Education is here placed among the articles of public care, not that it would be proposed to take its ordinary branches out of the hands of private enterprise, which manages so much better all the concerns to which it is equal, but a public institution can alone supply those sciences which though rarely called for are yet necessary to complete the circle, all the parts of which contribute to the improvement of the country and some of them to its preservation.[155]

Here Jefferson reiterated Washington's rationale for creating a national university. Moreover, Jefferson even suggested a specific method to establish such an institution, by asking the Congress to donate public lands to start a national educational institution.[156] Jefferson's interest in cultural improvement led him to patronize various intellectuals and engineers including Dr William Thornton, Benjamin Latrobe, Dupont de Nemours and Joel Barlow. Particularly, Barlow wrote a detailed plan for a national university at the urging of Jefferson, which Senator George Logan introduced to the Senate in 1806. Nevertheless, Congress showed no interest in the project. Thomas Jefferson lamented such 'narrow and niggardly views of ignorance' in his letter to Barlow a year later.[157] President Madison also supported the idea of a national university. In his second annual message on 5 December 1810, Madison stated, 'a well-constituted seminary in the center of the nation is recommended by the consideration that the additional instruction emanating from it would contribute not less to strengthen the foundations than to adorn the structure of our free and happy system of government'.[158]

Ultimately, Presidents Jefferson and Madison failed to implement such plans during their tenures because of the complicated international problems posed by the Embargo and War of 1812, which drained the resources and energies of the country.[159] Thus between 1810 and 1815, Madison's annual messages were silent on the cultural development of the country. It was not until Madison's seventh annual message on 5 December 1815, at the end of the War of 1812, that an American president revisited the establishment of a national university. At this time, the proposal became even more specific with the suggested university to be located in Washington DC.[160] Madison repeated the same call, in vain, in his following year's annual message as well.[161] So from Washington to Madison, American presidents expressed a repeated desire to establish a national university to spread knowledge and, more importantly, to increase national feeling among their fellow citizens. This was, not surprisingly, the same goal articulated by supporters of the American System, who, in the aftermath of the War of 1812, were beginning to organize their disparate ideas into a comprehensive political agenda.

2 THE GROWTH OF THE AMERICAN SYSTEM AND ITS CHALLENGES, 1815–24

The period from 1815 to 1824 saw the growth of the American System as both a political programme and a statement of American cultural nationalism. At the same time, however, a serious challenge to the American System also emerged as sectionalism increased in the wake of the Missouri Crisis from 1819 to 1821.

Post-War Nationalism and the 'Madisonian Platform'

Following the War of 1812, conditions in American society proved ripe for developing the idea of the American System. The successful conclusion of the war enhanced nationalistic feeling among Americans and increased their confidence in the potential of the new republic. Gallatin commented in a letter of 7 May 1816,

> [t]he war has renewed and reinstated the national feelings and character which the Revolution had given, and which were daily lessened. The people have now more general objects of attachment with which their pride and political opinions are connected. They are more Americans; they feel and act as a nation.[1]

President Madison stated in his annual message on 5 December 1815 that 'the nation [United States] finds itself possessed of a growing respect abroad and of a just confidence in itself'.[2]

Such nationalistic fervour caused many Americans to reflect on the recent war in which they had suffered from, among many things, the lack of a uniform national currency, and deficient roads and canals to mobilize the United States military. On the other hand, manufacturing grew rapidly during this period when foreign manufactured goods were prohibited because of the Embargo and British blockades. Americans in 1815 were thus more receptive to the establishment of another national bank, federally funded roads and canals, and protective tariffs than they had been previously. Capitalizing on such popular sentiment, James Madison, previously one of the most eloquent opponents of federal intervention in the economy, now came out in favour of protectionism. In his seventh annual and first post-war message to Congress on 5 December 1815 he proposed the incorporation of a national bank to restore 'uniform national currency' and 'public patronage [protective tariff]' for manufactures, which were necessary, not only for national defence, but also for American agriculture. Additionally, Madison voiced support for the construction of roads and canals under federal authority, which would have the political effect of 'binding more closely together the various parts' of the country.[3] In addition, Madison suggested the creation of a 'national seminary of learning within the District of Columbia'.[4] This plan, which historians would later call the 'Madisonian Platform'[5] was a succinct articulation of the goals and means of a political programme that would later evolve into the American System. However, he indicated that constitutional amendments might be necessary to initiate such a programme, stating that 'it is a happy reflection that any defect of constitutional authority which may be encountered can be supplied in a mode which the Constitution itself has providently pointed out'.[6]

Post-War Protectionism

Despite its rapid growth during the war, the American manufacturing industry faced a crisis at the onset of peace in 1815. Massive imports of British manufactured products, which had been denied entry into the American market since the Embargo, flooded the United States and hurt American manufactures by depressing the prices of manufactured goods.[7] In 1813 and 1814, American merchants imported $22 million and $13 million worth of goods respectively. In 1815 and 1816, imports rose to $85 million and $151 million.[8] In addition, post-war prosperity combined with an overextension of bank credits by state banks and the 2BUS inflated prices for raw materials, wages and rent, thereby increasing the costs of production for domestic manufactories. Domestic manufacturers quickly petitioned Congress to pass protective tariffs. Cotton merchants in Providence, Rhode Island petitioned Congress for protection on 22 December 1815.[9]

Following an outpouring of such petitions, Congress responded with the Protective Tariff Act of 27 April 1816. In the spirit of the President's message, Treasury Secretary A. J. Dallas proposed a sharp increase in tariff rates as part of a new tariff bill he proposed to Congress on 12 February 1816. This bill aimed at increasing the average tariff rate to 33 per cent, much higher than the minimum protective level of 25 per cent.[10]

However, a close analysis of the bill shows that protectionism was still not a dominant motive in the mind of its author. To start, Dallas candidly admitted that his main justification for the proposal was the need to raise revenue. In his financial report to Congress on 8 December 1815, Dallas stated that it was necessary to raise an additional $5 million in revenue to offset an expected financial deficit.[11] To raise the additional funds, Dallas wanted 'a competent addition to the permanent rates of the duties on merchandise imported'.[12] Yet the need to protect domestic industries was also a growing secondary concern for Dallas. While arguing for an increase in tariff rates, Dallas simultaneously proposed repealing all internal duties on domestically manufactured goods to help through 'the exoneration of domestic manufactures from every charge that can obstruct or retard their progress'.[13] In other words, Dallas's objective was to relieve domestic manufactures of the burden of internal duties, while making up the revenue loss by increased duties on imported goods.

Congressional debates on the bill also indicated a growing awareness in the minds of political leaders on the need to protect American industries as well as raise revenue. When Dallas's bill came to the House, William Lowndes of South Carolina and his Committee on Ways and Means approved of the protective principle, but reduced the rates suggested in Dallas's report.[14] Lowndes's committee wanted to raise the necessary revenue and provide moderate protection, without hurting the agrarian-based economy of his own home region. The committee therefore insisted on levelling average tariff duties of 25 per cent, the minimum level needed to protect domestic manufactures. Importers of cotton and woollen goods were to pay a 25 per cent import tax, which would be reduced to 20 per cent after three years, just long enough to replenish the depleted national treasury. The Tariff Bill of 1816 was thus a compromise between protective principles and a need to raise money.

Politicians drew upon post-war nationalism to promote protectionism with the stated goal of creating a home market that would make the United States economically and politically stronger in years to come. A Republican Representative from Pennsylvania, Samuel D. Ingham, declared in a speech on 22 March 1816 that 'the great principle involved in this bill was not a revenue proposition'. Rather, he stated, the 'primary object' was 'to make such a modification of duties upon the various articles of importation, as would give the necessary and proper protection and support to the agriculture, manufacture, and commerce of the country'. The revenue was thus only 'an incidental consideration'. Ingham asked, 'is it not most obviously the policy of the Government to insure to its agriculture the advantage of a home market, that cannot be affected by the caprice and vexatious impositions of foreign nations?'[15]

The logic of a 'home market' proved a very effective argument for protectionism. First, the home market argument could appeal to both manufacturing and agricultural interests, because agricultural interests would consider domestic manufactures as their home market. On the other hand, the 'infant industry' argument appealed only to manufacturing interests without suggesting benefits to agricultural interests. Second, the argument could demand a permanent, rather than a temporary, system of tariffs as a policy measure. Third, by depicting the creation of a home market as an exercise in nationalism, advocates of protectionism could appeal to post-war nationalism in a way that would transcend economic calculations. Ultimately the argument for a 'home market' rested upon the belief that the various sectional interests of the country could and should be united. In other words, proponents of protective tariffs sought to politically strengthen the bonds of union through the economic means of a home market. As historian Henry Carter Adams stated over a century ago, protective tariffs as part of the American System were 'a subordinate part of a prominent and strong political purpose' of throwing off completely 'the yoke of colonial dependence'.[16] This idea had far-reaching political implications. Proponents of a home market assumed that sectional differences could be reconciled. They also reasoned that sectional conflicts over economic policies were temporary and could be overcome in time. But increasing sectionalism eventually made this assumption precarious.

At least in 1816, however, the South was in a mood to support the protective principle. Not only did Chairman William Lowndes of South Carolina support the Tariff Bill of 1816, but John C. Calhoun, the future firebrand of Southern sectionalism, also defended the bill. With his eyes set firmly on future presidential elections, Calhoun reasoned that domestic manufactures were critically important to prepare the country for a possible war. In a House debate on 4 April 1816, Calhoun asserted that 'the subject before them was connected with the security of the country'.[17] Calhoun, like many other Americans at that time, considered another war with a foreign country, especially with Britain, very possible. As such, he agreed with the principles of a domestic market. He stated:

> Neither agriculture, manufactures, nor commerce taken separately, is the cause of wealth; it flows from the three combined, and cannot exist without each. The wealth of any single nation, or any individual, it is true, may not immediately depend on the three, but such wealth always presupposes their existence ... Without commerce, industry would have no stimulus; without manufactures, it would be without means of production; and without agriculture neither of the others can subsist. When separated entirely and permanently, they perish.[18]

Ultimately he argued that a protective tariff was necessary for a stronger national union, stating that 'it [the protection of domestic manufactures] is calculated to bind together more closely our widely spread Republic. It will greatly increase our mutual dependence and intercourse'.[19] Even Clay could not have better articulated the principles of the American System.

The bill passed the House on 8 April 1816 by a wide margin of eighty-eight to fifty-four. Support for the measure increased in the Senate, where the tariff bill passed by a more lopsided vote of twenty-five to seven on 19 April 1816. The decisive results of the votes were an indication of the strength of protectionist sentiment throughout the country.[20] Even Southern delegates, who would later turn solidly against protective tariffs, added votes to help pass the bill. In the House, the South voted seventeen to thirty-three against the bill. In the Senate, however, the South voted seven to three for the bill.

Table 2.1. Roll Call Analysis on the Tariff Act of 1816.

	Senate		House	
	Yeas	Nays	Yeas	Nays
New England	6	2	17	10
Mid-Atlantic	8	2	44	10
Northwest	4	–	10	1
South Atlantic	3	3	14	30
Southwest	4	–	3	3
Total	25	7	88	54

Source: *Senate Journal*, 14th Cong., 1st sess. (19 April 1816), p. 505; *House Journal*, 14th Cong., 1st sess. (23 January 1816), pp. 610–12.

As historian Norris W. Preyer pointed out, some Southern delegates supported the bill because of the prosperous economic condition of the country, the expected danger of another war with Britain and, ultimately, post-war nationalism.[21] There is a great deal of logic in these arguments. The post-war American economy had, after all, experienced an unprecedented burst of prosperity. American exports had dropped sharply during the War of 1812 from $61 million in 1811 to $39 million in 1812, $28 million in 1813 and $7 million in 1814. The figures bounced back to $53 million in 1815, reached $82 million in 1816, rose to $88 million in 1817 and then finally peaked at $93 million in 1818.[22]

As Calhoun's speech indicated, political elites supported protective tariffs throughout the 1810s based on a combination of economic jubilation and diplomatic fear of yet another war with Great Britain. In a letter to Benjamin Austin on 9 January 1816, Jefferson made the famous comment that '[w]e must now place the manufacturer by the side of the agriculturalist.'[23] He explained away his disparaging remarks against manufactures in his *Notes on the State of Virginia*, by arguing that 'experience has taught me that manufactures are now as necessary to our independence as to our comfort.'[24] In this sense, Jefferson, the standard bearer for states rights and agrarian interests in the 1790s now aligned himself with the idea of the American System.

The Incorporation of the 2BUS

Feelings of nationalism following the War of 1812 also provided impetus for the creation of a second national bank. Taking a cue from President Madison, Congress quickly reversed its position and incorporated another national bank on almost identical principles as those of the 1BUS in 1816.[25] The authorized capital of the 2BUS was even raised to $35 million, compared to $10 million of the 1BUS.[26] Currency problems provided much of the immediate justification for the establishment of the 2BUS. In his annual message of 5 December 1815, President James Madison explained the need of a national bank: '[i]t is ... essential to every modification of the finances, that the benefits of an uniform national currency should be restored to the community ... If the operation of the State banks cannot produce the result, the probable operation of a national bank will merit consideration.'[27] Secretary of Treasury A. J. Dallas concurred in his annual report to the Senate that '[i]t is a fact ... incontestably proved, that those institutions [state banks] cannot, at this time, be successfully employed to furnish a uniform national currency.'[28] On the contrary, Dallas argued, '[a] national bank will ... possess the means and the opportunity of supplying a circulating medium, of equal use and value in every State, and in every district of every State.'[29] Thus he proposed the establishment of a national bank.

Historical evidence supports Dallas's arguments. In the last year of its existence, the 1BUS issued fewer bank notes than the amount of specie in its vault, while state banks issued bank notes by more than double the amount of their specie holdings.

Table 2.2. Percentage of Specie to Notes for First BUS and State Banks, 1 January 1811.

	Specie ($)	Notes ($)	Specie to Notes
1BUS	5,800,000	5,400,000	107%
State Banks	9,600,000	22,700,000	42%

Source: 'Considerations on the Currency and Banking System of the United States', 1 January 1831, *The Writings of Albert Gallatin*, ed. H. Adams, 3 vols (New York: Antiquarian Press Ltd., 1960, original publication 1879), vol. 3, pp. 286, 291, 296.

Thus, the national bank provided the basis for a much sounder currency. In addition, both the first and second national banks were able to restrain the state banks' overtrading.[30] The following is a good example of the restraining effect of a national bank over state banks:

Table 2.3. Notes Issued by BUS and State Banks, in Dollars, 1811–29.

	1811	1816	1820	1829
1 and 2 BUS	5,400,000	–	4,221,770	13,048,984
State Banks	22,700,000	68,000,000	40,641,574	48,274,914
Total	28,100,000	68,000,000	44,863,344	61,323,898

Source: Gallatin, 'Considerations on the Currency and Banking System of the United States', 1 January 1831, *The Writings of Albert Gallatin*, vol. 3, pp. 286, 291, 296. Data for 1811, 1816 and 1820 is from 1 January; data for 1829 is from the end of that year.

Unrestrained by a national bank, state banks had from 1811 to 1816 sharply increased their supply of notes, from $22.7 million to $68 million. This in turn caused the suspension of specie payments by state banks during the War of 1812. The re-imposition of control by the 2BUS after 1816 resulted in a reduction of $40,641,574 in state banknotes issued in 1820. During a ten year period between 1819 and 1829, state banks increased their total note issues by less than $8 million.

By imposing strict currency controls, the 2BUS created a sound and uniform currency throughout the nation. A comparison of the currency prices in several cities in 1816 and 1829 conspicuously revealed the fact that the 2BUS had created a sound and uniform national currency.

Table 2.4. Comparison of Domestic Bank Note Exchange Rates, 1816–29.

Source of Notes	Boston 1816	Boston 1829	New York 1816	New York 1829	Philadelphia 1816	Philadelphia 1829
Boston	–	–	7½ – 8 dis	¼ dis-par	17–18 dis	¼ dis-par
New York	7 adv	par	–	–	–	par
Philadelphia	17 adv	par	9½ adv	par	–	–

Source: The first column represents the price of banknotes on 1 July 1816 and the second column the price of such notes on 5 December 1829. This table is only a part of a more comprehensive comparison of the prices of bank notes from many banks in two time periods, which can be found in 'Report of Committee, 1830', 13 April 1830, *Legislative and Documentary History of the Bank of the United States Including the Original Bank of North America*, eds. M. St. C. Clarke and D. A. Hall, (1852: 1st repr., New York: Augustus M. Kelley Publishers, 1967, original publication, 1832), pp. 762–3.

In 1816, Boston bank notes were traded at 7 or 17 per cent advances over par (100 per cent of the face value) because New England banks had not suspended specie payments. Other banknotes were discounted by various percentages in other cities. In 1829, banknote prices were either at par or very slightly discounted throughout the country. It was as sound and uniform a currency as possible in those days, and the 2BUS played a critical role in creating this system.

Dallas presented a detailed plan for a national bank in an 8 January 1816 letter to John C. Calhoun, the incoming chair of the House Select Committee on National Currency.[31] Calhoun's committee consisted of Nathaniel Macon of North Carolina, James Pleasants and Henry St George Tucker of Virginia, Thomas Bolling Robertson of Louisiana, Joseph Hopkinson of Pennsylvania and Timothy Pickering of Massachusetts. The Committee had already 'determined that a National Bank is the most certain means of restoring to the nation a specie circulation'. Despite the dominance of Southerners, the committee approved the establishment of a national bank. The bank issue was not, at least at this time, a sectional issue. Dallas proposed the bank to be capitalized at $35 million with a possible increase to $50 million based upon the bank's initial performance. He proposed that the President of the United States appoint five of the twenty-five directors of the board. To justify such a concentration of federal authority, Dallas stated that the national bank should not be regarded as merely a privately-owned commercial bank because it was funded with federal deposits as well as private stocks. Thus, Dallas concluded, 'it is not an institution created for the purposes of commerce and profit alone, but much more for the purposes of national policy, as an auxiliary in the exercise of some of the highest powers of the Government'. He also proposed to ask for a gift of $1.5 million from bank stockholders as a fee for a federal charter. Eventually this request became the basis of the Bonus Bill of 1817, which was intended to create a fund for internal improvements.

Calhoun presented a bank bill to the House which included every suggestion posed by Dallas on 8 January 1816.[32] During the ensuing debates in Congress, the currency problem dominated the discussion. Bank proponents used the problem to justify the establishment of a national bank. Calhoun, in his speech in the House on 26 February 1816, said, '[w]e have, in lieu of gold and silver, a paper medium, unequally but generally depreciated.'[33] The cause of this depreciation was the excessive issuing of paper money, which had in turn eventually led to a suspension of specie payments, argued Calhoun. The solution would be to establish a national bank, which would have a 'tendency to make specie payments general, as well by its influence as by its example'.[34]

Economic problems wrought by currency devaluation undercut enough public opposition to the bank bill to allow its passage. Even Clay, a key player in denying the recharter of the 1BUS in 1811 changed his constitutional view of a national bank. He defended his apostasy by stating that: '[t]he constitution ... never changes ... but the force of circumstances, and the lights of experience, may evolve to the fallible persons ... the fitness and necessity of a particular exercise of constructive power to-day, which they did not see at a former period.'[35] John Randolph lamented the 'apathy, the listlessness [of debates] on this subject [among the Congressmen]'.[36] The House passed the bill by a margin of eighty to seventy-one on 14 March 1816. Such a close vote suggested that the 'apathy' witnessed by Randolph, may have represented a stoic front put forward by legislators unwilling to publicly oppose the bank bill, yet still willing to silently cast votes against the measure. Only the clear recognition that something must be done to address the currency crisis persuaded enough Representatives to vote for the bill. The debates in the Senate were even less eventful. As in the House, the reference to the currency disorder was enough to silence any opposition.[37] The Senate passed the bill by the decisive vote of twenty-two to twelve.

Table 2.5. Vote Analysis on the 1816 Bank Bill.

	Senate		House	
	Yeas	Nays	Yeas	Nays
New England	5	4	13	21
Mid-Atlantic	5	5	26	27
Northwest	3	1	7	6
South Atlantic	5	2	30	16
Southwest	4	–	4	1
Total	22	12	80	71

Source: *Senate Journal*, 14th Cong., 1st sess. (3 April 1816), pp. 385–6; *House Journal*, 14th Cong., 1st sess. (12 March 1816), pp. 466–8.

In terms of sectional attitudes to the bank, there was no distinct correlation between the region representatives came from and their votes for or against the bank. The only section that showed any significant opposition was New England. Its Representatives voted thirteen to twenty-one against the bank. Its Senators, however, voted five to four for the bill. Because New England's banks did not suspend their specie payments during the war the currency issue was less salient to their voters. All other sections either supported the bank bill, or at least evenly divided their votes between yeas and nays. Interestingly, the South cast nine to two votes in the Senate and thirty-four to seventeen votes in the House for the bill. Overall the bank enjoyed widespread support throughout the country, particularly the South. The consensus on the need to bring some sort of stability to the currency helped protect the bank from politically motivated attacks.

The Defeat of the Bonus Bill of 1817

Although post-war nationalism had proved crucial in creating the protective Tariff Act of 1816 and establishing the 2BUS, such sentiment proved insufficient to launch a system of internal improvements. Echoing Madison's call for a national plan for internal improvement, Clay recommended a programme of internal improvements in his House speech on 29 January 1816, saying '[h]e desired to see a chain of turnpike roads and canals from Passamaquoddy to New Orleans, and other similar roads intersecting the mountains'.[38] To provide support for such an ambitious programme, Calhoun turned to the tried and true technique of beating war drums. He warned Congress about the possibility of war with either Spain or Great Britain,[39] even predicting that 'future wars with England are not only possible, but ... they are highly probable – nay, that they will certainly take place'. Calhoun then argued that '[w]e ought to contribute as much as possible to the formation of good military roads ... to enable us on emergencies to collect the whole mass of our military means on the point menaced.'[40]

For once, however, Calhoun and his supporters miscalculated the reaction of ordinary Americans to their political goals. Rather than rallying to support a comprehensive programme of internal improvements, a variety of opponents unleashed a volley of constitutional and political arguments against Calhoun's suggestion. The first casualty of this conflict was the defeat of the Bonus Bill. In 1816 the newly created 2BUS offered $1.5 million to the federal government as the bonus for its charter. On 16 December 1816, Calhoun moved in the House to set up a committee 'to inquire into the expediency of setting apart the bonus, and the net annual proceeds of the National Bank, as a permanent fund for internal improvement'.[41] A week later, his committee forwarded a bill to authorize a permanent fund to construct roads and canals to be paid for by the dividends of the federal government's subscription to the stocks of the BUS combined with the $1.5 million bonus.[42]

Up until this time, the focus of the internal improvement debate had centred primarily on the economic interests of specific states or regions. For example, opposition to the construction of the Cumberland Road revolved around the alleged partiality of the road's economic benefits to Maryland and the West over the interests of Pennsylvania and Virginia. John Randolph, who would later invoke constitutional and political objections against federally funded internal improvements, was no exception. On 11 January 1817, Randolph spoke in the House to oppose a proposal to consider surveys along the Tennessee, Coosa and Tombigbee Rivers. Randolph pointed out that such projects would benefit only Western states. As *Annals of Congress* recorded:

> [h]e [Randolph] saw ... with surprise and regret, the course the Government had taken and was taking. He did not refer to any Constitutional difficulties whatever; but he saw distinctively that the old United States, particularly that State [of Virginia] to which the Government owed almost all its territory east of the Mississippi and west of the Ohio, was not to be benefited by any expenditure in respect to canals and roads, except such benefit as that State would contingently receive by the [National] road from Fort Cumberland passing through a part of the State ... He could not see why all the benefits of an expense, equally borne by all, were to endure entirely to the Western States and Territories.[43]

However, starting with the Bonus Bill, the constitutional issue emerged as the centre of political discourses on internal improvements. On 4 February 1817, Calhoun invoked economic growth and military necessity in strenuously urging his colleagues to support passage of the Bonus Bill. But the main thrust of Calhoun's argument involved an appeal to nationalism, reasoning that the size of the country raised risks of '*disunion*'. To prevent such a catastrophe the country should be bound 'together with a perfect system of roads and canals. Let us conquer space'.[44]

In essence, Calhoun's speech amounted to a call to tie the country into a single political entity in substance if not in form. He also brushed away constitutional scruples over federal support for internal improvements. Calhoun said that '[h]e was no advocate for refined arguments on the Constitution. The instrument was not intended as a thesis for the logician to exercise his ingenuity on. It ought to be construed with plain, good sense.'[45] Calhoun's strong nationalistic appeal for the bill invited intense rebuttals from Southern Congressmen. Philip P. Barbour of Virginia made a frontal attack on the constitutionality of the bill in the House. He began by acknowledging the usefulness of internal improvements,[46] but quickly added that 'he should feel himself constrained to vote against the bill, upon the ground, that it embraced objects not within the sphere of the Constitutional powers of Congress'.[47]

Senator Nathaniel Macon of North Carolina agreed that the authority to pass the bill seemed to derive from political and legal precedents rather than the Constitution. However, argued Macon, he did not agree that precedents could be the rule in the interpreting of the Constitution; otherwise, the Constitution could be altered at will without going through the amendment process.[48] Both Barbour's and Macon's comments foreshadowed both the decline in nationalist sentiment and the rise of constitutional arguments which would in future years dominate the controversy surrounding internal improvements.

The constitutional concern was the main reason for President Madison's veto of the bill on 3 March 1817. In this veto message, Madison expressed his approval for federal internal improvements on policy grounds. He noted 'I am not unaware of the great importance of roads and canals and the improved navigation of water courses, and that a power in the National Legislature to provide for them might be exercised with signal advantage to the general prosperity'. But he also expressed his disapproval of federally supported internal improvements on constitutional grounds, writing that '[b]ut seeing that such a power is not expressly given by the Constitution, and believing that it cannot be deduced from any part of it ... I have no option but to withhold my signature from it.'[49] Madison's veto was another indication that the issue of internal improvements was becoming a constitutional rather than a strictly economic issue. In fact, the debate over internal improvements had by 1817 produced the first sustained constitutional opposition to the very idea of the American System.[50]

Calhoun's 1819 Report on Internal Improvements

During James Monroe's presidency, the National Republicans sought to create a federal programme of internal improvements in one form or another. John C. Calhoun's 1819 report on roads and canals was an example of these efforts. Calhoun prepared the report in response to a request from the House for the Secretaries of War and the Treasury to report on constitutional ways for the federal government to support internal improvements. Although Secretary of the Treasury William H. Crawford failed to produce a report, Secretary of War Calhoun leapt at the chance to expound on a topic he found so important.[51] Calhoun's report was based on a broad construction of federal authority. He began with an innocuous example, that of public roads. He argued that it is impossible to distinguish between commercial, mail and military roads, pointing out that

> [a] judicious system of roads and canals, constructed for the convenience of commerce, and the transportation of the mail only, without any reference to military operations, is itself among the most efficient means for the more complete defence of the United States.

For, explained Calhoun, such a system of commercial and mail roads would greatly improve the country's resources in war 'by consolidating our Union, and increasing our wealth and fiscal capacity'.[52] By pointing out the intrinsic relationship between military, postal and commercial roads, Calhoun subtly advocated roads of 'all' purposes.

After having intermingled private and public interests in supporting internal improvements, Calhoun then laid out a cautious plan to construct roads and canals, which he claimed would be used to defend the three frontiers of the United States: 1) the eastern or Atlantic frontier; 2) the northern or Canadian frontier, and 3) the southern or the frontier of the Gulf of Mexico.[53] Calhoun did not recommend the immediate construction of canals and roads, rather he suggested a survey to serve as the '*basis*' for an eventual system of internal improvements by determining exact expenses and routes.[54] Drawing a lesson from the defeat of his Bonus Bill, Calhoun thus approached the issue cautiously. He also showed prudence in attempting to bypass the constitutional question on internal improvements; he wrote

> I have thought it improper, under the resolution of the House, to discuss the constitutional question ... the whole of the arguments which are used, and the means proposed, must be considered as depending on the decision of that [Constitutional] question [by the Congress.][55]

Calhoun chose a guarded approach to the constitutional question in deference to the known views of President Monroe and to avoid antagonizing more states'-rights-oriented members of the House.

But Calhoun's subtle approach could not hide the essentially aggressive nature of his report. His advocacy of the economic, political and military benefits of internal improvements, and his previous record of supporting such projects, indicated that he cared little for the constitutional orthodoxy of either his current superiors or former colleagues in the House. Moreover, his treatment of the constitutional issue was subtly, but significantly, different from the way Gallatin had discussed the matter in his report on internal improvement of 1808. In that report, Gallatin wrote '[i]t is evident that the United States cannot, under the constitution, open any road or canal, without the consent of the State through which such road or canal must pass.'[56] For Gallatin, state consent was a necessary prerequisite for giving federal support for internal improvements. On the other hand, Calhoun left the decision entirely to Congress, implying that such determinations could be made 'without' the consent of states. The specific words in Calhoun's report may sound cautious, but the overall impression of the report amounts to a strong defence for a federal programme of internal improvements.

The House failed to follow up Calhoun's report with any action. Economic difficulties spurred by the Panic of 1819 turned Congressional attention elsewhere.[57] The national treasury recorded deficits of $400,000 and $1.3 million in 1820 and 1821 respectively, which made it impossible for the government to substantially fund internal improvement projects.[58] But Calhoun's report contributed significantly to the cause of internal improvements by offering the scheme of a general survey, which eventually resulted in the passage of the General Survey Act of 1824. Calhoun's 1819 report on internal improvements was his last expression of nationalism. He would gradually and irreversibly turn into a state's-rights-advocate afterwards. This was a popular decision to make for a South Carolinian, for the Missouri Crisis of 1819-1821 shattered the post-war nationalism in the state.

The Missouri Crisis, 1819–21 and the Decline of Post-War Consensus

The crises that ensued over the admission of Missouri as a state in 1819 illuminated the trials and tribulations that brewed and simmered for forty years before boiling over into the Civil War. At the heart of the controversy lay the festering dilemma of coping with a nation founded on the espoused principles of freedom and equality yet all the while maintaining and expanding slavery. When the Missouri territory applied for statehood in 1819, Representative James Tallmadge Jr of New York proposed an amendment to the Missouri Enabling Act on 13

February 1819 for the gradual abolition of slavery in Missouri. Those born into slavery after statehood were to be freed upon reaching the age of twenty-five.

Eli Whitney's invention of the cotton gin in 1793 made it possible to profitably grow short-staple cotton in the lower South. The almost insatiable demand for American cotton in British factories accelerated the westward expansion of slave-based cotton plantations alongside a correspondingly dramatic increase in the slave population. In 1800, the Southern states combined had about 700,000 slaves. The number reached 1.25 million in 1820, and passed 2 million in 1840. Southwestern states experienced a much faster increase of slave population than South Atlantic states, as the Southwest became the centre of cotton production and utilized an increasingly large number of slavers.

Tallmadge's bill was met with great hostility from white Southerners who resented outside intervention in their peculiar institution. The rise of the fer-

Table 2.6. Slave Population in Southern States, 1800–60, in thousands.

	1800	1810	1820	1830	1840	1850	1860
South Atlantic	684	863	1,038	1,249	1,303	1,534	1,686
Southwest	17	97	229	436	800	1,137	1,480
Total	701	960	1,267	1,685	2,103	2,671	3,166

Source: R. Sutch and S. B. Carter (eds), *Historical Statistics of the United States: Earliest Times to the Present, Millennial Edition*, 5 vols (New York: Cambridge University Press, 2006), 2:375–7.

Figure 2.1. Slave Population Growth, 1800–60.

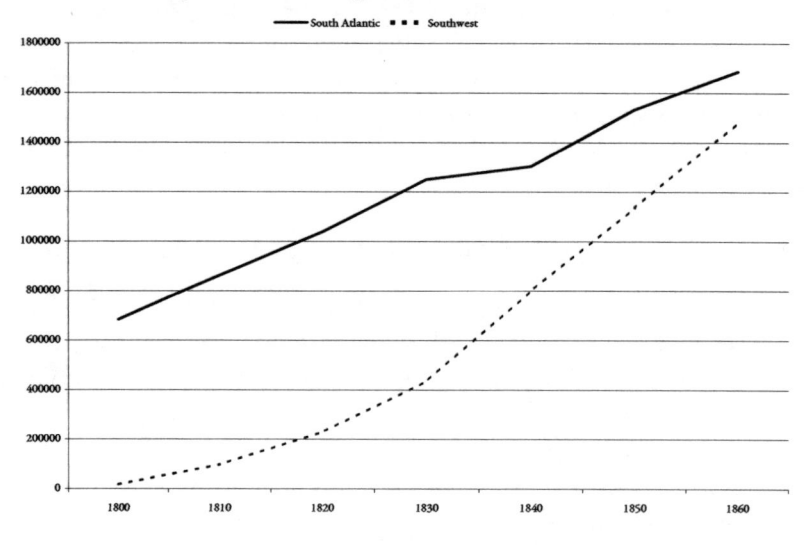

tile Southwest not only opened up new cotton farms and plantations but also a market in which South Atlantic slave owners could sell off their extra slaves as a source of additional income. This came at an important time, when the overused soil of the South Atlantic states was yielding increasingly smaller tobacco profits. Planters also feared racial tensions might arise if large numbers of slaves were freed.[59] In addition, if Congress ended slavery in new states and territories, it could move in time to eradicate the institution throughout the nation.

In this context, slave owners stressed the danger of a broad construction of the 'necessary and proper' clause of the Constitution that might be construed to give the federal government the power to pass laws regulating slavery within states.[60] Also at stake was the balance of political power in Congress. The three-fifths clause of the United States Constitution granted Southern states extra representation, enabling slave states to secure seventeen additional House seats in 1819.[61] Yet the balance of political power in the Senate was even more important.[62] For if control of the House eventually fell to the fast-growing Northern population, then Southern Senators could bottleneck any threatening bills and check abolitionist proposals only when slave states maintained at least parity with Northern states.

Tallmadge's proposal illustrated the threat facing the Southern status quo as events unfolded. The House passed the Missouri Enabling Act, including the Tallmadge amendment, by an eighty-two to seventy-eight vote, with eighty yeas coming from Northern Representatives and sixty-four nays from Southerners. However, the bill was defeated in the Senate by a twenty-two to sixteen vote with five Northern Senators siding with the solid Southern opposition.[63]

Eventually this deadlock was broken by the Missouri Compromise of 1820. Another region seeking entrance into the union as a state in 1819 was the Massachusetts district of Maine. Maine's admission was quickly linked to the entrance of Missouri. By allowing both states to enter the union at the same time the Senate balance would be maintained. In addition, another compromise limited the northern boundary of slavery in the remaining Louisiana Purchase territories. Illinois Senator Jessie Thomas proposed a compromise deal that declared all territories above Missouri's southern border to be free and all land below that point open to slavery.[64] The nation thus averted a political crisis over slavery.

However, the political struggle over the Missouri Compromise affected the future tone of Southern politics, pushing the South into a more determined defence of slavery. For example, in the 1822 Congressional election, 70 per cent of the congressmen from the South Atlantic states who had opposed the Thomas Proviso returned to the next Congress, while only 39 per cent of those who had supported the proviso were re-elected.[65] Thus, the slavery issue came to occupy Southern politics front and centre, and eventually dominated national politics, seriously jeopardizing the future of the American System. The constitutional doctrine of broad construction undergirding the policies of the American System was considered potentially threatening to slavery. Thus constitutional issues and the American System became intertwined even more tightly. One example of this trend was President James Monroe's veto of the Toll Gate Bill in 1822.

The Panic of 1819 and the 2BUS

While the Panic of 1819 made the idea of a domestic market more favourable to Western farmers, it made banks in general and the 2BUS in particular more unpopular. From 1816 to 1819, the 2BUS, along with other banks, lavished credit in the West and Southwest to profit from the speculative boom. When the Panic hit the country, banks rapidly reduced the total volume of loans to save themselves. This resulted in bankruptcies for many, who in turn blamed banks for their difficulty. The 2BUS did not escape this criticism. Jefferson explained the causes of such hostility towards the 2BUS.

> The operation of the United States Bank for the demolition of the State banks obliged these suddenly to call in more than half their paper, crushed all fictitious and doubtful capital, and reduced the prices of property and produce suddenly to one-third of what they had been.[66]

Criticism towards the 2BUS was most loudly heard in the West and South.[67] Several indications of criticism towards the bank were the resolutions introduced in the House on 19 January 1819 by David Trimble of Kentucky and on 9 February 1819 by James Johnson of Virginia, demanding the repeal of the bank's charter.[68] The House, however, rejected both resolutions decisively by a vote of thirty-nine to 116 (Trimble's resolution) and by a vote of thirty to 121 (Johnson's resolution) on 25 February 1819.[69] The House's decisive willingness to maintain the bank's charter indicates that its members still believed in the necessity of a national bank. But the undercurrent of antagonistic feelings against the bank provided fuel to sustain Andrew Jackson's attacks on the bank during the Bank War.

The Land Act of 1820

One of the reasons that the 2BUS and state banks increased loans after 1816 was strong demand for credit for land purchases. Post-war prosperity lured more and more people to purchase public lands. The federal government met such demand by facilitating public land sales. The Land Act of 22 February 1817 reduced the minimum size of land sales from quarter sections (160 acres) to half quarter sections (eighty acres) but did not reduce minimum land prices further.[70] By the act of 1817, a farmer could now buy a lot with an initial payment of just $40, while the same individual would have needed a minimum of $160 in 1800 and $80 in 1804. In passing a new land act the federal government sought to balance two goals. It tried to lure people to the West by making it easier to buy land while carrying out its main goal of raising revenue. The growing public interest in western settlement was reflected in the Land Act of 1820.[71]

The 1820 act sought to reform the national land system by the abolition of the credit system. But attempts to end the credit system faced stiff opposition from Western interests, which saw it as central to facilitating their desire to acquire land. Under the act of 1817, once a Western farmer paid his initial fee of $40 he then had to pay another $40 instalment within two years. The credit system thus seemed to enable even the poorest farmers to own their own farms. When the purchasers could not meet their obligations, they then pressured Congress to extend the due dates for credit.

Niles' Weekly Register explained the details of the situation. According to the journal, men purchased lands beyond their means. If they could not sell the extra land before the second payment became due, the settlers would pressure Congress to pass special acts to postpone the periods of the contracts. *Niles' Weekly Register* charged that 'this has been done so often that it seems only necessary to ask for an extension of credit and receive it – which is, in a fact, to offer a bounty to *speculation*'.[72] Congress passed thirteen relief acts between 1806 and 1820, and eleven more between 1821 and 1832.[73] This legislation gave farmers additional reasons to be speculative in their behaviour and appreciative of the credit system.

Congress also had an interest in maintaining the credit system. The system made it possible to charge higher minimum prices and sell larger lots than would otherwise be available. Thus, even though six Congressional Committees from 1804 to 1819 recommended the abolition of the credit system, Congress did not heed their recommendations.[74] Congress's desire for revenue and the speculative zeal of the American people conspired to keep the credit system afloat.

Maintaining the credit system resulted in further speculation in land. This increased dramatically after the War of 1812 as this was when British factory demand for American cotton created a subsequent desire for more available land on the frontier.[75] Land speculation was most severe in 1818 and 1819, especially in Alabama, Mississippi and Illinois.[76] Land sales passed the annual one million acre mark in 1814 and remained above that level until 1819. What was most striking was the dramatic increase of land prices claimed at public auctions – people paid unbelievably high prices for land. Federal government's land office at Huntsville, Alabama sold lands for over $30 per acre in 1818.[77] In 1820, Senator John W. Walker of Alabama stated that he had known land purchases as high as $78 per acre.[78]

The explosive sale of lands in terms of higher prices and increases of acres resulted in a large amount of debt. As of 31 December 1819, the total balance from individuals stood at a staggering $22 million.[79] About half of this debt was accumulated during the period of 1818–19. In 1820, Secretary of Treasury William H. Crawford stated that '[d]uring the excessive circulation of bank notes not convertible into specie ... and the high price which every description of domestic produce commanded, large quantities of public lands were sold at public auction at prices greatly beyond their real value.'[80] A Western newspaper explained the situation as follows: '[c]apitalists, both real and fictitious, have engaged very extensively in this business [of land speculation]. The banks have conspired with the government to promote it; the former by leading money to the speculators, and the latter by its wretched system of selling the lands on credit.'[81]

The Panic of 1819 finally prompted Congress to abolish the credit system. The accelerated land speculation before 1819 was based on public expectations that high post-war agricultural prices would continue. But the Panic of 1819 brought down those rosy expectations. According to then-Secretary of Treasury William H. Crawford, in early 1819, the price of Western produce fell so low that it created the 'most serious distress at the moment, and excited alarming apprehensions for the future'.[82] Because of these 'alarming apprehensions for the future', Western farmers demanded a restructuring of the land system. The *St Louis Enquirer* wrote that 'the government debtors become too numerous and too powerful to be controlled by the government'.[83] Edward Tiffin, the Surveyor General Northwest of the Ohio, wrote to Josiah Meigs, Commissioner of the General Land Office, that 'I much fear a Spirit of disaffection &&& [*sic*] towards the general government is arising in the West sufficient to alarm its fast friends and certainly requires vigilance in watching its Offenders among us'. In addition, 'it is enough to admonish the government to make no more Debtors, but change the system of disposing of the public lands'.[84]

As a result of these concerns, Congress abolished the credit system in the Land Act of 24 May 1820. As Treasury Secretary Crawford noted, the most prominent consideration in the abolition of the credit system was 'the necessity of preventing the further increase of a debt, then about $22,000,000, strongly affecting the interests and feelings of a great number of citizens'.[85] As a corollary to the elimination of this system, the government reduced minimum land prices from $2 per acre to $1.25.[86] The size of minimum land tracts was also reduced to half quarter sections (eighty acres) from quarter sections (160 acres) for all federal lands.[87] Now farmers would have to scrape together only $100 to afford an eighty-acre farm.

Congress hoped that by repealing the credit system it could secure revenue safely, while settling the West gradually. Congressional debates clearly reveal this conclusion. The initiative for the Land Act of 1820 began in the Senate.

On 20 December 1819, Walter Leake of Mississippi (Republican) introduced a resolution to the Committee on Public Lands to inquire into the expediency of dividing lands into half quarter sections and ending the credit system.[88] Thomas H. Williams of Mississippi (Republican), the Chairman of the Senate Committee on Public Lands, reported a bill on 11 January 1820.[89] The bill incorporated Leake's recommendations. The ensuing struggle centred on a sectional conflict between Northeastern and Western Senators, rather than along party lines. Northern Senators, led by Rufus King of New York (Federalist), tried to end the credit system that had embarrassed the national government so much. Western members were divided between those who wanted to keep the credit system and those who wanted to abolish it. Most Senators from South Atlantic states remained aloof during the debates. But it was noticeable that Nathaniel Macon of North Carolina sided with diehard Federalists like King of New York and Harrison Gray Otis of Massachusetts. Eastern states, including South Atlantic, opposed a credit system that enabled farmers to purchase Western lands too easily, thus inducing them to migrate west.[90] The bill passed the Senate by thirty-one to seven on 9 March 1820.[91] Out of the seven negatives, six came from the Northwest and the Southwest.

Table 2.7. Vote Analysis on the Land Act of 1820.

	Senate		House	
New England	10	–	33	1
Mid-Atlantic	7	–	56	3
Northwest	3	4	9	7
South Atlantic	5	1	33	6
Southwest	6	2	2	6
Total	31	7	133	23

Source: *Senate Journal*, 16th Cong., 1st sess. (9 March 1820), p. 223; *House Journal*, 16th Cong., 1st sess. (20 April 1820), pp. 436–7.

The Senate debates over the Land Act of 1820 illustrate that Western politicians pursued two objectives regarding the West. They considered the land not so much as the property of the United States government, to be sold at will, but as a common resource for all, to be 'distributed'. Western members thus wanted to use the land to attract settlement as expeditiously as possible. The problem of debts, for them, was no more than a technical matter. It could and should be easily overcome by the generosity of the federal government in the form of relief acts or outright cancellation. On the other hand, Northeastern politicians saw public lands as a revenue source that should be carefully guarded. They also did not want to depopulate the Northeast.

These two different conceptions of the role of public lands in the development and expansion of the country were repeated more forcefully and eloquently in the House debates over the Bill. In the House, a combined force of the Northeast and some Westerners supported the bill, while other Western representatives strenuously opposed the proposal. Representatives from South Atlantic states were as lukewarm during the debates as their counterparts were in the Senate. But it is also noteworthy that Philip P. Barbour of Virginia sided with Henry R. Storrs of New York, a Federalist, against Western Republicans. As in the Senate, House Republicans voted on the issue of credit abolition based on their sectional interests.[92] The House passed the bill by the overwhelming vote of one hundred thirty-three to twenty-three.[93] About half of the votes against the bill came from the Northwest. All sections, including the Southwest, overwhelmingly voted for the bill. Only the Northwest remained divided almost evenly on the bill. Overall, the consensus was that the country needed a new land act.

The Land Act of 1820 was a compromise over the disparate objectives of revenue and settlement. The foremost objective of the Land Act of 1820 was to abolish the credit system and thus eliminate debts from land purchases and avoid political danger. To realize this objective through the Land Act of 1820, however, Congress made concessions to the West by lowering minimum land prices and promising relief acts.[94] These concessions were to appease the West whose objective in land policies was settlement, not revenue. This explains the final passage of the Land Act of 1820 by a large margin.

James Monroe's Administration and the Failure of the Tariff Bill of 1820

Despite the protective intent of the Tariff Act of 1816's promoters, the result of the act was a mixed one, failing to protect domestic manufactures. First of all, the act itself could be considered as much a revenue act as a protective measure. The bill reduced the average rates from 33 per cent, as suggested by Dallas, to 25 per cent. Considering that 25 per cent was deemed the maximum rate for a revenue tariff, one could argue that the Tariff Act of 1816 was on the borderline between a protective and a revenue tariff. Not only were most of the rates lower than those recommended by Dallas, but the protection was not to be permanent. For instance, the 25 per cent duties on cotton and woollen goods mandated by the tariff were to last only two years, after which the rates would be reduced to 20 per cent.[95]

In this sense, one could argue that the bill was more a revenue act to help retire the huge debts accumulated during the War of 1812 than a protective measure. In fact, Representative Henry Baldwin (Federalist), the Chairman of the House Committee on Manufactures, said on the floor of the House on 21 April 1820 that the act of 1816 was 'a revenue bill ... more to aid the Treasury than to protect the industry of the country'.[96] Thus the act of 1816 was not protective enough to stem constant influxes of British manufactured goods. President Madison, in his eighth annual message to Congress, delivered on 3 December 1816, expressed regret that domestic manufactures had suffered a 'depression' due to an 'excess of imported merchandise'.[97] The Pennsylvania Senate echoed these sentiments, stating early in 1817 that 'in all parts of the country our manufactures are rapidly declining and sinking under a foreign combination and forced importation, and the unwillingness of the government to protect and uphold them'.[98]

After becoming President in 1817, James Monroe tried to redress this problem. Monroe was an Old Republican who emphasized states' rights over federal power. Like his predecessors, however, he also acknowledged the necessity of protection. In his first inaugural address, he asserted, '[o]ur manufactures will ... require the systematic and fostering care of the Government.'[99] He defended his positions via the arguments of war preparation and home market:

> [w]hile we are thus dependent the sudden event of war, unsought and unexpected, can not fail to plunge us into the most serious difficulties ... Equally important is it to provide at home a market for our raw materials, as by extending the competition it will enhance the price and protect the cultivator against the casualties incident to foreign markets.[100]

But Monroe's protective spirit was not implemented until the Protective Tariff Act of 1824.

There was, however, a serious attempt to implement protection through the failed Tariff Bill of 1820. The Panic of 1819 helped the notion of protection become popular not only with manufacturers but with farmers as well. The panic hit the American economy hard. In Philadelphia, workers lost manufacturing jobs in great numbers. The cotton industry employed 2,325 hands in 1816, but by 1819, that number had dropped to 149. Woollen manufactures witnessed a decline in workers from 1,226 in 1816 to 260 in 1819. Iron-casting jobs likewise fell from 1,152 in 1816 to fifty-two in 1819.[101] In Pittsburgh, total employment dropped from 1,960 in 1815 to 672 in 1819. Local manufactured goods also decreased in value from $2.6 million in 1815 to $832,000 in 1819. In addition, farmers suffered plunging prices for foodstuffs. The price of flour in Philadelphia was $14.75 per barrel in March 1817. By March 1821 it had dropped to $3.62.[102] Many farmers, rightly or wrongly, concluded that dependence on foreign manufactured products and the lack of a home market for agricultural produce had caused the panic. As a result, public support for protective tariffs increased among farmers. The main items that they demanded protection for were cotton, woollen and wrought-iron goods.[103]

The popularity of the protective cause strengthened pro-protection forces in Congress. When the Sixteenth Congress convened in December 1819, Henry

Clay retained his position as Speaker of the House. Congress showed signs of genuinely supporting permanent protective tariffs. House members established a new standing committee, the Committee on Manufactures, and selected Federalist Congressman Henry Baldwin of Pennsylvania as its chairman.[104] Baldwin was well known as a protectionist. In fact, the principle issue in his election had been the protective tariff. Clay packed the committee exclusively with friends of protectionism.[105] The committee recommended an increase of tariff rates on practically all articles. For example, the duties on basic items such as cottons and woollens were to increase from 25 to 33 per cent; clothing, hats, caps and ready-made bonnets, from 30 to 44 per cent; iron in bars and bolts, from $.75 to $1.25 per hundredweight, and hemp, from $1.50 to $2.50 per hundredweight. Duties on almost all other articles were to be increased as well.[106]

During the ensuing debates over the Tariff Bill of 1820, sectional divisions appeared prominently. In general, Northern congressmen defended the bill, while Southerners opposed it. New England Federalists remained divided. In contrast, mid-Atlantic states like Pennsylvania and Maryland solidly supported the bill.[107] On 21 April 1820, Congress opened the debate with Baldwin's report of the bill to the Committee of the Whole. The main defence of the bill lay in arguments for national defence and independence.[108]

Opposition to the bill mainly focused on whether it would affect the federal treasury and/or upset various economic interests throughout the country. For example, John Tyler, a Jeffersonian Representative from Virginia, attacked the bill in a lengthy speech by arguing that rather than offering a home market for farmers, protective duties would operate merely as 'a direct tax on them [farmers]' by increasing the prices of necessities. In conclusion, the bill would 'diminish the value of our land; it will shut us out from the foreign market; it cannot substitute a home market ... and ... it subjects us to a heavy burden of taxation'.[109]

The bill passed the House by a vote of ninety-one to seventy-eight on 29 April 1820. However, the Senate postponed debate on the measure until the next session by a twenty-two to twenty-one vote on 4 May 1820. What was noticeable was the strong hostility to protective tariffs displayed by the South. In the House, the Southwest and South Atlantic solidly voted three to fifty-one against the bill. In the Senate all fourteen members from the delegation save one voted yea on the motion to postpone the bill.

Representative William Lowndes of South Carolina, who had prepared and supported the Tariff Act of 1816, voted against the Tariff Bill of 1820. His action symbolized the changes wrought in Southern political circles over a four-year period. Representatives Philip P. Barbour and William McCoy of Virginia, and Felix Walker of North Carolina also reversed their positions between 1816

Table 2.8. Roll Call Analysis on the Tariff Bill of 1820.

	Senate*		House	
	Yeas	Nays	Yeas	Nays
New England	4	6	18	17
Mid-Atlantic	1	8	58	8
Northwest	2	6	12	4
South Atlantic	8	–	3	42
Southwest	7	1	–	7
Total	22	21	91	78

Source: *Senate Journal*, 16th Cong., 1st sess. (4 May 1820), p. 376; *House Journal*, 16th Cong. 1st sess, (29 April 1820), pp. 466–8.
*NB: The Senate vote was on the motion to postpone the bill.

and 1820, as did Senator James Brown of Louisiana, suggesting that sectionalism was trumping nationalism in the South.

Southern legislators had supported the Tariff Act of 1816 out of fears over the perceived possibility of war, the desire for economic prosperity and, most importantly, post-war nationalism. But the first of these factors evaporated by 1820 as another war with Britain seemed unlikely. In January 1820, John Quincy Adams, the Secretary of State, informed President Monroe that 'in our foreign relations, we stood upon terms with England as favorable as can ever be expected'.[110] Economic prosperity likewise disappeared with the Panic of 1819.[111] Finally, the Missouri Crisis increased Southern sectional unity over the slavery issue.[112]

Although the opponents of protection successfully stifled the tariff bill of 1820, supporters of the American System could still look to the future with optimism. Northern political power, which favored protectionism, was already overwhelming the House in 1820. The South barely defeated the bill in the Senate by a single vote. After the census of 1820, the Northern states increased their representation in the House by twenty (from 126 to 146), compared to the addition of only seven delegates (from sixty to sixty-seven).

Table 2.9. Representatives under Each Apportionment.

	2nd Census 1800	3rd Census 1810	4th Census 1820	5th Census 1830
New England	35	41	39	38
Mid-Atlantic	51	67	76	83
Northwest	7	18	31	45
South Atlantic	46	51	51	52
Southwest	3	9	16	24
Total	142	186	213	242

Source: *Biographical Directory of the American Congress 1774–1961* (Washington DC: United States Government Printing Office, 1961), p. 45.

Toll Gate Bill of 1822

The cause of internal improvements suffered another defeat when President Monroe vetoed a bill to erect tollgates on the Cumberland Road on 4 May 1822. In 1818, the Cumberland Road reached Wheeling, Virginia. Yet heavy travel by settlers moving westward eroded much of its eastern expanse.[113] On 29 April 1822, the House, by a vote of eighty-seven to eighty-six, passed a bill to erect toll gates on the Cumberland Road. Four days later, the Senate affirmed the measure by a twenty-nine to seven vote.[114]

President Monroe vetoed this bill the next day.[115] His short veto message and his much longer exposition on the issue of internal improvements entitled 'Views of the President of the United States on the Subject of Internal Improvements', Monroe made it clear that the main reason for his veto was his 'conviction that Congress do[es] not possess the power, under the Constitution, to pass such a law'.[116] He reasoned:

> [a] power to establish turnpikes with gates and tolls, and to enforce the collection of tolls by penalties, implies a power to adopt and execute a complete system of internal improvement ... A right to legislate for one of these purposes is a right to legislate for the others. It is a complete right of jurisdiction and sovereignty for all the purposes of internal improvement, and not merely the right of applying money under the power vested in Congress to make appropriations, under which power, with the consent of the States through which this road passes, the work was originally commenced, and has been so far executed. I am of opinion that Congress does not possess this power; that the States individually can not grant it, for although they may assent to the appropriation money within their limits for such purposes, they can grant no power of jurisdiction or sovereignty by special compacts with the United States. This power can be granted only by an amendment to the Constitution and in the mode prescribed by it.[117]

Monroe's veto carried a complex constitutional theory. Monroe argued that Congress's appropriation power included the ability to appropriate for the construction of roads such as the Cumberland Road. On the other hand, the power to erect tollgates was a separate power that did not fall under Congress's constitutional power to 'appropriate'. Monroe gave a more detailed analysis of the difference between these two powers in the long document: 'Views of the President of the United States on the Subject of Internal Improvement', which accompanied his veto message.[118]

The fact that Monroe's veto message and his 'Views' dwelt so much on the constitutional arguments surrounding internal improvements rather than policy issues revealed how serious the legal debate over federal support of such projects had become over the past two decades.[119] When Thomas Jefferson had signed the original Cumberland Road bill into law neither he nor his congressional allies had paid much attention to the constitutionality of their actions. As Madison later recalled, 'the question of constitutionality [of the bill] was but slightly if at all examined by [Congress]' and that Jefferson's 'assent was doubtingly or hastily given'.[120] But by 1822, the constitutional issue had become central and a serious obstacle to implementing such projects, because opponents of national internal improvement programmes, particularly the South, took the implications of its constitutional issues on slavery much more seriously than previously.

Survey Bill of 1824

The debate over the constitutionality of internal improvements resurfaced during the Congressional debates over the General Survey Bill of 1824 and helped make the American System a definitely sectional issue. In 1824, Congress passed and President Monroe approved a bill appropriating $30,000 for a general survey of road and canal routes. The debates over the bill reflected not only the constitutional significance of internal improvements but also the emergence of uncompromising Southern sectionalism against such projects.

On 2 December 1823, Congress authorized the US Corps of Engineers to examine possible canal routes to connect the Chesapeake with Ohio River and in turn the Ohio with Lake Erie. Monroe also requested that Congress authorize the Executive to negotiate with the states, through which the Cumberland Road passed, to establish tolls to defray repair expenses.[121] Following Monroe's suggestion, Joseph Hemphill of Pennsylvania (Federalist), chair of the Committee on Roads and Canals, nominate a bill entitled proposed an 'act to procure the necessary surveys and estimates on the subject of roads and canals' on 15 December 1823.[122] As a 'preparatory step', Hemphill argued that the President should employ both the Corps of Engineers and civilian engineers to survey possible canal routes.[123]

This was a new strategy. Mindful of the strong constitutional opposition to internal improvements, Hemphill chose a piecemeal approach. Instead of demanding millions of dollars for a system of internal improvements, which Gallatin's Report had called for, they chose to follow Calhoun's suggestion of demanding a smaller appropriation for a survey.

This strategy illustrates the persistence and ingenuity of American System proponents. When the Bonus Bill of 1817 failed, they did not give up their overall goal. Rather, they proposed a smaller project of surveys instead. But what is important is that both the larger Bonus Bill project and the much smaller general survey were in fact based on the same constitutional principle, namely that the federal government wielded sufficient authority to sponsor internal improvements.

Understanding this underlying issue in the bill, Representative Philip P. Barbour of Virginia, a consistent opponent of internal improvements, moved to strike out the enacting clause, arguing that 'the sense of the House might first be obtained on the general principles involved in the bill, before any thing should be determined as to its details'.[124] Henry Clay repeated Barbour's call, however, with another motive.[125] Clay tried to use the debates on the General Survey Bill of 1824 to portray himself as a champion of internal improvements, with his eye towards the Presidential election of 1824.

On 13 January 1824, Barbour gave a relatively short but forceful speech against the General Survey Bill. Barbour began by arguing that 'all powers which had relation to matters of internal regulation, all that might be denominated municipal powers [,] were reserved to the States'.[126] Commissioning internal improvements was a municipal power that belonged to the state governments.[127] It was a nicely reasoned syllogism, but it was based on the premise that 'all' municipal powers were within the jurisdiction of states' rights.

Barbour claimed that constitutional objections were not the only reason for the South's opposition. He also mentioned the fact that internal improvements favoured some regions, primarily the West, over others.[128] Clay countered by pointing out that some powers, like taxation and the ability to establish post offices and post roads, were still municipal yet unquestioningly belonged to the federal government. After countering Barbour's constitutional interpretation, Clay continued to expound on the Constitution to prove that Congress had power over internal improvements. This power could be inferred from the right of Congress to 'establish' post offices and post roads. He argued the meaning of 'establish' was 'to fix, to make firm, to build'. Thus Congress had the power to 'construct' roads. Regarding canals, Clay reasoned that the authority to open them stemmed from Congress's power to 'regulate commerce' with foreign nations and among the several states. If canal construction was unconstitutional, then so were federally funded buoys, beacons and lighthouses. Every House member knew, as well as Clay, that Congress had never objected to the erection of buoys, beacons and lighthouses, which had been built mainly for commercial purposes.

But the real thrust of Clay's speech lay in its defence of the bill via an appeal to nationalism. He stated: '[b]ut, sir, the bill on your table is no Western bill. It is emphatically a national bill, comprehending all, looking to the interests of the whole'. Clayed warned that 'if they [federal programme of internal improvement] be withheld from such objects, the Union ... may ... be endangered and shaken at its centre'. He was countering Barbour's claim that internal improvements were parochial in their benefits.[129] All in all, the clash between Barbour and Clay represented the clashes between strict and broad interpretations of the constitution – economic sectionalism and an appeal to forceful nationalism.

John Randolph added another important element to the debates: the implication of the internal improvements issue on slavery. Randolph made a speech on 30 January 1824 arguing that '[i]f Congress possesses the power to do what is proposed by this bill ... they may emancipate every slave in the United States.'[130] His point was that federally supported internal improvements might create a precedent for Congress to meddle with slavery as well. As early as 1818, Nathaniel Macon of North Carolina, a good friend of Randolph, wrote '[i]f Congress can make canals they can with more propriety emancipate [the slaves] ... Your error in this will destroy our beloved mother, North Carolina, and all the South Country.'[131] But while Macon used the private medium of a letter, Randolph was the first to publicly point out on the floor of Congress the danger the American System might pose to slavery. However, Randolph had never argued against the constitutionality of federally funded internal improvements or suggested a connection between slavery and internal improvement prior to 1824. The heightened sectional feeling since the Missouri Crisis of 1819-21 prompted Randolph to associate the issue of internal improvements with the issue of slavery.

Clay responded that Congress should not be restricted in its ability to interpret the Constitution based upon the conditions under which the document had been originally written:

> [a]re the narrow limited necessities of the old thirteen States, of indeed parts only of the old thirteen States, as they existed at the formation of the present Constitution, forever to remain a rule of its interpretation? Are we to forget the wants of our country? Are we to neglect and refuse the redemption of that vast wilderness which once stretched unbroken beyond the Allegheny? I trust not, sir. I hope for better and nobler things.[132]

Clay also stated that the expanded size of the United States demanded the extraction of 'every dormant power' in the Constitution. In essence, Clay argued that the Constitution was an organic document, which should be interpreted depending on changing circumstances.[133] Such logic could be used to expand federal power indefinitely, because one could simply argue that new power was necessary to accommodate changing situations.

Randolph and Clay were in fact projecting two different visions of national development, offering two different perceptions of federal power. Clay's vision of the country included the settlement of the West with the help of an energetic general government. On the other hand, Randolph sought to protect the old notion of the American union with the original balance of power agreed to in the Constitutional Convention. If the energy of the general government was a dreadful danger to Randolph, it was a blessing to Clay. In this sense, two different visions of the future clashed over the issue of internal improvements. On one side was the vision of a country restrained by the original agreement, while the other side envisioned a much more expansive and dynamic country with a variety of industries. After the eloquent speeches of Randolph and Clay, other members of the House tried in vain to emulate them. Western members eagerly defended the bill, while the South, especially Virginia delegates, was most vocal in their opposition.[134] The House finally passed the bill on 11 February 1824 by a margin of 115 to eighty-six.[135] Senate debates also showed the same sectional pattern of support and opposition.[136] The Senate passed the bill on 24 April 1824 by the vote of twenty-four to eighteen.[137] New England states opposed the bill, while mid-Atlantic States were, overall, in favour of the bill except for New York – whose delegates voted against the bill by a vote of seven to twenty-four in the House and zero to two in the Senate.[138] As they had already built superior systems of roads and canals by themselves, these states were not inclined to support national expenditures for other states. All Northwestern and Southwestern Representatives and Senators, except one, voted for the bill. Compared with the votes on the Bonus Bill of 1817, the South Atlantic States were more organized in their opposition to the Survey Bill of 1824. This reflected the growing sectionalism of the region. Interestingly, however, South Carolina voted one to one in the Senate and five to four in the House. After all, the idea of a general survey was the brainchild of John C. Calhoun, a famous native son. As far as internal improvements were concerned, the state of South Carolina in general, and Calhoun in particular, were not completely sectional in 1824. As late as 3 July 1824, Calhoun wrote that 'I think, it cannot be doubted that ... the power exists in Congress to appropriate money for internal improvements.'[139] Adams commented on the constitutional views of Calhoun during Monroe's administration as follows: 'Calhoun has no petty scruples about constructive powers and State rights'.[140] George McDuffie of South Carolina, who Adams called 'Calhoun's friend, protégé, and partisan',[141] gave a brilliant speech in the House to support the survey bill. It was Virginia and North Carolina that led opposition to nationalistic economic programmes until 1824. What is interesting is that then-Senator Andrew Jackson of Tennessee voted for the Survey Act of 1824.

Table 2.10. Votes on the Bonus Bill and Survey Bill by Region.

| | Bonus Bill of 1817 |||| Survey Bill of 1824 ||||
| | Senate || House || Senate || House ||
	Yeas	Nays	Yeas	Nays	Yeas	Nays	Yeas	Nays
New England	1	9	5	34	2	9	12	26
Mid-Atlantic	9	1	47	17	6	4	45	26
Northwest	6	–	10	5	9	–	28	–
South Atlantic	4	4	23	24	1	7	15	34
Southwest	2	2	1	4	7	1	15	–
Total	22	16	86	84	25	21	115	86

Source: D. Feller, *The Public Lands in Jacksonian Politics* (Madison, WI: University of Wisconsin, 1984), pp. 52, 61.

Tariff Act of 1824

The appearance of sectional politics evidenced in the fights over the Survey Bill of 1824 was more pronounced over the Tariff Bill of 1824. The Act signalled the return of the protective principle which had been building in power since its defeat in 1820. In 1824, protectionism had support from both the executive and legislative branches of the federal government. In his annual messages of 1822 and 1823, President Monroe recommended increasing tariff duties. He also suggested a review of existing tariff legislation with the intention of making it more protective.[142] Henry Clay was chosen as the Speaker of the House when the 18th Congress met in December of 1823. Representative John Todd, a protectionist from Pennsylvania, presided over the Committee on Manufactures.[143] In his report to the House on 19 March 1824, Stephen Van Rensselaer of New York, Chair of the House Committee on Agriculture, wrote that '[y]our committee consider [sic] the increase of duties on many foreign articles now imported into the United States would promote the agricultural prosperity of the nation.'[144] Van Rensselaer continued that '[t]he home market ... is at all times to be preferred to the foreign market ... it would seem wise and prudent to promote its [home market's] extension by every rational means within the sphere of legislation.'[145] The fact that the chairperson of the Committee on Agriculture supported protectionism indicated the strength of the home market argument.

On 9 January 1824, Todd delivered a report from the Committee on Manufactures, recommending increased duties on cotton and woollen goods, as well as raw wool, iron, hemp, flax and molasses.[146] As the federal treasury showed revenue surpluses of more than $5 million each in 1822 and 1823, the current bill was entirely protective in purpose.[147] Todd admitted up front that even if the new tariff bill cost revenue, 'that would be no reason against increasing the real wealth of the country by protecting domestic industry'.[148]

The New England states opposed the bill. Although Massachusetts was turning to manufactures, Boston financiers, shippers and merchants did not yet wholeheartedly embrace protectionism. They objected most strenuously to the proposed increase on iron, hemp and flax, which would increase shipbuilding costs, and the duties on molasses, which New Englanders distilled into rum for sale in the West Indies.[149] Federalist Daniel Webster from Boston argued ably against the bill, saying that he was willing to support a moderate but not a prohibitive protective tariff.[150]

The strongest opposition to the bill, however, came primarily from the South. What was alarming was the constitutional dimensions the debates over a protective tariff took. Until the Tariff Bill of 1820, Congressmen and Senators had focused on the economic and financial expediency of tariffs. However, in 1824 James Hamilton Jr and George McDuffie of South Carolina, and Philip P.

Barbour of Virginia argued against the bill on constitutional grounds.[151] In particular, Barbour argued that Congress's power of taxation could only be used to raise revenue. If Congress passed a tariff bill to encourage manufactures, Barbour continued, it transcended the limits of its legitimate authority.[152]

Defenders of the 1824 Tariff Bill were thus forced to develop their own constitutional counterarguments. It was Henry Clay who saved the Tariff Bill of 1824 before the onslaught of Southern opponents. Clay had several motives to strongly promote domestic manufactures. Protection was a popular cause in the West, especially in his state of Kentucky. By 1810, Kentucky, Ohio and western Tennessee were establishing sizable cotton-mills, wool-mills, iron furnaces and distilleries. Ohio produced about $2 million worth of goods, and western Tennessee $1.5 million. Kentucky led the Western states in manufacturing: the first in the number of powder mills, second in salt production, third in distilleries, fourth in the number of cotton and woollen looms in 1810.[153]

In addition, Kentucky was the centre of the hemp industry. Hemp was used for rope and ship sailcloth and as a fabric for bagging cotton.[154] In 1810, Kentucky produced all the cotton bagging in the United States.[155] It was the hemp manufacturers of Lexington, the district Clay represented in the House, who had sent the Congress a memorial in 1811, demanding protection by arguing for the necessity of a home market.[156] Clay himself was a stockholder of a hemp and cotton-spinning mill.[157] He also wanted to use the cause of protection to launch a run for the White House in 1824. The policies of the American System, including the protective tariff, would serve as a springboard for such a campaign.[158] Speaking after Barbour, he argued Congress's power to regulate commerce with foreign nations could form the constitutional basis for a protective tariff.[159] According to Clay, the power was 'plenary, without any limitation whatever, and includes the whole power of regulation, of which the subject to be regulated is susceptible. It is as full and complete a grant of power, as that is to declare war'.[160] But the real thrust of Clay's argument lay in his appeal to nationalism by his use of the term the 'American System'.

Until 1824, early exponents of the American System presented it mostly as a programme to help ensure American independence from European influence, with some potential for commercial independence as well. Clay, however, proposed an effective method of achieving such a goal. It was only after Clay's speech of 1824 that the American System became identified with the protection of domestic manufactures. He stated,

> [a]re we doomed to behold our industry languish and decay yet more and more [because of a restrictive European market]? But there is a remedy, and that remedy consists in modifying our foreign policy, and in adopting a genuine American System. We must naturalize them ... by adequate protection against the otherwise overwhelming influence of foreigners.[161]

If the political objective of the American System was the demand of political independence, the economic objective of the American System was the creation of a domestic market. Clay sought to elevate the home market argument to the level of nationalism, to appeal to a broader segment of the American people. He stated that 'The object of this bill under consideration is to create this home market, and to lay the foundations of a genuine American policy.'[162] In this sense, the idea of the American System was based on nationalism both politically and economically.

The vote on the bill was close, passing in the House, on 16 April 1824, by 107 yeas to 102 nays, and in the Senate by a margin of twenty-five to twenty-one on 13 May 1824. Representatives and Senators from the South voted five to seventy-eight against the bill, while mid-Atlantic and Northwestern delegates stood solidly behind the bill. As over the Survey Bill of 1824, Andrew Jackson cast his vote for the bill.

Table 2.11. Roll Call Analysis on the Tariff Act of 1824.

	Senate Yeas	Senate Nays	House Yeas	House Nays
New England	9	3	15	23
Mid-Atlantic	5	4	60	15
Northwest	9	–	29	–
South Atlantic	–	8	1	50
Southwest	2	6	2	14
Total	25	21	107	102

Source: *Senate Journal*, 18th Cong., 1st sess. (15 May 1824), p. 401; *House Journal*, 18th Cong., 1st sess. (16 April 1824), pp. 428–9.

The Tariff Act of 1824 turned out very protectionist in its final form. Iron, lead, wood, hemp, cotton bagging and textile fabric manufacturers were all protected by increased duties, and the minimum value principle was extended from cotton to woollen goods. Woollen manufacturers, however, found themselves almost in the same position as before. It is true that the duty on woollen imports was increased from 25 to 33.33 per cent. But the duty on raw wool also increased from 15 per cent to 30 per cent, raising its market price. Overall the act broke with the traditional balance between revenue and protection purposes in tariff legislation. The act was purely protective in purpose.

Together, the debates over and the passage of the General Survey Act of 1824 and the Tariff Act of 1824 showed several new developments. First, proponents of the American System now had a complete package of critical elements of their programme: specific policies of protective tariff and federally sponsored internal improvements; assumption of the shared interests of all sections of the union; the goal of the creation of a national domestic market, and a liberal construction of the United States Constitution to back up their policies. Second, support for the idea of the American System proved strong enough to pass both the General Survey Act and Tariff Act. Third, the political behaviour of the South, influenced by the Missouri Crisis, turned more sectional, the Southern delegates using the constitutionality of protective tariffs and federal improvement projects to attack the General Survey and Tariff Bills of 1824.

James Monroe and Cultural Improvements

President Monroe, like his predecessors, was also interested in promoting education. As early as 1801, while Governor of Virginia, Monroe stated the importance of education in a democratic polity in his annual message to the state legislature:

> In a government founded on the sovereignty of the people the education of youth is an object of first importance. In such a government knowledge should be diffused throughout the whole society, and for that purpose the means of acquiring it made not only practicable but easy to every citizen.[163]

Given Monroe's proposed establishment of a state-supported educational system,[164] he saw no problem with state involvement in education. He, along with ex-presidents Jefferson and Madison were members of the Board of Visitors when the University of Virginia opened in the spring 1825.[165] Madison commented in 1822 that learned institutions were 'the best security against crafty and dangerous encroachments on the public liberty.' He continued:

> A popular government, without popular information, or the means of acquiring it, is but a prologue to a farce or a tragedy; or perhaps both. Knowledge will govern ignorance: and a people who mean to be their own governors, must arm themselves with the power which knowledge gives.[166]

It is very clear that from Washington through to Monroe all Presidents shared a basic appreciation of education, which they considered necessary to spread knowledge and ensure democracy.

Thus it was no surprise that Monroe initially advocated establishment of a national university after becoming President. In his first annual message on 2 December 1819, Monroe recommended a constitutional amendment to grant the federal government the right to fund roads and canals.[167] He continued:

> I think proper to suggest also, in case this measure [constitutional amendment] is adopted, that it be recommended to the States to include in the amendment sought a right in Congress to institute likewise seminaries of learning, for the all-important purpose of diffusing knowledge among our fellow-citizens throughout the United States.[168]

However, like the messages of his predecessors, this recommendation also fell on Congressmen's deaf ears. Why wasn't a national university established after so many recommendations? The presence of a large national debt was initially the main problem. Then the Jeffersonian principle of strict construction of the United States Constitution was also a formidable obstacle. All three Jeffersonian presidents considered a constitutional amendment as a prerequisite for establishing such an institution.[169] What complicated the problem were the increasing sectional tensions in post-war politics. Both Presidents Jefferson and Madison urged the Congress to pass a Constitutional amendment several times each. However, Monroe made the appeal only once, in 1817. His annual messages were silent afterwards, reflecting the recognition of the impracticability of such an amendment in the midst of growing sectionalism. However, the last push toward a cultural improvement of the country was well on its way.

3 REFORM MENTALITIES AND IMPLEMENTATION OF THE AMERICAN SYSTEM, 1825–9

The social reform movements of the early republic paralleled and reinforced the philosophical assumptions behind the American System. Encouraged by reform-minded ideas, the concept of the American System helped promote protective tariffs and internal improvements during the administration of President John Quincy Adams. The 2BUS also flourished. However, opposition to the American System also became more intense during this time period, preparing for the eventual downfall of the system after 1829.

Henry Clay, John Quincy Adams and the 'Corrupt Bargain'

John Quincy Adams was elected as the fifth President by a final vote in the House of Representatives in the turbulent presidential election of 1824, despite the fact that he was second both in the popular and Electoral College votes to Andrew Jackson. It was Clay who pulled strings in the House, where he was Speaker, to elect Adams to Presidency. Adams reciprocated by appointing Clay Secretary of State, the traditional stepping stone to Presidency. Their political enemies called this a 'corrupt bargain', a charge that fundamentally crippled the effectiveness of the Adams administration and haunted Clay's future political career.[1]

However, Clay's support for Adams stemmed as much from their mutual political outlook as from the concurrence of their personal ambitions. By 1824, Clay's growing sense of nationalism had shown through in his strenuous support of the General Survey Act and Tariff Act of 1824. Adams, through his career as a diplomat and Secretary of State, came to consider the entire North American continent as the stage on which to play out his political vision by 1824. Adams brilliantly helped create the signing of a Transcontinental Treaty with Spain in 1819, acquiring Florida from Spain and expanding America's western boundaries to the Pacific Ocean.[2] Adams also formulated the Monroe Doctrine in 1823, which declared Central and South America off limits to European control, and a de facto sphere of American influence.[3] So when Adams launched his own administration in 1825, he and Clay shared much of the same grandiose nationalistic vision for the United States, and thus mutually supported the policies of the American System.

The Second Great Awakening, Reform and the American System

Clay and Adams shared not only a common political vision for the country, but also similar beliefs in the improvement of society through human efforts. Thus instead of following traditional patterns of a subsistence- or market-based agrarian economy, supporters of the American System like Adams and Clay sought to diversify the national economy with an emphasis on a domestic market. Through economic means, they also sought to enhance national unity among different sections of the country. As such, their motives were quite similar to those of social reformers who sought through temperance laws, expansion of the suffrage and abolitionism to create a more politically and socially diverse nation.[4]

Underlying the Reform Movements was the Second Great Awakening, an outbreak of religious revivalism that swept across the United States from 1800s to the 1830s. The first wave of revivalism wound through the southwestern frontier of the United States.[5] Later it moved northward, hitting western New York with such force that the region became known as the 'burned-over district', due to the intensity of local religious fervour.[6] Steering away from traditional Calvinist doctrines of predestination, the Second Awakening emphasized individual perfectionism and millennial optimism.[7] The millenialists believed that the Kingdom of God on earth was imminent, and moreover human beings can hasten its coming. Thus the Second Great Awakening promoted social reform as a way to speed up the coming of the millennium.[8]

This breakdown between the sacred and secular worlds was nothing new in American society. In her study of eighteenth century Baptist churches in Virginia, North Carolina, Kentucky and Tennessee, historian Monica Raja convincingly argued that Baptist churches in the Upper South exercised authority both in religious and secular matters including marriage, slavery and commerce. They therefore exercised authorities over parishioners not merely in church but also in their 'neighbourhoods, business places, courthouses, and homes'. Ultimately Baptist churches tried to create 'pure covenanted communities that could guide members to live God's commands and that could shine as beacons to unbelievers.'[9]

The case of Charles G. Finney succinctly exemplifies the close connection between the Second Great Awakening and Reform Movements in the early nineteenth century. Born in western New York in 1792, Finney gave up a legal apprenticeship to become a Presbyterian minister. He later became a prominent abolitionist, distinguished professor and president of Oberlin College. He argued that human beings can contribute to God's plan by voluntarily submitting to divine authority. Thus he stated that '[a]ll Holiness ... must be voluntary.'[10] He devoted considerable time and energy to condemning what he saw as the scourge of humanity, slavery. His idea was called 'Christian perfection', an attempt to improve Christians' conduct and purify their lives.[11] The social implications of this rational theology to society were obvious: humans had the power to actively improve society. As a Mississippi politician John Quitman stated in July 1831 on a visit to New York State:

> Among the masses in the Northern States, every other feeling is now swallowed up by a religious enthusiasm which is pervading the country ... I have found preachers holding three, four, six, and eight days' meeting, provoking revivals, and begging contributions for ... the negroes, ... temperance societies, societies for the education of pious young men, religious libraries, etc., etc.[12]

Reformers thus saw it as a sacred duty to end slavery, improve prisons, poorhouses and sanatoriums, promote temperance and empower women.[13] As author John L. Thomas pointed out the reformers believed that '[a]s the sum of individual sins social wrong would disappear when enough people had been converted and rededicated to right conduct.' They assumed that 'when a sufficient number of individual Americans had seen the light, they would automatically solve the country's social problems.'[14]

The religious zeal that spurred the Second Great Awakening also provided a psychological drive that allowed ordinary Americans to risk physical, emotional and financial sacrifices, even risk their own lives, to pursue their goals. Abolitionists such as William Lloyd Garrison and Lydia Child often risked their lives when speaking before hostile crowds. Susan B. Anthony practically dedicated her life to the cause of women's rights. When asked why she never married, she would respond 'when I am crowned with all the rights, privileges, and immunities of a citizen, I may give some consideration to this social institution; but until then I must concentrate all of my energies on the enfranchisement of my own sex.'[15]

The emphasis on social perfection that characterized the Second Great Awakening also fuelled nationalist sentiment among many Americans. As historian John L. Brooke pointed out, 'the national conventions and assemblies of the Presbyterian, Baptist, Methodist, and Episcopal churches stood among the very few truly national structures linking [American] people.'[16] Although reformers were more influential in northern states, certain reform-minded movements such as the Bible Society were disproportionally powerful in southern states.[17]

Proponents of the American System shared many of the same beliefs as social reformers. Those that favoured internal improvements were determined to pursue their policies despite strenuous opposition, and believed that such projects would better American society and economy. For instance, Southern reformers were individuals interested in 'turnpikes, canals, and banking, and perhaps were inclined toward the moderate National Republicans, but most certainly to the Whigs; they advocated thorough modernizing reform for southern society and reform'.[18] Nathaniel Macon, a shrewd Southern politician, aptly expressed the connection between the religious fervour of the Second Great Awakening, reform movements, and the American System:

> We have abolition, colonization, bible and peace societies ... the character and spirit of ... all – it is a character and spirit of perseverance bordering on enthusiasm. And if the general government shall continue to stretch their powers [through economic policies], these societies will undoubtedly push them to try the question of emancipation ... The states having no slaves may not feel as strongly as the states having slaves about stretching the constitution, because no such interest is to be touched by it. The camp that is not always guarded may be surprised.[19]

This religious zeal of the Second Great Awakening created an intellectual milieu which inspired proponents of the American System to achieve their goals.[20] John Quincy Adams represented an obvious example of this trend. His whole presidential programme revolved around the idea of 'improvement'. In his first Presidential address to Congress on 6 December 1825, Adams invoked political and religious authority to argue for the social improvement of the United States. He stated that '[t]he great object of the institution of civil government is the improvement of the condition of those who are parties to the social compact.' For this purpose, he advocated the internal improvement of roads and canals. The second authority he alluded to was that 'moral, political, intellectual improvement' were 'duties assigned by the Author of Our Existence'.[21] In his speech in 1828 on the occasion of the opening of the Chesapeake and Ohio Canal, Adams stated that 'Progressive improvement in the condition of man is apparently the purpose of a Superintending Providence.'[22]

The influence of religion upon John Quincy Adams, which historian Samuel Flagg Bemis called the 'smack of orthodoxy',[23] helped to define not only the scope of the internal improvement projects during Adams's presidency, but also his attitude when facing opposition to his projects. On 26 November 1825, while Adams and his cabinet members reviewed the draft of his Presidential message of 1825, Secretary of State Henry Clay calculated that a proposal for a national university was 'entirely hopeless'.[24] Adams replied that it was his 'indispensable duty' to make such suggestions. Adams confided in his memoir that 'the perilous experiment must be made. Let me make it with full deliberation, and be prepared for the consequences.'[25] Overall, Adams's religious beliefs made him inflexible on the issue of internal improvements.

Yet religious revivalism impressed even the cunning Henry Clay. Shortly after the inauguration of Andrew Jackson in 1829, Clay wrote that

> the number of changes, and of penitents, and the number who are on the anxious seat ... is quite considerable. Reform, real and substantial, very different from the mock reform at Washington, I believe to be now going on throughout the whole Country. Its progress may be slow, for some time, but its ultimate accomplishment I believe to be certain.[26]

When Clay proposed a land reform measure known as the Distribution Bill of 1832, he sought to use the land revenue not only for internal improvements, but also for the education and colonization of free blacks outside the United States. He argued that that 'the General Government ... will feel, from the expenditure of the money ... the benefits of moral and intellectual improvement of the people, of greater facility in social and commercial intercourse, and of the purification of the population of our country'.[27] It is clear that Clay was also expanding the scope of his concept of the American System to include what he saw as 'cultural improvement'.

In addition, Clay stood by his version of the American System throughout his national political career even when such a position proved unpopular with his constituents. He reduced his chances of becoming president by opposing the idea of reducing public land prices, a very popular proposal in the West. Certainly, however, Clay was more calculating than Adams in using reason and political calculation to improve society gradually.[28] For example, after the decisive loss of Adams to Jackson in the presidential election of 1828, Clay was not discouraged. Rather he predicted that given time, the American people would come to their senses and accept the nationalistic policies Adams and he had so strenuously advocated. He, along with other National Republican leaders, believed that Adams's aloofness and Jackson's aggressive campaigning techniques had triumphed over the President's reasoned policy proposals. He wrote to James Barbour of Virginia, the Secretary of War under President Adams, that he saw 'nothing in their [national political] condition to discourage the hope of a speedy restoration of the reign of reason and common sense'.[29] In the 1832 presidential election, Clay stubbornly refused to capitalize on anti-mason feeling in Pennsylvania and New York, despite the fact the Anti-Masonic Party showed signs of serious political power in these two critically important states.[30] Although more secular and calculating than Adams, Clay was not less committed to the notion of progress as exemplified in the American System.

Public Land Policies

The unique political culture shared by the proponents of the American System appeared most prominently in the way they approached the public land issue. From 1824 to 1828, the most important aspect of this issue was the notion of graduation presented by Senator Thomas Hart Benton of Missouri. Benton's objective was to sell public lands to Western farmers as cheaply as possible, or even to donate lands to Western settlers if possible. Benton asserted 'that sales of land by a government to its own citizens, and to the highest bidder, was false policy; and that gratuitous grants to actual settlers was the true policy, and their labour the true way of extracting national wealth and strength from the soil'.[31] From 1824 to 1828, Benton tried repeatedly to push a graduation bill through Congress.

A native of North Carolina, Benton lived in Tennessee for fifteen years before moving to St Louis, Missouri in 1815. The Missouri State legislature sent Benton to the United States Senate in 1820. His association with the land issue was a long one. Both his grandfather and father had been land speculators. Benton, like many prominent Westerners, was also involved in land speculation. After moving to St Louis, his legal practice not surprisingly focused on land claims and titles, the most lucrative business on the frontier.[32] He explained the influences on his ideas on land issues in his memoir *Thirty Years' View*:

> [i]t might have been in childhood, when reading the Bible, and seeing the division of the promised land among the children of Israel: it might have been later, and in learning the operation of the feudal system in giving lands to those who would defend them: it might have been in early life in Tennessee, in seeing the fortunes and respectability of many families derived from the 640 acre head-rights which the State of North Carolina had bestowed upon the first settlers.[33]

His religious upbringing, interest in medieval history and frontier experience may have introduced Benton to the notion that land was to be distributed among, rather than sold to, the people. However, he also realized that his political future depended upon representing the demands of his constituents for cheap land.

Benton believed strongly in following the will of the people. Although he strongly supported Henry Clay in the presidential election of 1824, when an inconclusive Electoral College vote threw the contest into the House of Representatives, Benton did not follow the advice of Clay to support John Quincy Adams. Rather he publicly supported Andrew Jackson, his one time opponent in a duel. He explained later why he had decided to support Jackson: 'I preferred the General, because he was preferred ten to one by the people of Missouri'.[34] He thus urged John Scott, the only Missouri House member, to cast his precious vote for Jackson. When Scott indicated that he would still support Adams, Benton wrote him, '[t]he vote which you intend to give is not your own. It belongs to the people of the state of Missouri. They are against Mr. Adams. I, in their name, do solemnly protest against your intention, and deny your moral power thus to bestow their vote.'[35] Benton's democratic idealism was also tempered by the practical fact that Jackson advocated the cheap land for Western settlers.

It was indeed the will of Westerners to get land as easily as possible. For example, in January 1824 the Indiana General Assembly petitioned the United States Congress to provide relief for public land purchasers. Legislature also requested that Congress reduce land prices from a dollar or fifty cents per acre. The legislatures of Illinois and Alabama quickly followed suit.[36]

On 28 April 1824, Benton proposed a Senate bill entitled 'A bill to sell and dispose of the refuse lands belonging to the United States'. The bill had two main elements. First, if public lands could not be sold at the market price of $1.25 per acre in five years they would be deemed of poor quality and offered to settlers at a reduced price of fifty cents per acre. Benton argued that land prices should be apportioned to land quality. Second, household heads, adults over twenty-one, or widows who had inhabited such discounted lands would receive an additional half quarter section (eighty acres) of land for free.[37]

Benton's logic seemed reasonable but had a serious flaw. In a real market situation, the salesperson would not announce his or her intention to radically discount land prices. He or she would simply lower the product's price when sales were slow. This is what the federal government had been doing through successive lands acts from 1796 to 1820 by gradually reducing the minimum cash price of public lands from $2 to $1.25 per acre. If potential purchasers had the exact information on a substantial discount of the product price, including the discount rate and the discount period, they could wait as long as possible until the price fell.

Senator David Barton of Missouri, the Chairman of the Senate Committee on Public Lands, pointed out this fundamental problem. He stated that Benton's bill was 'incompatible' with the purpose of raising revenue to retire the national debt. After all, few people would purchase lands at $1.25 per acre when they could simply wait a few years and buy them at fifty cents per acre.[38] The bill was thus 'premature and improper at this moment' and Barton proposed its indefinite postponement which the Senate promptly agreed to.[39] Over time Barton became the primary opponent of Benton's land policies until the elderly politician retired from national politics after an unsuccessful re-election bid in 1830. Several factors influenced Barton's position on land policies. First of all, Benton and Barton belonged to different political factions in Missouri state politics. Benton belonged to the 'junto' group that included Auguste Chouteau, Bernard Pratte, William Clark, Edward Hempstead and John Scott. Barton, however, belonged to the 'anti-junto' group that included William Russell, Rufus Easton, Judge John B. C. Lucas and his son Charles Lucas. The junto represented a group of French-descended business leaders and planters who possessed large estates under French and Spanish law. Anti-junto forces composed of American settlers who arrived in St Louis in the wake of the Louisiana Purchase.[40]

Second, Barton easily won his Senatorial seat in an election held in the Missouri general assembly in 1820. But he did not exert any of his powerful political influence for Benton's candidacy, despite the desperate urging of John Scott, who favoured Barton.[41] As such, Benton won his seat by a narrow one-vote majority.[42] Therefore it was not strange that Barton was ill inclined to support a bill that would aid his rival.

Third, Barton had a different approach to politics than Benton. If Benton's political motto was to follow the public will, whether right or wrong, Barton preferred to make decisions based upon his own judgments. During the 1824 election, Barton came out in support of Adams. He wrote to Scott that he supported Adams because 'he is superior as a theoretic and practical statesman, and diplomatist; is best acquainted with our foreign, and equally so with our domestic relations; and not inferior in talents, acquirements, patriotism and integrity to any of our public characters'.[43] He valued the qualifications of candidates more than their local popularity. Therefore Barton probably thought it irresponsible for a Senator, especially the Chairman of the Committee on Public Lands, to support a bill which could squander federal property, even though the bill represented the will of his constituents. Eventually Barton's opposition to the popular bill played a major role in ending his Senatorial career in 1831.[44]

Despite the Senate's initial rebuff of his bill, Benton did not give up. In December 1824 and January 1825, Illinois and Missouri petitioned Congress to reduce land prices and donate land to actual settlers.[45] The passage of these memorials prompted Benton to reintroduce his bill with modifications in December 1825. The modified bill contained a 'graduation' scheme to reduce minimum land prices by twenty-five cents every year from the current minimum price of $1.25 to twenty-five cents after four years. But Benton soon moved to table the bill, as he felt the Senate was still not ready to take up the measure.

On 16 May 1826, six days before the end of the legislative session, Benton reintroduced the bill with an extensive speech on the floor of the Senate.[46] He added a cession clause to the bill, in which all lands unsold after one year would be donated to individual states.[47] He argued that the bill would both raise revenue and help settle the West. Low land prices would speed land sales and increase revenue, which would allow the federal government to quickly retire public debts.[48] To convince recalcitrant senators Benton stated:

> I see, in the adoption of this great measure, consequences which connect themselves with the durability and prosperity of the Republic – the number of tenants diminished; the class of freeholders increased; the multiplication of that class of population

which is to pay taxes, bear arms, defend the country against foreign and domestic enemies, and to furnish the future statesmen and warriors of this Republic.[49]

Benton's argument resembled Jefferson's famous praise of yeoman farmers in his *Notes on the State of Virginia*.[50] The assumption behind this logic was that independent farmers were the backbone of the republic; therefore it was necessary to use economic policies to create such a class. The logical conclusion then was that the government should 'distribute' land to increase the number of yeoman farmers, rather than to 'sell' it to increase federal revenue. Benton appealed to his colleagues, 'I speak to Senators who know this to be a Republic, not a Monarchy; who know that the public lands belong to the People, and not to the Federal Government; who know that the lands are to be disposed of for the common good of all, and not kept for the service of a few.' He also uttered the memorable statement that 'the Earth is the gift of God to man'.[51]

Considering Benton's emphasis on 'distributing' over 'selling' federal land, his argument that the bill would help retire the national debt was political rhetoric designed to appeal to revenue-oriented Eastern Senators. His proposal to cede federal lands to states was also a political gesture to Southern legislators. Many Southern leaders believed that federal lands within state borders should be returned to their sovereign states. In this sense, Benton's graduation bill in 1826 was a sophisticated scheme to appeal to every section in the union. But Barton ridiculed the bill as an 'electioneering stump', considering that the Congressional election of 1826 was just a few months away. On a motion from Barton, the Senate once more tabled Benton's bill.[52]

Shortly after the convening of the Second Session of the 19th Congress on 4 December 1826, Barton gave a long speech against the bill.[53] His purpose was obviously to kill the bill for good, thus dealing a political blow to his rival.[54] Barton argued that the present land system had helped industrious people to settle Western lands. On the other hand, the proposed system of graduation placed lands into the hands of a small number of speculators. Barton predicted that the graduation scheme would, in five years, throw millions of acres of land into the market at twenty-five cents per acre, during which only few lots would be sold. The final result of the measure would be to reduce all land prices to twenty-five cents per acre after five years. It would encourage, argued Barton, the worst kind of speculation.[55]

The assumption behind Barton's argument was that if land prices fell, speculators would purchase large land parcels and re-sell or lease them to small farmers. Therefore a moderate price level was necessary to protect actual settlers. Barton thus praised the current land system: 'during the operation of this system, the great landholders in the valley of the Mississippi, or elsewhere, can never realize princely fortunes either by rent, lease, or re-sales to the actual cultivators of the ground'.[56]

Whether Barton was aware of it or not, the history of public lands supported his argument. For the purpose of generating quick revenue, Congress in 1787 had sold 1.5 million acres to the Ohio Company at less than ten cents per acre. In 1788, Congress sold 1 million acres to Judge John Cleves Symmes at a similar price. The Ohio Company and Symmes resold the lands to small farmers. Congress later had to pass a number of acts to clear up the mess left by the schemes of these two speculators.[57] Barton also opposed cession. He argued that state sovereignty did not warrant state control of federal lands. He asserted, '[t]he power to interfere with the United States' lands, was not among the sovereign powers to be granted to the new States, into which those lands were divided, but was expressly reserved to the United States.'[58]

Overall, Barton represented the traditional viewpoint of seeing public lands as a source of revenue. Benton, on the other hand, represented a new attitude, which saw Western land not as much as a source of revenue but rather as the basis for settlements. Barton argued that cheap land prices would create speculation, while Benton argued that it would expedite western settlement. Barton reasoned that cheap land would create large landowners and dependent small farmers, while Benton countered that it would create independent yeoman farmers. Unlike previous Congresses, the 19th Congress seemed ready to take up the graduation bill. This time a number of Senators rose to debate the bill.[59] But the controversy ended when Martin Van Buren of New York proposed tabling the bill until the Senate had more specific information on the size, sales and expenses of public lands.[60]

The Senate's readiness to agree to Van Buren's motion indicated that it was still not sure of the future of public land policy. The Senate further avoided confronting the issue by repeatedly tabling the bill. In this situation, the most interested party on land issue, the West, could eventually achieve its objective by being persistent in its demands. This was exactly what Benton did on behalf of the West.

Benton and the West, however, could not expect help from President John Quincy Adams. Adams felt the bill posed a serious threat to the American System. A federally sponsored programme of internal improvement, a pillar of the American System, was based on the availability of revenue from protective tariffs and land sales. For example, the Cumberland Road, the most famous federally sponsored internal improvement project, was based on a 'two per cent fund': 2 per cent of the revenue raised from the sale of federal lands in Ohio. Thus proponents of the American System, like Adams and Clay, could not support Benton's bill.

A case in point was Clay's response to a letter from Representative John Scott of Missouri late in 1826. In the letter, Scott asked Clay to urge Adams to recommend a graduation of land prices as per Benton's plan. Scott informed Clay that Benton's bill would create a 'madness for the public lands'. But Clay responded that such a proposal politically and financially contradicted the philosophy of the American System.[61] The American System sought to strengthen the union through the use of economic policies. Benton's bill, especially the cession clause, removed control of public lands, one of the ties of union, from federal hands and thus weakened the union. Clay therefore told Scott that Benton's proposals were 'to be considered only as a revival of Burr's enterprises – treasonable in their character'. This was a damning comparison as Aaron Burr had tried to separate western states from the union during the administration of President Thomas Jefferson.[62]

Seeking to downplay the matter, Clay told Adams that Benton's proposition had excited only Missourians, while sentiments in Ohio were 'sound'. Adams dismissed Benton's bill merely as 'one of his electioneering engines for securing his own re-election as a Senator'.[63] Later developments show that Adams and Clay had fallen out of touch with Westerners and fundamentally underestimated the popularity of Benton's bill in the West. This miscalculation would prove politically costly to Adams and Clay.

Contrary to Clay's estimation, Western settlers overwhelmingly wanted Benton's graduation bill. In addition to Indiana, Illinois and Alabama, which had already petitioned the Congress for a reduction of land prices, the Missouri, Arkansas and Louisiana legislatures also passed petitions similar in content to Benton's graduation bill.[64] In addition to Western legislatures, groups of settlers also directly petitioned Congress in support of Benton's bill. Benton himself introduced two petitions, which were signed by 200 and 300 Missouri citizens respectively.[65]

This outpouring of support gave Benton more impetus to push his bill in Congress. When the 20th Congress convened on 3 December 1827, Benton immediately reintroduced his proposal.[66] This time Benton argued that the bill would help quickly retire the national debt in five years and thus relieve the American people of an annual tax burden of $12 to 15 million. Benton argued in such a fashion to address the fiscal concerns of eastern Senators. By doing so, he negated the premise of his 1826 speech that his bill sought to distribute lands, 'the Gift of God', to the people.[67] Basically Benton wanted to secure cheap land for the West by any means possible. He could thus discuss Western lands as both a source of revenue and a means to encourage new settlements of yeoman farmers, even though both arguments conflicted with each other. In addition to Western farmers and state assemblies, Benton had an ally in Representative Joseph Duncan of Illinois, a Jacksonian Democrat and Chairman of the House Committee on Public Lands.[68] Undaunted by such support, Barton attacked the bill on the House floor.[69] He argued that graduation would simply delay sales for five years after which speculation would ensue. Barton's logic was equally reasonable to, if not more than, that of Benton. But it was Benton who was earning political capital among Westerners. Frontier residents were not interested in logic, but in who could benefit their section. As historian Daniel Feller has pointed out, it was difficult to discern actual settlers from speculators in the West. Small farmers as well as capitalists speculated in land. As long as a boom did not burst into a panic, Westerners welcomed speculation.[70]

Barton directed his harshest criticism towards the graduation clause in Benton's bill, claiming that 'graduation' was a deceptive title. Barton argued that the bill would create a rapid depreciation of public land prices and an increase in speculation, because the demand from the immigrants to the West could not exceed 2 million acres over the next three years. The other lands would be appropriated by capitalists. In other words, there was insufficient demand to meet the supply of land under the graduation scheme.[71]

But Barton argued that he was 'friendly' to the idea of donation and promised to suggest '[a] judicious plan of donations of lands' of his own. He also claimed to support cession as well, although he did not elaborate on the matter.[72] Such stalling tactics revealed that Benton and his graduation bill were clearly popular amongst both Congress and the general public.

But when Barton eventually presented amendments to Benton's bill, they did not include a cession clause. The amendments instead proposed reducing the price of all lands to $1 per acre, from the current $1.25. Barton also suggested allowing any person to settle on a quarter section (160 acres) and to receive the land if he or she inhabited and cultivated it for five successive years.[73] Overall, Barton's amendments attempted to preserve the structure of the old land system by making some concessions to Western interests.

When compared to Barton's amendments, the radical nature of Benton's bill became more evident.[74] These speculators would not improve the value of the lands through residency, but would simply sell the property in question when the residency requirement expired. In this case, the federal government would not benefit from the donation at all. Moreover, cession of public lands to states would cost the federal government not only financially, but politically by eliminating an important symbol of federal presence in states. Overall Benton's bill was more beneficial to the West and had the potential to create speculation.

The ensuing Senate debates echoed the arguments of Benton and Barton. Supporters of Benton's bill argued: 1) land was a gift of God which belonged to the people, not to the government; 2) land had to be sold quickly to pay off the national debt by reducing land prices and that the current system had failed as a revenue measure,[75] and 3) the real purpose of the current land system was to stem western migration.[76]

The last argument was a politically explosive one. Western congressmen pointed to statements made by President Adams and Treasury Secretary Richard Rush in their 1827 annual message and report to Congress as evidences of a conspiracy. In his annual message, Adams had stated, '[t]he acquisition of them [public lands], made at the expense of the whole Union, not only in treasure but in blood, marks a right of property in them equally extensive.' Adams used the word 'blood' to strengthen federal land claims. He also stated that the current land system 'has been hitherto eminently successful'.[77] He did not make any direct reference to Benton's graduation bill, but it was clear that the President considered public lands to be the common property of the Union. He had no intention of changing the land system in the way desired by proponents of the graduation bill.

Like Adams, Rush also did not address the graduation bill directly in his report, instead arguing for the protection of domestic manufactures by increasing tariff rates. As a part of this argument, Rush remarked that land prices should not be lowered to prevent westward migration and to protect the labour pool available to manufactures.[78] The combination of these two statements by Adams and Rush gave the impression that the current administration would defend the current land system against Western interests

Overall, Western legislators had certain facts on their side. It was difficult to deny cheap or free land to the West when more than 20 million acres of federal lands were lying unappropriated. The current land system had furthermore failed to generate substantial revenue. From this perspective, selling or donating land to settlers made a certain sense. Not surprisingly, Barton's amendments eventually failed in the Senate by a vote of fourteen to twenty-eight.[79] The fact that the Senate rejected Barton's substitute bill so decisively indicates that legislators were aware of the need to radically alter, not simply modify, the current land system.

Despite the changing mood in the Senate, the idea of cession faced stiff opposition. Northeastern Senators understandably opposed the cession of federal lands to the states. Mahlon Dickerson of New Jersey argued that state sovereignty, the theoretical basis for cession, was a 'modified one', because 'a portion [of state sovereignty] has been yielded to the United States [when states entered the Union]'. Thus, argued Dickerson, states could not claim complete control over land within their borders. He continued, 'when we speak of the sovereignty of the people, we mean the people of the United States, not the People of New York or Pennsylvania'.[80] In this way, Dickerson denied the compact theory of the union, which had been the staple of Southern constitutional interpretation.

What is interesting is that although Benton included the idea of cession in his graduation bill to attract Southern support, South Atlantic states' senators opposed the notion. During congressional debates Thomas W. Cobb of Georgia, John Tyler of Virginia and Nathaniel Macon of North Carolina vehemently opposed cession. The reason for this discrepancy stems from the fact that as agricultural regions, the Southeast and the West were rivals in the competition for land and population.[81] South Atlantic states had a large stake in preventing the migration of their population westwards. Such opposition to his bill must have puzzled and frustrated Benton. Some politicians, at least, sought a sectional alliance between the South and West over the land issue. In a letter written on 27 May 1829, Clay wrote that 'An influential Southerner lately asked a western friend of mine. Will you of the West give up the Tariff if we give up to you the public lands?'[82]

Table 3.1. Vote Analysis on the Graduation Bill of 1828.

	Senate Yeas	Nays
New England	–	12
Mid-Atlantic	1	7
Northwest	9	1
South Atlantic	3	5
Southwest	8	–
Total	21	25

Source: *Senate Journal*, 20th Cong., 1st sess. (22 April 1828), p. 323.

The division clearly reflected an East–West divide. All Western delegates, except Barton of Missouri, voted for the bill. Barton's vote against the bill cost him his office in the election of 1830.[83] These votes were as expected. Tennessee, Alabama, Mississippi and Louisiana Senators voted unanimously for the bill. As far as the land issue was concerned, Suthwestern states sided with their Northwestern friends, rather than with their South Atlantic brethren. On the other hand, New England Senators voted against the bill. Middle states voted one to seven and the South Atlantic states three to five against the bill.

Historian Raynor G. Wellington argued that in sectional struggles after 1828 'the South Atlantic States would help the West to obtain what it wanted on the public lands, while the Northwest would assist in its effort to pass a lower tariff'.[84] In fact, there were efforts in this direction. Benton added the cession clause in his graduation bill in 1828 as a way to unite the Northwest and the South on the basis of states' rights. But Senators from the South Atlantic states refused this offer. They instead attacked the idea of cession so vigorously that Benton dropped this clause from the bill. In addition, the majority of Senators from the South Atlantic states also voted against Benton's bill. There was a chance to create a 'logical' sectional alliance between the South and the Northwest. But the South refused to take the offer.

Throughout the early republic, demands for land reform came from the West. Westerners argued that land was a gift from God to be distributed to the people. The Graduation Bill of 1828 was the culmination of Western efforts to acquire cheap land.[85] Proponents of the American System like Adams, Clay and Rush fought such designs. They argued that public lands were national property; that they should create revenue to repay the national debt and sponsor internal improvements. Adams in particular felt that moderate land prices would regulate the flow of settlers westward, guaranteeing a cheap labour pool for east coast manufacturers. They thus failed to produce any comprehensive land policy that could be accepted by the Western people.

The attitude of Adams and Clay to Benton's bill shows one important aspect of the political culture shared by supporters of the American System. They tried to push what they believed was good for the union, rather than what was popular with their constituents. Their politics were not the politics of possibility but of righteousness under any circumstances. Thus rather than supporting Benton's graduation bill, which was extremely popular in the West, they tried to hang on to the old land system.

Internal Improvements under the Adams Administration

The idea of internal improvements met with limited success under John Quincy Adams's administration. Adams did not hesitate to express his enthusiasm for internal improvements from the moment he took the presidential oath of office. In his inaugural address, Adams emphasized the benefits, stating that, 'internal improvement ... is that from which ... unborn millions of our posterity who are in future ages to people this continent will derive their most fervent gratitude to the founders of the Union'.[86]

Adams was also less concerned with the constitutional problems raised by internal improvements than his predecessors. He acknowledged the 'diversity of opinion' on the matter in his address, but expressed hope that 'by the ... process of friendly, patient, and persevering deliberation all constitutional objections will ultimately be removed'.[87] Adams's remarks were well meant but naïve. The President failed to understand the strength of constitutional opposition on this issue throughout the country, especially in the South.

Adams's first annual message, on 6 December 1825, revealed his fundamental beliefs on internal improvements and his unique perception of federal power. Adams's vision of internal improvements encompassed far more than simple roads and canals. Rather it included the establishment of a national university in Washington DC, an astronomical observatory, the construction of a ship for the exploration of the whole northwest coast and the creation of a new Department of the Interior.[88] Such a conception of internal improvements relied not so much on physical improvement, but on the intellectual or spiritual refinement of the American people. Adams stated that '[r]oads and canals, by multiplying and facilitating the communications and intercourse between distant regions and multitudes of men are among, the most important means of improvement.' But, Adams continued, 'moral, political, intellectual improvement are duties assigned by the Author of Our Existence to social no less to individual man'.[89] What really made Adams's message unique was his imperative for the use of federal power. He stated that federal support for internal improvements was a 'duty as sacred and indispensable as the usurpation of powers not granted is criminal and odious'.[90]

Adams's positive perception of power culminated in his understanding of 'liberty'. He stated that 'liberty is power; that the nation blessed with the largest portion of liberty must in proportion to its numbers be the most powerful nation upon earth'.[91] The federal government could thus engage in any project that might elevate all physical or cultural aspects of human life in the United States. Under Adams's auspices, internal improvements could open the door to any project, which might theoretically include the abolition of slavery. George Washington had already expressed similar attitudes towards the relationship of federal power and liberty. He stated that 'your union ought to be considered as a main prop of your liberty, and that the love of the one ought to endear to you the preservation of the other', in his famed Farewell Address.[92] Adams's presentation of this grand scheme of internal improvements rang an ominous echo in the ears of Southern congressmen. But Adams added more fuel to the fire in his message, displaying a dismissive attitude towards those who might fear expansive federal power. He rhetorically asked:

> [w]hile foreign nations less blessed with that freedom which is power than ourselves are advancing with gigantic strides in the career of public improvement, were we to slumber in indolence or fold up our arms and proclaim to the world that we are palsied by the will of our constituents, would it not be to cast away the bounties of Providence and doom ourselves to perpetual inferiority?[93]

Adams, unlike his predecessors, furthermore demonstrated his audacity by conspicuously omitting a recommendation for a constitutional amendment which would grant Congress the power to fund internal improvements.

Adams's grandiose plan for federally supported internal improvements was a politically difficult proposition. Jefferson, Madison and Monroe all failed to implement the construction of roads and canals via federal sponsorship (except the Cumberland Road), let alone found a national university. More practically minded politicians had already warned of the futility of such an attempt. Commenting on the draft of Jefferson's annual message of 1806, in which the third president proposed to apply federal revenue from import duties to public education, Gallatin commented that the proposition on the improvement of roads, rivers and canals might 'probably be popular', but the proposition on a university would 'certainly be unpopular'.[94] Henry Clay, Adams's Secretary of State and the godfather of the American System, who Adams had promoted in his message, also did not approve of such an expansive scheme of internal improvements.[95]

Why did Adams not learn from the failures of his predecessors and insist on submitting the message? He seemed optimistic about the acceptance of his views by Congress and the nation. He concluded his address with the upbeat observation that

> I shall await with cheering hope and faithful cooperation the result of your deliberations, assured that ... you will, with a due sense of your obligations to your country and of the high responsibilities weighing upon yourselves, give efficacy to the means committed to you for the common good.[96]

It is difficult to believe that such a skilled diplomat and politician would really believe that Congress would approve his projects, which did not even receive Clay's support. Adams might have realized the impossibility of his proposals. However, he seems to have had a long-term plan in mind, which made him ignore the more immediate dangers. Adams admitted that he presented his proposals with a view of 'a practicality of a longer range than a simple session of Congress'. His analogy was that the 'plant may come late, though the seed should be obtained'. As such, he considered it an 'indispensable duty' to make his suggestions. Therefore, Adams claimed, it was 'not very material' for him to suggest it now or later, in other words, it was his 'duty', despite any foreseeable negative reception.[97] Here one can witness Adams's somewhat religious character: obedience regardless of political consequences.[98]

Adams was completely mistaken in his political calculations, particularly in regard to how Southerners would react to his internal improvement plans. To start, Southern politicians judged Adams's proposal to be both unconstitutional and a bold attempt at federal consolidation. William H. Crawford of Georgia thought that the message was 'replete with doctrines which I hold to be unconstitutional'.[99] Nathaniel Macon of North Carolina commented that '[t]he message of the President seems to claim all the power to the federal government.'[100] Thomas Jefferson saw Adams's message as a Federalist attempt to establish 'a single and splendid government of an aristocracy'.[101] Martin Van Buren, a New Yorker sympathetic to Southern concerns, felt that 'not one of the followers of the old Republican faith ... could fail to see in them [Adams's proposals] the most ultra latitudinarian doctrines'.[102]

Southern state legislatures also criticized Adams's message. On 4 March 1826, the Virginia General Assembly passed a resolution denying Congress's power 'to adopt a general system of internal improvement in the States, as a national measure'. A second resolution stated simply 'the appropriation of money by the Congress of the United States, to construct roads and canals in the States is a violation of the Constitution'.[103] The legislature of Georgia resolved on 24 December 1827 'to *oppose,* in every possible shape, the exercise of the power, on the part of the General Government, to encourage domestic manufactures or to promote internal improvement'.[104]

Even the South Carolina legislature, whose congressional delegates had supported the Survey Bill in 1824, opposed Adams. On 16 December 1825, ten days after Adams's message to Congress, both houses of the South Carolina legislature '*Resolved*, That Congress does not possess the power, under the constitution, to adopt a general system of internal improvement as a national measure'.[105] This change reflected the growing sectionalism in the South, which coincided with the economic deterioration of the region after 1815. South Carolina also followed a path similar to those of other Southern states, becoming more sectional by 1825.[106]

Given such organized resistance, Adams' proposals for 'moral and intellectual' improvements received no Congressional support.[107] By 1826, Adams himself recognized the impossibility of creating a national university. On 26 August 1826, Emma Hart Willard, a famous proponent of women's education, called on him to request Congressional patronage for an institution of female education. Adams told her that he was 'convinced' that Congress would do 'nothing'. Nor would Congress educate boys except to make them soldiers. Therefore her application for Congressional support of female education 'must be fruitless'.[108] His proposals for an astronomical observatory and a survey of coastlines fared no better.[109]

Even though Adams's moral and intellectual projects received no help from Congress, more practical projects received a measure of legislative attention. In fact, the yearly average appropriation during Adams's administration surpassed those of his predecessors.

Table 3.2. Federal Government Expenditures for Internal Improvements.

Administration	Totals	Annual Average
Thomas Jefferson (1801–9)	$14,201.90	$1,775.24
James Madison (1809–17)	$875,825.54	$109,478.19
James Monroe (1817–25)	$1,612,634.66	$201,579.33
John Q. Adams (1825–9)	$2,808,333.96	$702,083.49

Sources: J. G. Van Deusen, *Economic Bases of Disunion in South Carolina* (New York: Columbia University Press, 1928), p. 128, fn. 2.

How do we explain the increased amount of appropriations for internal improvement projects during Adams's administration amid increasing sectionalism? Congress approved such funds because proponents of these projects neutralized constitutional and ideological attacks by urging subscriptions to state-chartered internal improvement companies.[110] During the Adams administration, the federal government subscribed to the following projects:

Table 3.3. Subscriptions to Internal Improvement Projects by the Federal Government.

Subscription for Stocks Projects	Date of Act	Amount
Louisville and Portland Canal Company	13 May 1826	$100,000
Dismal Swamp Canal Company	18 May 1826	$150,000
Chesapeake and Ohio Canal Company	24 May 1828	$1,000,000
Chesapeake and Delaware Canal Company and Dismal Swamp Company	2 March 1829	$200,000
Louisville and Portland Canal Company	2 March 1829	$135,000
	Total	$1,585,000

Source: *Statutes at Large* 4:162, 4:169, 4:293–4, 4:350, 4:353.

The totals for such subscriptions amounted to $1,585,000 or 56.4 per cent of the total appropriations for internal improvements during Adams's tenure as President.[111] For example, the federal government's subscription of $1 million worth of stock in the Chesapeake and Ohio Canal Company, the largest amount to a private company up to that time, received both Senate approval, by the vote of twenty-nine to seventeen, and the support of the House, by the vote of 107 to seventy-one, with large margins. In both of these battles, the South was denied its tried and true constitutional attacks and thus failed to stage an effective opposition to those appropriations.[112]

2BUS and its Business

Another area of the American System that enjoyed a measure of temporary success was the 2BUS. After the Panic of 1819, the 2BUS performed well, especially under the leadership of Nicholas Biddle, who became president of the institution in 1823. He pursued a cautious plan of supplying large sums of money and credit to the economy and government, while preventing state banks from overextending their credit.

The 2BUS admirably achieved its economic and financial objectives: supplying money to the national treasury and establishing a sound and uniform currency by regulating the loans granted by other financial institutions. The average amount of notes of the 2BUS in circulation and deposit were as follows:

Table 3.4. Notes and Deposits of the Second Bank of the United State.

Year	Notes ($)	Deposits($)	Total ($)
1817	3,658,000	13,413,000	17,071,000.00
1818	8,461,000	11,173,000	19,634,000.00
1819	4,809,000	5,800,000	10,609,000.00
1820	4,491,000	6,693,000	11,184,000.00
1821	5,654,000	6,917,000	12,571,000.00
1822	5,306,000	7,491,000	12,797,000.00
1823	4,487,000	11,075,000	15,562,000.00
1824	5,791,000	12,779,000	18,570,000.00
1825	8,825,000	12,736,000	21,561,000.00
1826	9,635,000	13,385,000	23,020,000.00
1827	9,780,000	14,342,000	24,122,000.00
1828	11,067,000	15,427,000	26,494,000.00
1829	13,102,000	15,516,000	28,618,000.00
1830	15,067,000	16,059,000	31,126,000.00

Source: The data on the amounts of notes and deposits of the Second Bank of the United States are yearly averages from R. C. H. Catterall, *The Second Bank of the United States* (Chicago, IL: The University of Chicago Press, 1903), p. 512.

To be certain, the bank had large amounts of note circulations and deposits for the years 1817 and 1818. This was due to excessive and careless discounting during the administration of William Jones, the first president of the Second Bank of the United States, which eventually put the bank in a dangerous situation.[113] However, the bank saved itself by reducing its circulation between 1819 and 1822. Afterwards the circulation of the bank increased again – but gradually.

The significance of the money supplied by the 2BUS can be verified by comparing the 2BUS's business with that of the state banks. Although we lack complete yearly data on the business of state banks, we have information for two specific occasions during the 2BUS's existence, which gives us a general idea of the relative importance of the 2BUS in its capacity to supply money to the American economy.

Table 3.5. Notes and Deposits of State Banks and the Second Bank of the United States (1 January 1820).

	Notes ($)	Deposits ($)	Total ($)
307 State Banks	40,641,574	31,244,959	71,886,533
Second BUS	4,221,770	4,705,511	8,927,281
Total	44,863,344	35,950,470	80,813,814
Percentage Belonging to the Second BUS	9.41%	13.09%	11.05%

Source: 'Considerations on the Currency and Banking System of the United States', 1 January 1831, *The Writings of Albert Gallatin*, vol. 3, p. 291.

Table 3.6. Notes and Deposits of State Banks and the
Second Bank of the United States (End of 1829).

	Notes ($)	Deposits ($)	Total ($)
329 State Banks	48,274,914	40,781,119	89,056,033
Second Bank	13,048,984	14,778,809	27,827,793
Total	61,323,898	55,559,928	116,883,826
Percentage Belonging to the Second BUS	21.28%	26.60%	23.81%

Source: 'Considerations on the Currency and Banking System of the United States', 1 January 1831, *The Writings of Albert Gallatin*, vol. 3, p. 296.

In 1820, the 2BUS only supplied 11.05 per cent of the total amount of credit to the American economy in general. However, in 1829, this figure had risen to 23.81 per cent. The data agrees with the generally accepted interpretation of the business trends of the 2BUS. Historian Ralph C. H. Catterall wrote that Langdon Cheves, the President of the 2BUS from 1819 to 1823, curtailed the business of the 2BUS to protect the institution from difficulties caused through overtrading by the bank during the administration of his predecessor.[114] On the other hand, Nicholas Biddle, Cheves's successor, pursued a policy of expanding bank business – although in a controlled way.[115]

We also have data on the average yearly discount of the 2BUS and the new loans of the 2BUS to the Treasury Department.

Table 3.7. Discounts and Loans of the Second Bank of the United States.

Year	Discounts ($)	New Loans ($)
1816	–	500,000
1819	32,211,674	–
1820	28,808,267	2,000,000
1821	27,099,050	4,000,000
1822	28,574,893	–
1823	30,584,919	–
1824	29,478,255	5,000,000
1825	29,327,219	5,000,000
1826	29,592,103	–
1827	27,948,592	–
1828	30,820,944	–
1829	32,703,280	–

Source: The data on discounts is from Gallatin's 'Considerations on the Currency and Banking System of the United States', 1 January 1831, *The Writings of Albert Gallatin*, vol. 3, p. 363. The data of new loans of the Second Bank of the United States are from Catterall, *The Second Bank of the United States*, p. 471.

The data above allows us to draw a couple of conclusions. First, the bank, during its existence, was important as the sole supplier of bankloans to the treasury.

The bank supplied all loans between 1816 and 1836, the period of its charter.[116] But the amount of money supplied by the bank was not indispensable from the government's perspective. The total amount of bankloans from the 2BUS to the general government was $16.5 million. This amount was even less than the average yearly expenditures of the general government, which was $18,172,000.[117] When we divide the total amount of bank loans from the bank by the number of years between 1816 and 1830, we get the figure of $1.1 million, which is no more than 6 per cent of the average yearly expenditure of the general government during that time. When compared with the percentages of the 1BUS loans to the general government during the first two presidential administrations (65 per cent) and the early years of the Jeffersonian administrations, 1801–7 (15 per cent), the 2BUS does not appear to have been critical in financing the government.[118]

The 2BUS was less important as a source of income for national finance than its predecessor. This was largely due to the general prosperity of the country, which in turn resulted in sufficient revenue for the national treasury after the end of the War of 1812. This made it possible for the American government to avoid borrowing money and to retire public debts quickly.[119] Second, the bank supplied about 17 per cent of the total loans and discounts of the United States at its peak strength. In 1830, the combined total for bank loans and discounts reached $41 million while that of all other banks combined was $200 million.[120] Probably this share was somewhat larger than that of the 1BUS at the peak of its power, considering the relative strength of the 2BUS over the 1BUS (in its business of note circulation in all banking: 23.81 per cent vs 19.22 per cent), because discounts were related to the amount of bank notes and deposits.[121] Overall, the 2BUS was losing its importance as a source of money for national government's finances.

Nevertheless, it was still an important source of money to the national economy of the United States. First, the 2BUS was critical in the establishment of a sound and uniform currency. Second, and more importantly from the perspective of a national economy, the 1BUS had restraining powers against the overtrading of state banks, making the latter's notes sound, to the point of producing the closest uniform national currency system possible at the time.

It is important to remember that the national bank's currency, especially with regard to its banknotes, was insured by the acts of incorporation. Such acts guaranteed that all 2BUS banknotes 'shall be receivable in all payments to the United States, unless otherwise directed by act of Congress'.[122] State banks could not boast this legal guarantee for their notes. Another important legal mechanism, ensuring the soundness of the national bank's currency, was the limitation of the bank's liabilities, guaranteed by its charter. The maximum amount of debt that the bank could owe at any given time was never to exceed the bank's capital, over and above the amount currently deposited in the bank. In cases of excess the directors were to be held personally liable.[123] This clause prevented the bank from issuing excessive amounts of bank notes. In addition, the charter of the 2BUS positively stated that the bank could not suspend specie payments.[124] Obviously, this was inserted into the charter to prevent another financial disaster like the specie suspension crisis during the War of 1812. During most of its existence, the national bank had a much higher ratio of specie/notes and specie/deposits compared to state banks. We do not have complete and yearly data on the comparative ratios of specie/currency between the 2BUS and state banks, but a general picture can be drawn by analysing the available data on two points of time: 1819 and 1829.

Table 3.8. Percentage of Specie to Notes and Specie to Deposits from the 2BUS and State Banks.

	Notes ($)	Deposits ($)	Specie ($)	Specie to Notes	Specie to Deposits
January 1820					
Second BUS	4,221,770	4,705,511	3,147,977	75%	67%
State Banks	40,641,574	31,244,959	16,672,263	41%	53%
End of 1829					
Second BUS	13,048,984	14,778,809	7,175,274	55%	49%
State Banks	48,274,914	40,781,119	14,939,643	31%	37%

Source: The amounts of notes, deposits, and specie are from Gallatin's 'Considerations on the Currency and Banking System of the United States', 1 January 1831, *The Writings of Albert Gallatin*, vol. 3, pp. 286, 291, 296.

On both occasions, the national bank had consistently higher ratios of specie to notes and deposits, when compared to those of state banks. In addition, the yearly data, from 1818 to 1841, comparing the ratio between the specie of the 2BUS (and its total currency) against those of the New York and Massachusetts banks, the two strongest banking states, shows that the ratio of the 2BUS was almost always higher.[125]

The national bank was able to restrain the state banks' overtrading because the former was almost always the creditor in relation to state banks. On forty occasions between February 1817 and March 1836, the 2BUS was the debtor to state banks only six times.[126] Also from time to time, the national bank presented state banknotes for payment, as this would enforce restraint.[127] The result of this restraining power was the creation of a dependable currency throughout the country. In 1829, the prices of banknotes were either at par or very slightly discounted throughout the country. It was a sound economic arrangement, and the national bank played a critical role in creating this system.

Overall, the 2BUS was important in supplying money and credit to the American economy and in meeting the financial needs of the federal government. But its importance in supplying money to the national government decreased over time as the national debt was paid off. Nevertheless, the 2BUS supplied a significant portion of the total US currency. In fact, during the third decade of the nineteenth century, the 2BUS was expanding its money supply much faster than state banks. This expansion was possible because the national bank had the power to restrain the overtrading of state banks.

Tariff Act of 1828 and Its Political Repercussions

The idea of the American System scored another important victory with the passage of the Tariff Act of 1828. Protectionists pushed for a protective tariff act in 1828, because high tariffs imposed four years earlier failed to protect domestic manufactures. This made it possible for British wool manufacturers to sell their products more cheaply in America. As a result, British goods once again flooded the American market, devastating domestic manufactures.[128] The *Philadelphia Gazette* reported that about three-quarters of 4,000 handlooms went unused between 1825 and 1826.[129] New England woollen manufactures also greatly suffered and thus pressed for higher tariff rates.[130] Responding to such demands, Congressman Rollin Mallary of Vermont, the Chairman of the House Committee on Manufactures, introduced a woollen bill in January 1827. The measure did not recommend changing the duty rates on woollen goods, but instead suggested three minimum values for wool and woollen goods. The bill passed the House on 19 February 1827, by a vote of 106 to 95, only to be killed in the Senate, by the tie-breaking vote of Vice President John C. Calhoun.[131] Calhoun's motives in opposing the Woolen Bill were not hard to determine. Calhoun's initial support of protective tariffs and internal improvements after the end of the War of 1812 had almost ruined his political career. He and his friends temporarily lost control of the South Carolina legislature to the faction of William Smith, who opposed Calhoun's nationalism. By 1824, the South Carolina planters, like their counterparts in other slave states, had given up the hope of developing their own industrial base. The South lacked both a skilled factory labour force and sufficient waterpower to run mills. But the most critical factor in the dearth of industry in the South was the supreme profitability of slavery over all other industries. Slave-based cotton farms or plantations proved much more profitable than any other industry.[132] Calhoun killed the protective bill of 1827, regained his local political influence and, in 1828, wrote the *South Carolina Exposition and Protest,* arguing that a state's right to declare protective tariffs was unconstitutional. South Carolinians rewarded Calhoun's political turnabout by granting him and his supporters control of the state legislature in the election of 1828.[133] Calhoun's defection to the anti-protection side was a clear sign of growing Southern sectionalism.

Not discouraged by this setback, however, the proponents of protectionism called for a national tariff convention in Harrisburg, Pennsylvania on 30 July 1827. The convention proposed a programme to Congress and to the general public for higher duties on wool, woollen goods, cotton goods, hemp, flax, iron and glass.[134] The political situation was auspicious for supporters of protection. President John Quincy Adams's cabinet contained several members who believed strongly in such measures. After all, Adams's Secretary of State Henry Clay was the architect of the American System. Treasury Secretary Richard Rush was likewise a strong protectionist.[135] In addition, by 1828 the New England economy was shifting from navigation to manufacturing.[136]

As much as the forces of protectionism became better organized, in and out of the federal government, Southern opposition to internal improvements was likewise unifying.[137] Southerners resented the increase in prices on imported manufactured goods caused by additional duties. They also were worried about possible European refusals to buy southern cotton in retaliation for American protective tariffs. But Southern planters primarily feared protective tariffs because they relied upon a broad construction of the Constitution that could lead to the abolition of slavery. In his inflammatory pamphlet published in 1827, *The Crisis*, Robert J. Turnbull, a South Carolina tidewater planter, pointed out the dangers of broad construction. He stated that '[t]he question ... is not ... whether we are to be taxed without end'. Rather the real question was 'whether the institutions of our forefathers ... are to be preserved ... free from the rude hands of innovators and enthusiasts, and from the molestation or interference of any legislative power on earth but our own?'[138] Turnbull advocated resistance to protective tariffs and threatened disunion as an answer to the question. He demanded that Southern states wage 'not a resistance by resolutions of town meetings, but by such acts and measures of the local Legislatures, as shall curse the usurpers at Washington, to tremble at what they are doing, and to pause, ere they plunge this people, hitherto so happy and so united, into discord and disunion'.[139]

Thomas Cooper, the President of South Carolina College, agreed with Turnbull. On 2 July 1827, Cooper gave a powerful speech, pointing out the economic disadvantages the South would continue to suffer from a protective tariff and raising the spectre of secession. He argued that the effects of the system would be:

> to sacrifice the south to the north, by converting us into colonies and tributaries – to tax *us* for their own emolument – to claim the right of disposing of our honest earnings – to forbid us to buy from our most valuable customers – to irritate into retaliation our foreign purchasers, and thus to confine our raw materials to the home market – in short to impoverish the planter, and to stretch the purse of the manufacturer.[140]

Cooper ominously argued that '[t]he question is ... fast approaching to the alternative, of submission or separation.'[141] By 1827, the tariff issue had therefore become completely linked to the sectional interests of slavery and states' rights.

By 1827, the issue of tariffs became a political controversy between the North and the South. It also became a political wedge between the supporters of President Adams and General Andrew Jackson in the presidential election of 1828. As the election approached, it became clear that, whereas the New England states supported Adams, the South would rally behind Jackson. The election thus depended upon Northwestern states that had thrown their votes to Henry Clay in the election of 1824.[142] At this juncture, Jackson's supporters used the tariff issue to promote his candidacy. They hoped to propose a bill with tariff rates so high that only the combined votes of the South and New England would kill the proposal. When the bill was defeated, Adams's New England supporters would be held responsible, which would turn pro-protection Western voters away from Adams.[143]

However, the tariff bill did not satisfy anyone. It asked for increased duties on woollen products. But the rates of proposed duties did not reach the prohibitive levels demanded at the Harrisburg Convention. The bill also asked for a high duty on raw wool to increase its price for domestic manufacturers. Finally, the bill also placed new duties on iron, hemp and molasses, which would in turn hurt New England ship owners, merchants and distillers. Representative John Bailey of Massachusetts criticized the bill as a tool to embarrass the Adams administration. He stated that the tariff bill 'was framed precisely to defeat itself'.[144] Despite this criticism, enough New England delegates, including Daniel Webster, eventually voted for the bill to allow its passage. The bill passed the House, by a vote of 105 to 94, on 22 April 1828, and the Senate, by a vote of twenty-six to twenty-one on 14 May 1828. The sectional pattern of voting continued. Fifty-nine of the sixty-two Southern Representatives voted against the bill along with fourteen of the sixteen Senators from the South. The mid-Atlantic States and the Northwest were solidly for the protective bill.

Table 3.9. Roll Call Analysis on the Tariff Act of 1828.

	Senate		House	
	Yeas	Nays	Yeas	Nays
New England	6	5	16	23
Mid-Atlantic	8	2	57	11
Northwest	10	–	29	1
South Atlantic	–	8	3	43
Southwest	2	6	–	16
Total	26	21	105	94

Source: *Senate Journal*, 20th Cong., 1st sess. (14 May 1828), p. 410; *House Journal*, 20th Cong., 1st sess. (22 April 1828), pp. 607–9.

The Tariff Bill of 1828 was the culmination of the protective principle inherent in the American System. At the same time, it was also the high-water mark for the politicization of the tariff issue in national politics. Proponents of the protective tariff argued that their initiative would harmonize sectional interests through the creation of a home market and the promotion of nationalism. Rather than harmonizing different economic and sectional interests, however, the tariff issue escalated sectional conflicts. Voting records show the deepening patterns of sectional voting. In the debates over tariff bills, constitutional rather than economic arguments emerged as central concerns. These were the omens of what was waiting in wings following the election of President Andrew Jackson in 1829.

4 DECLINE OF THE AMERICAN SYSTEM, 1829–37

The idea of the American System suffered a decline during the two terms of President Andrew Jackson. When Jackson took the oath of office to become the seventh President of the United States on 4 March 1829, his opinions on the policies of the American System remained elusive. While serving as a senator from Tennessee in the 18th Congress from 1823–5, he had voted for a number of internal improvements bills, including a scheme for the federal government to purchase stocks in private companies, most notably the Delaware and Chesapeake Canal Company.[1] However, he mostly refrained from participating in such debates.

Jackson also voted in favour of the Protective Tariff Act of 1824. He remained silent during Senate debates over the bill. The former general also elusively expressed his opinion on tariffs in a letter, aimed at his constituents during the presidential campaign in 1824.[2] 'It is, therefore', Jackson wrote, 'my opinion that a careful and judicious Tariff is much wanted to pay our national debt and afford us the means of defence within ourselves on which the safety of our country and liberty depends.'[3]

Andrew Jackson: Frontiersman, Soldier, Presidential Contender

Although Jackson's ideas on the American System remained mysterious, his upbringing and career path seemed to indicate that he was not in its favour.[4] He was born to a Scots-Irish family in Waxhaws, then a frontier region on the border between South Carolina and North Carolina. His father died three weeks before Jackson was born. Jackson became an orphan at the age of fourteen during the American Revolution, as his mother and two brothers succumbed to diseases and hardship.[5] He then lived with relatives in Charleston, South Carolina and read law in Salisbury, North Carolina.[6] Admitted to the North Carolina bar in 1787, Jackson then moved to Nashville, Tennessee the following year to find a job as a public prosecutor.[7] Jackson thrived as a frontier lawyer, land speculator and merchant, eventually acquiring the Hermitage, a large plantation outside Nashville.[8]

As much of his law business in frontier Tennessee involved land title disputes, Jackson quickly understood the strong desire of Western settlers for cheap land and the complex legal issues that surrounded such demands. Jackson also became aware that just as settlers fought over often overlapping land titles, frontier residents and Native Americans still vied for control of the Old Southwest.

Even Jackson's marriage reflected the complexities of frontier culture. Upon arriving in Nashville, Jackson took up residence in the prominent boarding home of the widow Rachel Stockley-Donelson. The young attorney fell in love with the widow's daughter, Rachel Donelson Robards, who was in an estranged marriage with Lewis Robards. Jackson and Rachel began living together as a couple in Nashville in 1791, well before Rachel's official divorce from Robards in September 1793.[9] Four months later, Jackson and Rachel were officially married. Law was not as important as the harsh realities of frontier life and could be easily ignored.

Jackson also learned a bitter lesson on the dangers of complicated financial transactions involving banks. In March 1795, Jackson sold 68,750 acres of land to David Allison of Philadelphia. Using three promissory notes gained from Allison, Jackson purchased supplies for a general store he was opening in conjunction with his trading operations on the Cumberland River. Because the notes were now endorsed under Jackson's name, he became liable for payment if Allison defaulted on his payments. When Allison went bankrupt in 1795, Jackson sold his general store and a large amount of land in desperation to cover his debts.[10] After several years of legal and financial wrangling, Jackson avoided debtor's prison but acquired a lifelong hatred of paper money and banks. Although Jackson rebuilt his fortune as a successful attorney, land speculator and planter and launched a successful career as senator and eventually President, he never lost his identity as a small Western farmer. He understood Western anger towards east coast bankers and politicians and approved of the desire for Indian land in the West.

Jackson became President of the United States in 1829, mainly on the strength of his military record. As Commander of the Tennessee militia, he first demonstrated his military leadership against Red Stick Creek Indians during the Creek War in Alabama, 1813–14, which formed part of the larger War of 1812. After defeating the Creeks, Jackson forced them to cede twenty million acres of land in present-day Alabama and Georgia.[11] While Jackson's opening of so much land to white settlement made him a hero among white Southerners, his decisive victory over British forces at the Battle of New Orleans in January 1815 secured his national reputation. After the War of 1812, Jackson continued in his military exploits, pursuing Seminole war bands into Spanish Florida in March 1818.[12] Although Jackson's action set off an international crisis, Secretary of State John Adams adroitly turned the situation to America's advantage by brokering the

Adams–Onís Treaty (Transcontinental Treaty) in 1819, which brought all of Spanish Florida into the United States and extended America's western boundary to the Pacific Ocean for the first time.[13] The rigours of military life and experience of serving with Americans from different regions kindled in Jackson a deep sense of nationalism.

In 1822, the Tennessee legislature nominated Jackson for President in the upcoming 1824 election. To keep their candidate in the national limelight, state officials also sent Jackson to Washington DC as a United States senator. Less than two years later, Jackson fought John Quincy Adams, William H. Crawford and Henry Clay for the presidency. Jackson won a plurality of popular and Electoral College votes. However, with only ninety-nine electoral votes, he did not have enough votes for a majority win; the final decision was thus relegated to the House of Representatives. Crawford suffered from a stroke that year which hurt his candidacy. This gave Henry Clay, as Speaker of the House, the opportunity to engineer Adams's election to Presidency over Jackson.[14] As has been noted, Jackson interpreted the political compromise struck between Adams and Clay as a usurpation of the elite against the people and identified his personal fate with that of American people in general.[15]

Jackson used aggressive advertising and an army of loyal political spokesmen to take 178 Electoral College votes, against eighty-three for Adams, in the presidential election of 1828. Such widespread public support undoubtedly reinforced Jackson's belief that he was not just the representative of the people but their voice personified. Although Jackson was elusive on specific issues, his private life and public career revealed a certain amount of hostility towards federal intervention in American economic and social life.[16] In his first inaugural address, Jackson stated 'Internal improvement and the diffusion of knowledge, so far as they can be promoted by the constitutional acts of the Federal Government, are of high importance.'[17] This was the whole extent of his reference to the policies of the American System and was nothing but a perfunctory reference to the topic. Jackson was not interested in the American System. His interest lay in the westward expansion of American settlements.

Indian Removal

During the 1830s, Jackson led federal efforts to remove major Indian tribes from the Old Southwest to present-day Oklahoma, opening large tracts of land for white farmers and planters. Historian Daniel Walker Howe argues that the nature of so-called Jacksonian Democracy was 'the extension of white supremacy across the North American continent'. Thus, Indian Removal was the most important policy of Jackson's administration and it ensured his popularity in Western and Southern states, except in South Carolina.[18] Devastating for Native

American tribes who struggled to maintain their ancestral lands east of the Mississippi, Jackson's Indian Removal policy spurred the development of a 'cotton kingdom' across the Deep South. As far as the American System went, such reliance on large-scale agriculture caused white Southerners to doubt the need for a diverse national economy supported by protective tariffs and internal improvements.

Throughout his career as a frontier lawyer, politician and militia leader, Jackson had repeatedly called for federally sponsored Indian Removal.[19] In fact, white Southerners strongly supported Jackson for president in 1828 due in no small part to the widespread perception that the former General supported Indian Removal.[20] Jackson's election as President in 1828 sent a strong signal that southern state officials could begin to move against Native Americans with little worry of federal interference.[21] The state of Georgia aggressively led efforts to dispossess Native Americans and showed a willingness to use force if necessary.[22] This was hardly a new development, for Georgians had diligently tried to acquire fertile Cherokee lands, ideal for cotton production, since the 1780s.[23] In addition, the discovery of gold deposits in the Cherokee territory rumored since 1815 made them even more attractive.[24] As author James Mooney puts it, 'the doom of the [Cherokee] nation was sealed' with the discovery of gold.[25]

White people, in general, also saw Indians as 'savages' – sometimes as noble ones and other times as dangerous ones. Many whites thought that the only hope for Indians was, thus, to adopt the ways of white civilization.[26] Paradoxically, many whites feared that the Native Indians were becoming too civilized. Whites felt threatened by the image of untamed savages lurking at their back door, but the threat of a *civilized* native cultivating or herding on good cotton land, or trading with slaves and potentially harbouring runways was an equal anathema to Southern planters.[27]

Upon becoming President, Jackson began orchestrating political and public support for Indian Removal. In his inaugural address, he attempted to sound sympathetic towards Indians. He stated: 'It will be my sincere and constant desire to observe towards the Indian tribes within our limits a just and liberal policy, and to give that humane and considerate attention to their rights and their wants.'[28] However, as early as in his first annual message of 8 December 1829, Jackson had suggested that Congress set apart 'an ample district west of the Mississippi' for Indian Removal.[29] Heeding Jackson's message, the 21st Congress passed the Indian Removal Act on 26 May 1830 authorizing the President to give Indians territory west of the Mississippi River in exchange for their eastern lands. Although Section I of the Act specifically stated that it applied to 'such tribes or nations of Indians as may *choose* to exchange land where they now reside, and remove there', Jackson and his supporters in Congress clearly intended for all Native Americans be removed to frontier land in the West.[30] The

Senate vote was twenty-eight to nineteen. In the House of Representatives, the bill passed by a narrower margin of 102 to ninety-seven.[31] Southern delegates were solidly behind the bill.

Table 4.1. Vote Analysis of the Indian Removal Bill in 1830.

	Senate Yeas	Senate Nays	House Yeas	House Nays
New England	1	11	9	28
Mid-Atlantic	4	5	28	40
Northwest	7	3	13	17
South Atlantic	8	–	39	10
Southwest	8	–	13	2
Total	28	19	102	97

Source: *Senate Journal*, 21st Cong., 1st sess. (24 April 1830), p. 268; *House Journal*, 21st Cong., 1st sess. (26 May 1830), pp. 729–30.

Once the bill passed Jackson quick sought to implement it in a way that would stifle public dissent and encourage all of the tribes to quickly move beyond the west bank of the Mississippi River.

To expedite this policy Jackson dispatched Secretary of War John Eaton to negotiate with Choctaw leaders, who had already expressed a willingness to capitulate in hopes of a better deal. Eaton hoped to formulate a treaty that would exemplify Jackson's touted claims of quick, cheap and humane procedures for dealing with Native Americans, silence opposition to such policies and encourage cooperation among the remaining tribes.[32] The first deportation of Native Americans from the Mississippi Valley was fraught with human failures compounded by the harsh winter of 1831–2.[33] When corrupt civilian agents proved unable to feed and supply the native refugees, Jackson placed the removal policy in the hands of army officers. Although the military improved rations for the displaced tribes, funding removal policies proved difficult. To save expenses the federal government offered a small stipend to Native Americans who voluntarily migrated westward. This policy, however, left individual families vulnerable to white traders eager to snatch up the specie they were carrying.[34]

In 1835, Jackson backed a treaty signed with supposed 'representatives' of the Cherokee nation, who in reality represented only one seventeenth of the tribal population, to take possession of all Cherokee land east of the Mississippi within two years. Even whites were dubious of the treaty for it passed only by a single vote in the Senate. Not surprisingly, only 2,000 Cherokees voluntarily departed for Oklahoma before the two-year deadline. The round-up, detention in concentration camps, and exodus of 15,000 remaining Cherokees occurred during President Martin Van Buren's administration. The removal of the Cherokees became known as the Trail of Tears due to the brutality, hardship and high casualty rates of its victims.[35] By the end of the 1840s, the United States had removed most of the eastern Indian tribes west of the Mississippi River.[36]

Expansion into the Southwest and Isolation of the South from National Economy

Indian removal affected the rejection of the idea of the American System in the South. One of the results of Indian Removal was the rapid settlement of the southwestern territories by white farmers and planters eager to plant cotton. This development vitiated the need for a diversified economy. As the following table reveals, the population in the Southwestern states rose very sharply, from 115,000 in 1800 to 2.1 million in 1840. It grew faster than the population in South Atlantic states. Alabama and Mississippi experienced a phenomenal rise in population, particularly during the 1830s. Alabama's population doubled from 1830 to 1840 while Mississippi's nearly tripled within the same decade.[37]

Slave population in the Southwest increased very rapidly as well. For instance, Alabama's slave population rose 215 per cent and Mississippi saw a 300 per cent increase from 1830 to 1840, while North Carolina's slave population remained the same and Virginia's dropped 5 per cent. As the United States Constitution banned slave import as of 1808, a large-scale domestic slave trade developed to meet planters' demand for slave labour on Southwestern plantations. About two thirds of a million slaves were sold from the upper South to the lower South between the writing of the Constitution and the outbreak of the Civil War. Large numbers of these slaves moved to new cotton plantations in Alabama, Mississippi and Louisiana: 288,000 in the 1830s, 189,000 in the 1840s and 250,000 in the 1850s.[38] Slavery was thus being entrenched in the Southwest more tenaciously than in the South Atlantic States.

The expansion of cotton plantations and slavery throughout the Southwest resulted in increasing the South's economic distance from the rest of the country. Cotton production increased very rapidly. In 1790, the United States produced a mere 3,000 bales. By the time of the start of the Civil War, the United States produced more than 4 million bales. About three quarters of the cotton went to the European market, particularly British factories, thus making Britain more important to the Southern economy than the Eastern or Northwestern United States.[39] For decades, the port city of New Orleans had received a substantial amount of the south-flowing western goods. These goods were shipped down the Mississippi River and unloaded in the Crescent City only to be re-exported for international markets along with the cotton, sugar and rice grown in the South.[40] Yet, by 1850 this flow became marginal in comparison to the amount of goods travelling from the Northwest to East along canals and public roads.[41] By 1860, northeastern states received $146.5 million worth of produce from

Table 4.2. General Population in Southern States
from 1800 to 1860, in thousands.

	1800	1810	1820	1830	1840	1850	1860
South Atlantic	**1,795**	**2,101**	**2,421**	**2,880**	**3,063**	**3,563**	**3,974**
Georgia	163	252	341	517	691	906	1,057
North Carolina	478	556	639	738	753	869	993
South Carolina	346	415	503	581	594	669	704
Virginia	808	878	938	1,044	1,025	1,119	1,220
Southwest	**115**	**379**	**779**	**1,345**	**2,148**	**2,900**	**3,573**
Tennessee	106	262	423	682	829	1,003	1,110
Alabama	1	9	128	310	591	772	964
Louisiana	–	77	153	216	352	518	708
Mississippi	8	31	75	137	376	607	791
Total	1,910	2,480	3,200	4,225	5,211	6,463	7,547

Source: R. Sutch and S. B. Carter (eds), *Historical Statistics of the United States: Earliest Times to the Present, Millennial Edition*, 5 vols (New York: Cambridge University Press, 2006), 1:180–359; census data unavailable in 1800 for LA.

Figure 4.1. General Population Growth in the South between 1800 and 1860.

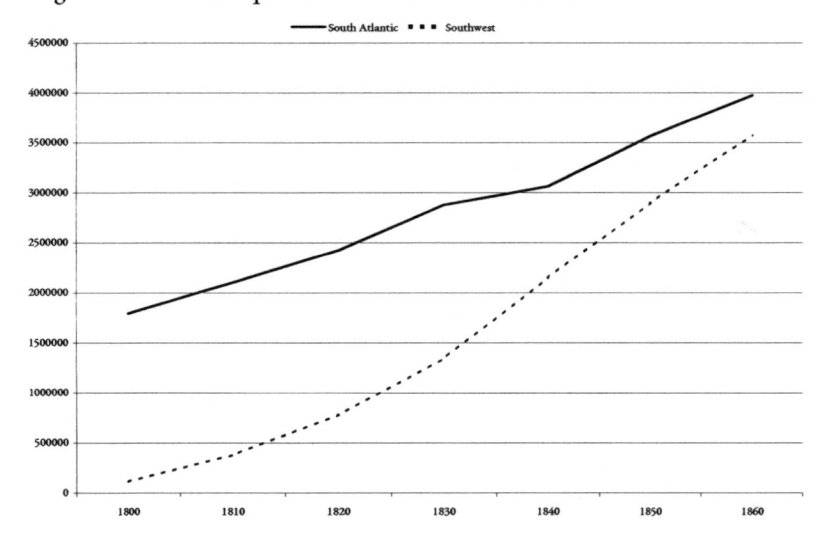

the Northwest while the South only received $42 million worth of similar foodstuffs.[42] The Northeastern and Northwestern states were developing an extensive trade relationship, while the South pursued its own economic interests alone.

Far from displaying hostility at such an economic development, the isolated South felt no need to be part of the national economy.[43] Cotton production was extremely lucrative but took considerable investment, particularly in slaves and land, in order to succeed. As such, Southern planters had little ability, and even less incentive, to diversify their economy or entertain notions of promoting domestic manufactures. Cotton came to define the contours of the Southern life. Plantation owners dominated the political and economic power in the South. Urban life was confined to the commercial centres of cotton trade: New Orleans, Mobile, Savannah and Charleston.[44] The South was indeed developing in its own unique manner.

Economic Growth of the Northwest

Contrary to what was happening to the South, the Northwest was developing a closer relationship with the Northeastern states. Cheap transportation encouraged western settlement and increased connections between the Northwest and Northeast. Immigration into the western territories beyond the Appalachian Mountains after the American Revolution led to the admission of a number of Western states into the union. Between 1792 and 1837, six Northwestern states were added to the union.

Table 4.3. Northwestern State Admissions into the Union.

State	Date
Kentucky	1 June 1792
Ohio	1 March 1803
Indiana	11 December 1816
Illinois	3 December 1818
Missouri	10 August 1821
Michigan	26 January 1837

Source: M. Leepson, *Flag: An American Biography* (New York: St. Martin's Press, 2005), pp. 268-9.

The population in the Northwestern states rose very sharply, from 272,000 in 1800 to 4 million in 1840.

Table 4.4. Population in Northwestern States, 1800–60, in thousands.

Northwest	1800	1810	1820	1830	1840	1850	1860
Illinois	2	12	55	157	476	851	1,712
Indiana	3	25	147	343	686	988	1,350
Kentucky	221	407	564	688	780	982	1,156
Michigan	4	5	9	32	212	398	749
Missouri	–	20	67	140	384	682	1,182
Ohio	42	231	581	938	1,519	1,980	2,340
Total	272	700	1,423	2,298	4,057	5,881	8,489

Source: R. Sutch and S. B. Carter (eds), *Historical Statistics of the United States: Earliest Times to the Present, Millennial Edition*, 5 vols (New York: Cambridge University Press, 2006), 1:180–359; census data unavailable in 1800 for Missouri.

The relative importance of Northwestern states increased dramatically as time progressed. In 1800, the Northwest represented only 5.1 per cent of the United States population, compared with 23.8 per cent in 1840 and 27 per cent in 1860 of the total American population.

Table 4.5. Northwestern Population Growth Within the United States.

Year	Total US Population	Northwestern Population	Per cent
1800	5,308,000	272,000	5.1%
1810	7,240,000	700,000	9.6%
1820	9,238,000	1,423,000	15.4%
1830	12,861,000	2,298,000	17.9%
1840	17,063,000	4,057,000	23.8%
1850	23,192,000	5,881,000	25.4%
1860	31,443,000	8,489,000	27.0%

Source: R. Sutch and S. B. Carter (eds), *Historical Statistics of the United States: Earliest Times to the Present, Millennial Edition*, 1:180–359; Total US population is from the United States Census Bureau, http://www.census.gov/population/www/censusdata/files/table-2.pdf (accessed 27 March 2009).

Western migration became easier because of the transportation revolution, which resulted in the reduction of freight rates and increase of the speed of movement. The freight rate of overland wagon transportation between 1800 and 1819 was thirty to seventy cents per ton.[45] Just before the Civil War, the charge on all-rail freight of wheat from Chicago to New York dropped to about 1.2 cents per mile, about a 95 per cent reduction compared to the rate of 1800 to 1819.[46] The freight rates on water travel also decreased dramatically. For example, the rate along Hudson River was 6.2 cents a ton per mile in 1814. It dropped to 0.7 cents in 1854, a decline of nearly 90 per cent.[47] The freight rate in 1817 from Buffalo to New York was 19.12 cents per mile. After construction of Erie Canal, ton–mile average for the period from 1857 to 1860 was mere 0.8 cents, a reduction of more than 95 per cent.[48]

The speed of transportation also increased as well. In 1817, goods sent from Cincinnati to New York would take more than fifty days. On the other hand, by the early 1850s, goods travelling the same terminals would take twenty-eight days by steamboat, eighteen days by canal, or only six to eight days by railroad.[49] The speed of transporting people also increased dramatically as well, particularly after the introduction of steamboats. On the Mississippi–Ohio system, keelboats took about three months to travel from New Orleans to the Ohio above Louisville, while steamboats reduced the time to eight days or less in the 1850s.[50]

This transportation revolution made it possible for a large number of people to move to and settle in the West beyond the Appalachian Mountains.[51] Cheaper transportation costs enabled Western frontier farmers to sell their wheat, corn and livestock at market and thus emerge from subsistence yeomanry into highly profitable enterprises with interregional and international destinations for their produce.[52] As New England's urban population rose, demand for Western foodstuffs increased, raising market prices and promoting Western settlement. The Erie Canal also stimulated Western settlement as it connected the Great Lakes to the heavily populated East.[53]

The Northwest diversified its economy rapidly with many growing cities. Dayton, Pittsburgh, Louisville, Nashville, Chicago, Detroit and St Louis developed into major urban and industrializing cities; Pittsburgh was a major food processing port and Cincinnati became 'the leading point of concentration for export of the surplus of the Ohio Valley'.[54] With support of solid internal improvements in place by the 1830s, Western urbanization rose from 3 per cent to 4 per cent in 1840, 9.5 per cent in 1850 and reaching 14 per cent by 1860. In comparison, the South's urban cities only contained 8.7 per cent of its population by 1860.[55]

Maysville Veto of 1830

While Jackson was very interested in effecting Indian Removal, he was not interested in promoting the American System. Rather he came to destroy all the pillars of the American System during his tenure as President. The first one to go was a federal programme of internal improvement. Jackson attacked a comprehensive and federal programme of internal improvements in the Maysville Road Veto of 1830. The Maysville Road Bill called for the federal government to buy 15,000 shares at $10 a piece in stock of Kentucky's Maysville Road Company. The company in turn would construct a sixty-five mile road between Lexington and Maysville in Kentucky.[56] The road would connect to the projected extensions of a national road running from Zanesville, Ohio to Florence, Alabama and from there on to New Orleans.[57] Despite his previous record of cautiously supporting internal improvements as a Senator, Jackson vetoed the Maysville Road bill on 27 May 1830.[58]

When Jackson came to power in 1829, he implied that he did not believe in the constitutionality of a federal programme of internal improvements. In his first annual message on 8 December 1829, he stated that 'Every member of the Union, in peace and in war, will be benefited by the improvement of inland navigation and the construction of high ways in the several States.' However, he expressed his wish to 'attain this benefit [of internal improvements] in a mode which will be satisfactory to all', indicating that he considered a constitutional amendment as precondition for the exercise of this power.[59] Jackson was more straightforward on this point in his Maysville Veto message. He stated that 'If it be the wish of the people that the construction of roads and canals should be conducted by the Federal Government, it is ... indispensably necessary, that a previous amendment of the Constitution ... should be made.'[60]

Jackson found another problem with the Maysville Road project. He acknowledged that all previous administrations had supported internal improvements. However, such aids were granted on projects '"of a general, not local – national, not State" character'.[61] On the other hand, the Maysville Road was 'a measure of purely local character'.[62] In his veto message, Jackson sought not merely to score political points with Southern voters but also to strike a personal blow against his long-time rival, Henry Clay, a strong supporter of the road intended to run through his home state.

The cause of internal improvements seemed to suffer a huge setback. John Quincy Adams confided in his diary that 'I suppose that the sacrifice of the Indians and the interest of internal improvement and domestic industry will strengthen, rather than weaken, the popularity of the present Administration ... The cause [of internal improvements] will no doubt survive me ... At present it is desperate.'[63] Martin Van Buren, Jackson's Secretary of State at the time of the veto stated in his autobiography that the general subject of internal improvements was 'banished from the halls of Congress' by the Maysville Veto.[64] On one level, both Adams and Van Buren were exaggerating the importance of Jackson's veto. Despite Jackson's veto, Congress appropriated more for internal improvements during Old Hickory's first term than they had done during John Quincy Adams's term. Jackson's second term witnessed even more federal funds for internal improvements. On another level, however, Adams and Van Buren were correct in the sense that future Congresses appropriated money for internal improvement projects on the merits of individual cases, not as part of a grand national programme of the kind of Gallatin's 1808 report on internal improvements or the General Survey Act of 1824. A *national programme* was gone. Remaining was only a number of disconnected projects. In addition, Jackson's veto completely blocked the most important method by which internal improvements were funded during Adams's administration: subscription to join stock companies. Jackson elaborated on the reasons why he objected to the federal government's subscription to private companies in his second annual message on 6 December 1830. He stated that such practice 'would ... change the character of this Government by consolidating into one the General and State Governments' and '[t]he power which the General Government would acquire within the several States by becoming the principal stock-holder in corporations' was 'dangerous to the liberties of the people'.[65] In addition, Jackson argued that subscription to stock companies would result in 'less security to the public interest' with wasteful spending of public money.[66] As a result, Congress began to end the practice of using private companies as proxies to build canals and road, while still quietly earmarking more money to directly fund regional improvement projects.[67] Jackson's policy on internal improvements made him ingratiated with the South, adding a building block to his tightly-knitted South–West political alliance.

Table 4.6. Federal Expenditure for Internal Improvements under John Q. Adams and Andrew Jackson.

	Rivers & Harbors	Roads & Canals	Lighthouses & etc.	Stock Subscription	Totals
Adams's Presidency	$928,700	$2,098,254	$1,025,861	**$2,185,000**	$6,237,815
Jackson's First Term	$2,468,012	$2,749,608	$1,124,284	$0	$6,341,904
Jackson's Second Term	$3,307,677	$4,261,704	$2,255,832	$0	$9,825,213
Jackson's Presidency Total	$5,775,689	$7,011,312	$3,380,116	$0	$16,167,117

Source: J. L. Larson, *Internal Improvement: National Public Works and the Promise of Popular Government in the Early United States*, (Chapel Hill, NC: The University of North Carolina Press, 2001), p. 191.

Figure 4.2. Federal Expenditure for Internal Improvements under Adams and Jackson.

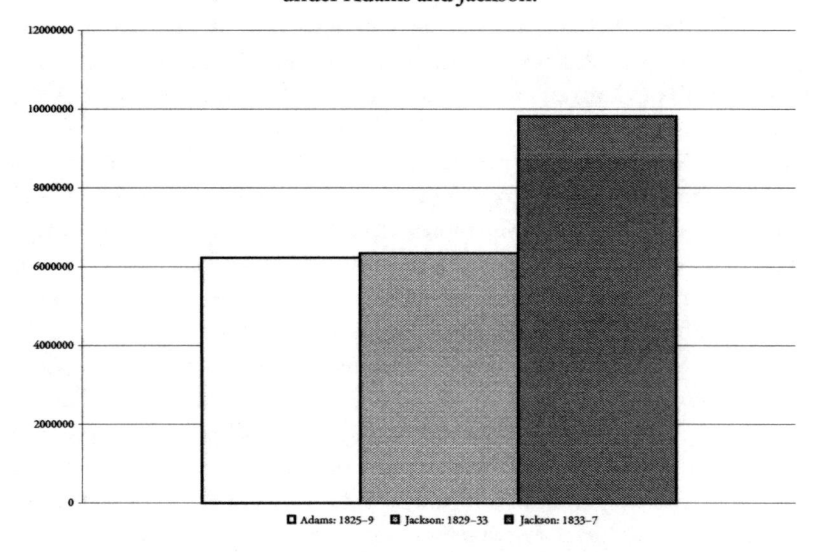

Failure of the Distribution Bills of 1832 and 1833

Another flashpoint in the ongoing debate over internal improvements occurred over the issue of distribution. The failure of the Disruption Bills in 1832 and 1833 was a setback to the cause of the American System. Distribution referred to the plan of distributing federal revenue from public land sales to the states, according to state population, for several causes including internal improvements.[68] Henry Clay unsuccessfully proposed Distribution Bills in 1832 and 1833.[69] This was in response to Thomas Hart Benton's graduation and cession schemes.[70] When the Maysville Road Veto blocked funding of internal improvements with the use of private corporations, Clay devised a plan to fund the internal improvements directly with federal revenue.[71] The distribution scheme would contribute to the cause of the American System on two levels. First, the revenue from land sales would contribute potential funding for internal improvements. Second, the distribution plan would undermine the rationale for cheap or free land in the West and justify protective tariffs. Opponents of the American System argued that tariff rates should be reduced with the retiring of the national debt. For example, Jackson stated in his third annual message of 6 December 1831 that '[i]t is therefore desirable that arrangements be adopted ... to relieve the people from unnecessary taxation after the extinguishment of the public debt.'[72] The only reason they swallowed high tariffs was the presence of national debt. With the distribution scheme, Clay could continue to justify protective tariffs and high land prices. Clay wrote in a letter on 4 October 1831 that

> [i]n some years, owing to the fluctuations of commerce, there may be a surplus ... Such an occasional surplus I would apply to the purpose of Int. improvements. But the Great resource on which I think we should rely for that object, after the payment of the public debt, is the proceeds of the sales of the public lands.[73]

Mixing three pillars of the American System together, the Distribution Bill seemed a political masterpiece. Clay also hoped to use the proposed system of internal improvements as the centrepiece for his campaign in the upcoming presidential election of 1832. While Clay could count on National Republicans to support his distribution plan, compromises were needed to lure additional patronage. Clay thus promised a 12.5 per cent rebate for lands sold within each state along with considerable land grants for internal improvement to Congressmen from Mississippi, Louisiana, Missouri, Alabama, Illinois and Indiana. Such brokering proved doubly advantageous to Clay, for he would need political support from these areas if he hoped to win the presidency.[74]

Unfortunately for Clay, the bill passed the Senate by a vote of twenty-six to twenty, only to be killed in the House.[75] Clay lost not only the Distribution Bill, but also his presidential bid in 1832 as well, carrying only Kentucky, Delaware, Connecticut, Rhode Island, Massachusetts and a majority of Maryland's vote.[76] He received a mere forty-nine Electoral College votes, while Jackson received 219 votes. The Bank War was doubtless a major factor for Clay's loss as he sided with the unpopular institution of the 2BUS. Of equal importance to the Bank War was the issue of the Distribution. Here again Clay fell onto the side of unpopularity when he proposed a scheme that many Westerners and Southerners disliked.

Western people wanted to have cheap land. The South wanted to get rid of protective tariffs and a federal programme of internal improvements. Many people in the South and West also hated the 2BUS. Jackson's scheme of cheap land, anti-2BUS, anti-protective tariffs and anti-federal programme of internal improvements was simple and very appealing to the South and West. On the other hand, Clay's plan of the American System was too complicated and did not appeal to the immediate interests of these two sections.[77] Clay was proposing a benefit plan for the future, while Jackson was promising immediate tangible results. Jackson interpreted the outcome of the election as a mandate for his political policies. As Jackson reminded Congress in his annual message in December 1832, the national debt would soon be paid off and revenue from land sales needed to be dealt with. He thus hinted that graduation and cession would be viable methods to dispose of excess federal revenue.[78]

Shortly thereafter, Clay countered by submitting a Distribution Bill to Congress for the second time, in early 1833. The Senate passed the bill by a vote of twenty-four to twenty-one on 25 January 1833, and the House followed suit on 1 March by a ninety-six to forty.[79] Debated alongside the Nullification Crisis, the Distribution Bill formed a symbolic relationship with the Compromise Tariff of 1833 and, not surprisingly, the voting pattern of regional support was identical for both.[80] The bill's success in the Congress owed mostly to the New England and Mid-Atlantic support it received. The Eastern states supported the bill because graduation, its alternative, threatened to lure their large populations to the West with very cheap land prices. Western legislators remained divided over the bill. Cheap land through graduation could make land ownership more available to a wider segment of the population. However, it could also allow speculators greater opportunities to gobble up large tracts of land, thus denying lands to poor western immigrants. On the other hand, although distribution would maintain somewhat higher land prices, it could also open up more land while replenishing the much-needed specie, which was drained from the West with every sale of land. These funds in turn would be spent on internal improvements that would encourage Western settlement and increase market access for blossoming agrarian communities. Southern delegates voted against the bill as they believed it threatened perpetual servitude under high tariffs.[81]

Table 4.7. Congressional Votes on the Distribution Bill of 1833.

	Senate		House	
	Yeas	Nays	Yeas	Nays
New England	10	1	21	2
Mid-Atlantic	7	2	43	6
Northwest	4	5	19	7
South Atlantic	–	8	9	16
Southwest	3	5	4	9
Total	24	21	96	40

Source: Senate Journal, 22nd Cong., 2nd sess. (25 January 1833), p. 138; House Journal, 22nd Cong., 2nd sess. (1 March 1833), pp. 460–1.

When the Distribution Bill reached President Jackson's desk, he left it there until the 22nd Congress expired, thus pocket-vetoing the proposal. The bill could not overcome the anti-American System feelings of the South and President Jackson.

The Nullification Crisis

The Nullification Crisis was a political showdown between the federal government and the state of South Carolina over the Tariff Acts of 1828 and 1832 which almost led to an armed confrontation. The Nullification Crisis destroyed the political prospects of the protective tariff in American politics until the coming of the Civil War. The origin of the crisis lay in the stagnation of South Carolina's overreliance on cotton as an export crop.[82] Following an international cotton boom in 1815, South Carolina became predominantly focused on the growth of this single cash crop. From 1800 through 1811, short staple cotton prices per pound averaged 17.8 cents. Rising from the low war years average of 10.9 cents, cotton prices rapidly climbed to an average of 26.9 cents per pound between 1815 and 1818.[83] The Panic of 1819 ended this prosperity. From 1819 to 1828 cotton prices fell to 12.9 cents per pound. From 1828 to 1832 short staple cotton averaged only 9.2 cents per pound.[84] Reeling from economic hardships, South Carolinians focused their fear and anger on protective tariffs.[85] They argued that such high tariffs raised the prices of manufactured goods in the domestic market, thus hurting their agricultural interests. In addition, a protective tariff punished planters twice over by reducing the purchasing power of British merchants, whose business was threatened by high tariffs of the United States.[86]

The protective tariff of 1824 raised duties on cotton and woollen goods to 33 per cent to combat the continued massive imports of British manufactured goods into the American market. The Tariff of 1828 contained 50 per cent duties on cotton and woollen goods. While South Carolina, along with other Southern states, supported the mildly protective tariff of 1816 out of post-war nationalism, the state was in no mood to support protectionism during a time of economic crisis. In addition, South Carolinians did not appreciate the goal of the American System, which was to create a domestic market, because only a small portion of their staples were traded within the United States.[87]

Just as the economic interests of their state prompted South Carolina's leaders to reject protectionism, the most important pillar of the American System, their political interests shifted to a strong states' rights ideology. When Congress passed the General Survey Act and Protective Tariff Act of 1824 with heavy Northern support, white Southerners began to realize the grim possibility of becoming a permanent minority in the union. Defeats over the Protective Tariff

Acts of 1828 and 1832 reinforced this feeling of weakness. In his inflammatory pamphlet published in 1827, *The Crisis*, Robert J. Turnbull, a South Carolina tidewater planter, argued that Southern 'uneasiness' stemmed from fears of a national majority opposed to Southern interests. He stated that

> [t]he cause is obvious. The more *National*, and the less *Federal*, the Government becomes, the more certainly will the interest of the great majority of the States be promoted, but with the same certainty, will the interests of the South be depressed and destroyed.[88]

In his speech of 1827 against protective tariffs, Thomas Cooper, the President of South Carolina College, also stated that 'the *American system*, is a system, by which the earnings of the south are to be transferred to the north – by which the many are sacrificed to the few; under which powers are usurped that were never conceded'.[89]

A symbol of declining Southern influence in national affairs was the 'End of the Virginia Dynasty'[90] in the presidential election of 1824. Virginia had produced four of the first five presidents of the United States, but in the presidential election of 1824, none of Virginia's sons ran for President. Moreover William H. Crawford, the candidate Virginia supported, came in third in the popular and Electoral College votes. None of the Southern states could afterwards fill the leadership void left by Virginia in either national or regional politics.[91] Commenting on the power of Virginia in the union in 1832, John Quincy Adams wrote, 'Virginia has now become a State of subservient policy, and is internally so much convulsed as to be deserving rather of compassion than of envy.'[92] Southerners became afraid for the future of slavery, the basis of Southern politics, economy and society.

In the wake of the passage of the Tariff Act of 1832, the newly elected legislature in South Carolina called a special convention, which quickly passed the Ordinance of Nullification on 24 November 1832, declaring the Tariff Acts of 1828 and 1832 null and void within the state's borders as of 1 February 1833. Despite his states'-rights leanings, Jackson denounced the Nullification Ordinance of South Carolina and threatened to personally lead a federal army to quell the rebellion. Jackson was after all a soldier who could not tolerate either a challenge to the integrity of the union or a challenge to his personal authority as President of the United States.[93] Eventually the Compromise Tariff Act of 1833 aborted a military clash between the United States and South Carolina. Senator Calhoun, who resigned his post of Vice-President to become a Senator from his home state, and Senator Clay orchestrated the deal. The final shape of the bill included a gradual yearly reduction of the percentage of duties paid over the next decade, until an average rate of 20 per cent was reached in 1842.[94]

The Nullification Crisis was an ominous event that took the nation to the brink of civil war and foreshadowed the harrowing events that came three decades later. It comes as no surprise that South Carolina was the first of the Southern states to break away from the Union in 1860. But before the secession of South Carolina occurred, the Compromise Tariff Act of 1833 effectively killed the principle of protectionism, the most important part of the American System. Despite several attempts at revival, protectionism remained dormant before the outbreak of the Civil War.

The Bank War

A major blow to the cause of the American System came with the Bank War of 1832–4. For nearly two years, Andrew Jackson battled Nicholas Biddle, the President of the 2BUS, over the re-chartering of the bank. Jackson eventually emerged victorious, killing one of the pillars of the American System and undermining American economic stability, which contributed to the coming of the Panic of 1837.

Nicholas Biddle, the bank's president during the Bank War, had been born into a wealthy Philadelphia family. As a youth, Biddle toured Europe before settling on careers as a lawyer and editor of a national magazine, the *Port Folio*, in which he translated poetry from Greek and French and analysed Machiavelli's *The Prince*. He also edited original journals of Lewis and Clark's expedition and served a term in the Pennsylvania legislature.[95] In 1819 President Monroe appointed Biddle as one of the five government-selected members of the 2BUS's Board of Directors. Succeeding Langdon Cheves, Biddle became the third President of the bank in 1823. During Biddle's tenure, the 2BUS began to assume the mantle of a central bank as focus drifted from purely profit-seeking to regulating and policing the banking practices of state banks.[96] Under Biddle's leadership the 2BUS influenced the amount of notes circulated by state banks through a fairly consistent process of redeeming state bank notes for specie, thus curbing state banks from overextending themselves.[97] It was an operation that had already worked locally within New England, where banking was more advanced and established. However, the strength and size of the 2BUS and its status as the receiver of notes from many different banks allowed it to operate on a national scale, making the bank perform the function of a central bank.[98]

When Andrew Jackson came to power in 1829, his ideas on the 2BUS were not well known. In his first annual address to Congress, however, Jackson argued that the bank was unconstitutional and that 'it has failed in the great end of establishing an uniform and sound currency'. He recommended that Congress devise a national bank 'which would avoid all constitutional difficulties and at the same time secure all the advantages to the Government and country that were expected to result from the present bank'.[99] Jackson returned to the issue in his second annual address in December 1830.[100] In his third annual address in 1831, Jackson proposed an 'investigation of an enlightened people and their representatives' on the 2BUS.[101]

The 2BUS's charter was set to expire in 1836. Yet, Nicolas Biddle petitioned Congress for a re-charter before the presidential election of 1832 was underway. This was one of the two most serious political mistakes the otherwise brilliant Biddle made during the Bank War. Henry Clay, the National Republican presidential candidate in 1832 supported Biddle's move. The cunning senator calculated that should the Bank be re-chartered then it would pave the way for the success of future federal programmes, namely the American System. Yet if Jackson vetoed the prosperous bank, it would anger the American people who would then turn on the President.[102] Such calculations proved costly to both Biddle and Clay.

On 9 February 1832, George M. Dallas, a Democrat Senator from Pennsylvania, presented Biddle's memorial for the recharter of the 2BUS to the Congress.[103] The bill for re-charter passed both houses, passing through the Senate on 11 June with a vote of twenty-eight to twenty and through the House of Representatives on 3 July with a vote of 107 to eighty-five. [104] After the re-charter bill passed through Congress, Biddle expressed relief but prophesied: 'My belief is that the President will veto the bill though this is not generally known or believed.'[105] As predicted by Biddle, Jackson's veto message was signed and delivered to Congress on 10 July.[106] In his veto message, Jackson argued that the bank was unconstitutional, despite the Supreme Court's affirmative decision on the constitutionality of the bank in the *McCulloch* v. *Maryland* case. He also argued that the bank was a monopoly and was under foreign influence, as about a quarter of the stocks were held by foreign stock holders, which ignored the fact the foreign stock holders were not allowed to cast votes on important decisions including the election of the president of the bank. Jackson also argued that the bank exercised a corrupting influence on Congress. In fact, the bank extended loans to important Congressmen including Clay and Daniel Webster, automatically renewing the loans. His veto message also condemned the bank for supposedly profiting the aristocratic few at the expense of ordinary Americans.[107] Jackson was thus fulfilling his role as the tribune defending the plebeians from exploitation by corrupt politicians. Biddle thought the veto message was self destructive and characterized it 'a manifesto of anarchy.' He even spent as much as $5,000 of his bank's funds to distribute printed copies of the veto message. Biddle also wrote and distributed letters, under the pen name Simon Snyder, to trumpet the virtues of the 2BUS.[108]

Within a few months after the bank veto, Jackson was re-elected to the presidency by 219 out of 286 Electoral College votes. Old Hickory interpreted the election results as support for his historic veto of the 2BUS. Anti-bank feeling did stem from working-class farmers who 'resented their creditors as much as they needed their financial services', Wall Street bankers eager to replace their Philadelphia counterparts as the economic brokers for the United States, and western 'wildcat bankers ... who resented the way the BUS monitored their behavior', and 'soft money entrepreneurs' looking for easy credit.[109]

This broad-based show of public support reassured Jackson as he now moved aggressively against the bank rather than just waiting for its charter to expire. Impatiently, he instructed Treasury Secretary Louis McClane to remove government funds from the 2BUS to several Democratic-leaning banks in several states. McClane officially responded that deposits could only be removed if they were in danger, which was obviously not the case.[110] Jackson snapped back that the bank had to be destroyed immediately or else 'with this hydra of corruption they will rule the nation, and its charter will be perpetual, and its corrupting influence destroy the liberty of our country'.[111] Although Jackson believed that he held the moral high ground, he was still forced to fire both McClain and William J. Duane, before Attorney General Roger B. Taney agreed to serve as Treasury Secretary and gradually remove the federal government's deposits to a number of selected state banks called 'pet banks'.[112]

Biddle responded by contracting the loans available and generating an economic crisis, his second grave political mistake that ultimately harmed his cause more than Jackson's. Biddle also lost many supporters when it was discovered that the specie reserves of the 2BUS had increased by 50 per cent, from $10 million to $15 million, while the bank was curtailing its loans by twenty-five per cent. Through hasty decision making, Biddle had ironically allowed the 2BUS to become the 'monster' portrayed in Jacksonian rhetoric.[113]

Jackson, on the other hand, was no closer to eliminating paper money or banks from the American landscape. Banks would continue to multiply and expand to facilitate the expansion of American economy. The number of pet banks rose to twenty-two by the end of 1833, with addition of more than ninety banks to the system by 1836.[114] What the Jacksonians were trying to do was not to stop all governments from interventioning in economy, but to block the 'federal' government from influencing the economy, thus opening opportunities to state governments. As in the case of internal improvements, Jacksonians were cutting the ties between the federal government and private companies. The Bank War thus destroyed another pillar of the American System, the 2BUS. Eventually the 2BUS folded its business as a federal bank in 1836 and operated as a state-chartered bank until 1841. Several attempts to charter another national bank all failed before the outbreak of the Civil War. Coinciding with the 2BUS's demise in 1836 was yet another economic downturn, the Panic of 1837.

The Panic of 1837

The Bank War and destabilization of the American economy did much to spark the Panic of 1837. Yet the crisis had its origins in fluctuating land prices which stretched back nearly twenty years. From 1820 to 1828 land sales stagnated at less than 1 million acres per year. Afterwards, however, land sales increased rapidly. Both settlers and speculators purchased large amounts of land in Michigan, Indiana, Illinois, Mississippi and Missouri.

Table 4.8. Public Land Sales, 1820–41.

Year	Acres Sold	Dollars Paid	Year	Acres Sold	Dollars Paid
1820	312,000	$435,000	1831	2,778,000	$3,557,000
1821	782,000	1,123,000	1832	2,462,000	3,115,000
1822	710,000	909,000	1833	3,856,000	4,972,000
1823	652,000	848,000	1834	4,658,000	6,100,000
1824	737,000	947,000	1835	12,564,000	16,000,000
1825	999,000	1,392,000	1836	20,075,000	25,168,000
1826	848,000	1,129,000	1837	5,601,000	7,008,000
1827	927,000	1,318,000	1838	3,415,000	4,306,000
1828	966,000	1,221,000	1839	4,976,000	6,465,000
1829	1,245,000	1,573,000	1840	2,237,000	2,790,000
1830	1,930,000	2,433,000	1841	1,165,000	1,463,000

Total Acres Sold: 73,895,000
Total Dollars Paid: $94,272,000

Source: B. H. Hibbard, *A History of the Public Land Policies* (New York: Peter Smith, 1939), table IX on page 103; all figures have been rounded to the nearest thousand.

Figure 4.3. Public Land Sales, 1820–41.

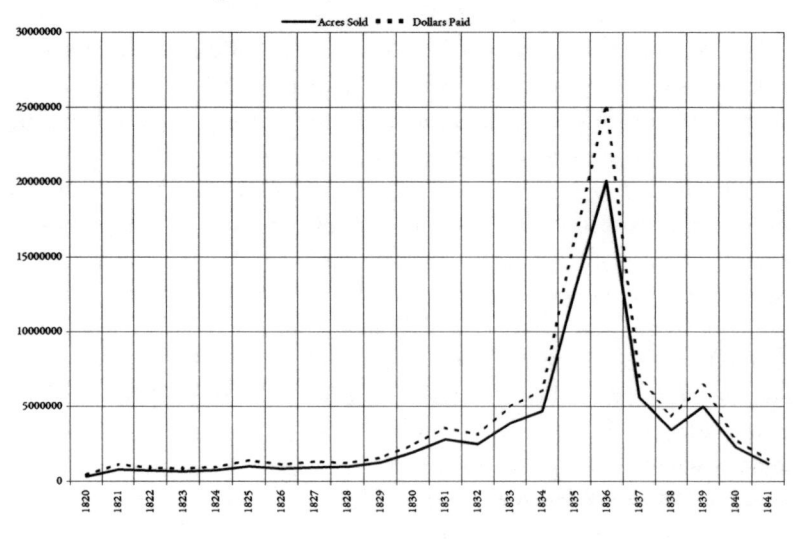

The causes for this increase in sales included the availability of easy loans by state banks, construction of internal improvement projects by states, influxes of immigrants to the West and high prices for agricultural produce. In addition, the Indian Removal policy removed an important obstacle for white settlement in the Southwestern frontier.[115]

To curb excessive land speculation, President Jackson issued the Specie Circular in July 1836, declaring that only gold and silver would be acceptable for the purchase of public lands.[116] Its goal was to curb speculation by reducing the amount of bank notes in circulation.[117] However, the Specie Circular did not produce the desired outcome. In 1836, public land sales reached $25 million, the record figure. Eventually this land speculation led to the Panic of 1837. As during the War of 1812, economic troubles began when state banks suspended specie payments. New York banks suspended specie payments on 10 May 1837. The crisis soon spread to other cities; Philadelphia, Baltimore, Albany, Hartford, Newhaven and Providence banks suspended specie payments the next day; Mobile and New Orleans banks on the twelfth; the District of Columbia banks on the fifteenth; Charleston and Cincinnati on the seventeenth.[118] Over the course of the following year, 194 of the 729 state-chartered banks across the nation were forced to close their doors. The prices of railroad, banking and industrial securities in the stock market plunged dramatically.[119]

Following the banking crisis of 1837, businesses throughout the US came to a standstill. A contemporary commented: 'A perfect apathy settled over the community. Barges and tow boats lay idle at the docks, building operations ceased, and thousands of laborers were thrown out of employment'.[120] Labour began to suffer immediately. In New York City alone 50,000 people went jobless and nearly another 200,000 lacked adequate means to support themselves and their families. In August of 1837, a New York journal carried a story describing how 500 men had replied in a single day to an advertisement for twenty positions as labourers at four dollars a day and board. It was also estimated that nearly nine tenths of the factories in the East were closed during the months immediately following the bank closures.[121]

In addition, the majority of existing coins disappeared from circulation. Specie was now at a premium and those who held it began to hoard it, thus making small bills the new method of currency.[122] During the following months, the banks worked to increase their specie reserves while at the same time curtailing their loans and discounts. Because of these tight fiscal policies, banks were able to resume specie payments in May of 1838. This was followed by a short period of increased economic growth. Yet public distrust in the economy made such growth short-lived.[123] The Panic of 1837 merged with the Panic of 1839 to create a prolonged period of hard times that continued throughout the Presidency of Martin Van Buren.[124]

Fall of the American System

By the end of the 1830s, all of the policy proposals of the American System had been categorically rejected by the President, the Congress and the majority of American voters. Clay himself bitterly accepted the fall of the American System which he had done so much to promote. In a letter to Judge Francis Brooke of Virginia written on October 9, 1838, Clay stated that '[a]t present ... it is useless to try to establish any Bank of the U.S. with any modification whatever'.[125] In his letter to the Virginian states' rights ideologue and secessionist Judge Beverly Tucker, written on 10 October 1839, the Kentuckian stated that he had abandoned the rest of the American System. He noted that '[i]n the origin of the protective policy, it was never supposed by me or by others of its friends ... that it was to be permanent'. He continued, 'I thought it inexpedient that Congress should continue to exercise that power [over internal improvements] by commencing any new work; and that all that I ever wished now to see done by Congress was ... Leaving to their [states'] exclusive care the general subject of internal improvements'. Clay even renounced the very basic principle of the American System: 'I have said, again and again, and most sincerely hold, that the patronage of the general government ... is fraught with imminent danger to the institutions and liberty of the country.'[126] It was hard times for the American System.

Jackson and Cultural Improvement

Just as the economic policies of the American System suffered blow after blow during the administration of President Jackson, cultural improvement also passed into complete oblivion during his tenure. During the eight years in office, Jackson made only two perfunctory references to education, in his first inaugural address on 4 March 1829 and in his first annual message on 8 December 1829. On the first occasion, he stated that 'Internal improvement and the diffusion of knowledge, so far as they can be promoted by the constitutional acts of the Federal Government, are of high importance.'[127] It was nothing but a general statement of principle. On the second occasion, he stated that 'The fiscal power of the States will also be increased [at the extinction of national debt in a few years], and may be more extensively exerted in favor of education and other public objects.'[128] He expressed his belief that education belonged to the state authority, not to the federal government. It is therefore not strange that Jackson did not even make a casual reference to education or other aspects of cultural improvements in his official statements during the next seven years. Jackson was interested in more immediate and practical issues such as Indian Removal, destruction of the 2BUS and lowering of tariff rates, rather than the establishment of a university or library.

CONCLUSION: THE AMERICAN SYSTEM AND AMERICAN SOCIETY AND ECONOMY, 1790–1837

The American System and American Politics

The American System was based on a nationalistic understanding of the country and served as a political centerpiece first for the National Republicans and later the Whigs. Both groups believed that the union was created by the American people, instead of the states, to last for all time. In addition, it was assumed that the federal government was to be more powerful than state governments.[1] A strong system of federally sponsored tariffs, roads and canals would permanently safeguard this political union and refine American culture. As such, many proponents of the American System were motivated by nationalistic zeal and moralistic passion as well as political ambition. Many historians have understated the moralistic and religious dimension of the American System, while overemphasizing the nationalistic side of the concept. The moralistic and religious aspects of the American System made the idea resilient and persistent in pursuing its goal of achieving a strong federal union through various economic and cultural projects.

Although Jackson and Southern political leaders each played crucial roles in the demise of the American System, the programme also failed due to an inherent contradiction. As scholars have consistently agreed, the American System was based on the assumption that diverse regional interests throughout the country *could* be reconciled through political and economic compromises. Also, it has been assumed that the nationalism felt among ordinary Americans would overcome sectional differences. However, such sentiments proved to be wishful thinking. There was not enough cohesiveness in the country to outweigh the persistent sectional jealousies in antebellum American society. State and regional loyalties proved too strong for the nascent nationalism of the period to coalesce around a system of internal improvements. The simple fact that Henry Clay from Kentucky, a pro-protection and pro-internal improvements state, could continue his support for the American System, while John C. Calhoun, from South

Carolina, ended up embracing states' rights ideas, indicated the strength of state loyalties. When the erratic Virginia Congressman John Randolph accepted a challenge from Henry Clay after insulting him in the House, Randolph insisted on a location 'within the State of Virginia' for the duel. Senator Thomas Hart Benton testified that Randolph's insistence on the Virginia location was because he represented Virginia, and if he died in the duel, 'Virginia soil was ... the chosen ground to receive his blood'.[2]

Ultimately, both the strengths and weaknesses of the American System were based on the underlying conviction that it was a policy package sufficient to unify different sections of the United States. However, its proponents could not persuade its opponents to overcome their sectionalism.[3] The result only served to exacerbate sectional tensions. As historian Thomas Brown aptly pointed out, '[i]ronically, the American System, which was to help unify the national existence, would itself become a source of dissension'.[4] The proponents of the American System underestimated the emotional intensity over sectional interests, including Southern slavery and cheap Western land. Basically the American System rested upon an overly idealistic understanding of American reality. It was a vision, but the lofty vision collapsed under the weight of the political conflicts of the 1830s and the Panic of 1837, without being able to develop its full potential.

The American System and American Economy

As historian Daniel Walker Howe pointed out, the plans of Henry Clay and John Quincy Adams to develop the American System could have diversified the American economy, liberating it from excessive dependence on slave-based plantation economics.[5] But its failure led to the continuous expansion of the 'Cotton Kingdom' in the Old South. The failure of the American System kept tariff rates low in the 1840s and 1850s, never to rise to the level of a protective tariff until after the outbreak of the Civil War. As a result of the failure of the American System, internal improvement initiatives passed from national to state governments and private investors. According to economic historian Walter Licht, about 70 per cent of the total costs for canal construction before the Civil War were assumed by state and municipal governments, while private capital made up 70 per cent of railroad construction costs during the same period.[6] In addition, several attempts to establish a national bank also failed until the start of the Civil War. As such, the failure to implement a national programme of internal improvements hindered the emergence of a national domestic market, which was the aim of the American System.[7]

As economic historians Albert Fishlow and Diane Lindstrom have shown, a national domestic market had not emerged even as late as the 1850s.[8] Lindstrom in her study of Philadelphia's economic development shows that it was an intraregional market rather than an interregional market that sustained the economic development in antebellum United States.[9] According to economic historian David Meyer, the South took no more than 8 per cent of the East's production and the Midwest even less as of 1840. In the next two decades, the share of Eastern manufactured products exported to the South and Midwest ranged between 10 per cent and 15 per cent.[10]

Ironically, federal land reforms continued to survive, albeit mainly in the form of relief acts rather than a complete overhaul of the system. Land policies based on the principle that land was a common property of the United States persisted for many years, until replaced by the Homestead Act of 1862, which granted free land to long-term resident settlers in western territories and states.

The American System and American Society

Although the American System had failed as a political programme by 1837, it survived to some degree as a programme for promoting social reforms. Commenting on the presidential campaign of 1828, an antebellum newspaperman wrote that the Adams campaign had 'dealt with man *as he should be*', while the Jackson campaign had 'appealed to him *as he is*'. This description can be applied to the whole idea of the American System. The supporters of the American System were idealists who sought to better American society according to their design of how the United States should be.

Ironically, the failure of the American System in a political and economic sense helped the reform movements to succeed. Without the central control by the federal government in political and economic realms, social changes in culture, transportation, communication and technological innovations occurred in a more free society. Reform associations pushed the agenda for social change to the forefront of public discussion. Better communication and transportation helped to spread the news of reform throughout the country.[11]

The antebellum American economy and society became increasingly liberal and capitalistic during the Jacksonian period, not necessarily because Jackson and his followers were pursuing such goals.[12] In fact, Jacksonians could be quite anti-capitalistic at times. Benton's scheme of graduation of land prices was a good example of such a trend in that it compromised the proprietary rights of the United States. Jacksonian Indian Removal policy simply brushed aside the property rights of Native Indians and violated the sanctity of contracts, the basis of capitalism, by violating numerous treaties signed with Native tribes. The Bank War might have been a good political move, but could hardly be considered conducive toward the capitalistic development of the American economy. In a sense, antebellum American capitalism grew, despite such fundamental problems. It would take many more years before such hurdles to capitalistic improvement could be overcome in American society.

The proponents of the American System had a clear vision for the United States: politically united, economically prosperous, internationally independent and culturally advanced. They were forward-looking and progressive people. On the other hand, Jacksonians were afraid of the radical changes that might be brought about by the policies of the American System and successfully halted such changes in antebellum America. The main issue for the proponents of the American System was how to improve the United States. The main issue for the Jacksonians was how to stop the federal government from meddling in their lives and economics. Jacksonians had better success in appealing to the minds of American people in general before the Civil War. That, however, is not enough of an excuse to underestimate the value of the vision of the American System.

Epilogue: The Revival of the American System

Although the American System died during the Jacksonian era, it was revived during the Civil War. After the massive resignation of Southern delegates from the United States Congress, the Republican Party held 102 out of 146 House seats and twenty-nine out of thirty-six Senate seats in 1861. With the urging of the Executive branch, the Congress enacted a series of policies, composed of the relics of the American System. First, the Morrill Tariff Act of 1861 raised the average tariff rate by 5 to 10 per cent. This tariff sought to protect domestic manufacturers as well as raise revenue for the war treasury. Representative Justin Smith Morrill, who initiated the Tariff Act of 1861, argued in the House that the new Tariff Bill would benefit not only manufactures but also agriculture, commerce and mining. Other Republican Representatives and Senators also argued that the Tariff Bill would lead to an expanded domestic market, and a prosperous and independent country. The Congress continued to raise tariff rates in 1862 and 1864 for the dual purpose of revenue and protection.[13]

In addition, the Republican Congress also passed a National Bank Act on 25 February 1863 and brought a large number of state banks under the umbrella of a national banking system. Banknotes produced under this system provided a uniform currency nationwide. President Abraham Lincoln and Treasury Secretary Salmon P. Chase strongly promoted a national bank law.[14] Yet it was Senator John Sherman from Ohio who initiated the bill in Congress. While urging passage of the bill, he stated that notes issued by the national banking system would strengthen the federal government's authority, and enhance 'a sentiment of nationality' in the union.[15]

The Republican Congress also passed the Pacific Railroad Act in 1862, which incorporated two railroad companies, the Union Pacific Railroad and Central

Pacific Railroad. Congress awarded these corporations land grants of more than 60 million acres and $20 million to help them build a cross-continental railroad from Omaha, Nebraska to San Francisco, California. The railroad was completed in 1869, thus creating a genuine national economy and expanding immigration and investment into the West. The economic side of the American System was thus completed.[16]

The cultural nationalism of the American System was also realized during the Civil War. The Congress passed Morrill Land Grant Act in 1862, which granted large tracts of lands to states. State governments were to use the revenue from the land sales to start colleges focused on agricultural and mechanical arts.[17] George Washington, John Adams, Thomas Jefferson, James Madison, James Monroe, Henry Clay and John Quincy Adams would have been pleased to know that their dream of national improvement was on its way towards implementation, despite the tumults of the Civil War.

NOTES

Introduction: What Was the American System?

1. C. Sellers, *The Market Revolution: Jacksonian America 1815–1846* (New York: Oxford University Press, 1991).
2. S. Wilentz, *The Rise of American Democracy: Jefferson to Lincoln* (New York: W. W. Norton & Company, 2005).
3. D. W. Howe, *What Hath God Wrought: The Transformation of America, 1815–1848* (New York: Oxford University Press, 2007).
4. Ibid., p. 62.
5. Ibid.
6. In fact, this merging of social and cultural history with political and economic history was the main theme of his earlier article: D. W. Howe, 'The Evangelical Movement and Political Culture in the North During the Second Party System', *The Journal of American History*, 77:4 (March 1991), pp. 1216–39.
7. M. G. Baxter, *Henry Clay and the American System* (Lexington, KY: The University Press of Kentucky, 1995), p. 27.
8. B. F. Wright (ed.), *The Federalist* (Cambridge, MA: The Belknap Press of Harvard University Press, 1966), p. 141.
9. 'Mr. Jefferson and the Tariff', *Niles' Weekly Register*, 38 (12 June 1830), p. 294, italicization by Jefferson.
10. *Annals of Congress*, 16th Cong., 1st sess. (10 May 1820), p. 2228.
11. 'Seventh Annual Message', 2 December 1823, *A Compilation of the Messages and Papers of the Presidents*, ed. J. D. Richardson, 11 vols (New York: Bureau of National Literature, 1911), vol. 2, p. 787.
12. 2 December 1823, *Memoirs of the John Quincy Adams*, ed. C. F. Adams, 12 vols (Philadelphia, PA: J. B. Lippincott & Co., 1875), vol. 6, p. 224.; R. V. Remini, *Henry Clay: Statesman for the Union* (New York: W. W. Norton & Compnay, 1991), p. 221.
13. *Annals of Congress*, 18th Cong., 1st sess. (1 March 1824), p. 1978.
14. Ibid. (31 March 1824), pp. 1978, 1963.
15. For some of the contemporary debates on the American System, see D. Raymond, *The American System* (Baltimore, MD: Lucas & Deaver, 1828); *The Southern Excitement, Against the American System* (Poughkeepsie: Platt & Parsons, 1829); W. B. Giles, *Mr. Clay's Speech upon the tariff, or, The 'American system', so called, or, The Anglican System, in Fact Introduced Here, and Perverted in its Most Material bearing upon Society, by the Omission of a System of Corn Laws, for the Protection of Agriculture: Mr. Giles' Speech upon the Resolutions of Inquiry in the House of Delegates of Virginia, in Reply to Mr. Clay's Speech:*

also, his *Speech in Reply to Gen. Taylor's, Accompanied with Sundry Other Interesting Subjects and Original Documents: the Whole Containing a Mass of Highly Useful Information at the Present Interesting Crisis* (Richmond, VA: Thomas W. White, 1827). For later studies on the American System, see G. G. Van Deusen, *The Life of Henry Clay* (Boston, MA: Little, Brown and Company, 1937), p. 215; R. W. Binkley, Jr., 'The American System: An Example of American Nineteenth-Century Economic Thinking Its Definition by Its Author Henry Clay' (PhD dissertation, Columbia University, 1949); S. F. Bemis, *John Quincy Adams and the Union* (New York: Knopf, 1956), p. 33; M. L. Wilson, *Space Time and Freedom: The Quest for Nationality and the Irrepressible Conflict 1815–1861* (Westport, CT: Greenwood Press, 1974), pp. 49–72; D. W. Howe, *The Political Culture of the American Whigs* (Chicago, IL: University of Chicago Press, 1979); D. Feller, *The Public Lands in Jacksonian Politics* (Madison, WI: University of Wisconsin Press, 1984), p. 59; *The Jacksonian Promise: America, 1815–1840* (Baltimore, MD: The Johns Hopkins University Pres, 1995), pp. 66, 71; M. D. Peterson, *The Great Triumvirate: Webster, Clay, and Calhoun* (New York: Oxford University Press, 1987), pp. 68–84; Remini, *Henry Clay*, pp. 210–33; Baxter, *Henry Clay and the American System*; D. P. Currie, *The Constitution in Congress: The Jeffersonians 1801–1829* (Chicago, IL: University of Chicago Press, 2001), p. 250; J. L. Larson, *Internal Improvement: National Public Works and the Promise of Popular Government in the Early United State* (Chapter Hill, NC: The University of North Carolina Pres, 2001); J. R. Van Atta, 'Western Lands and the Political Economy of Henry Clay's American System, 1819–1832', *Journal of the Early Republic* 21:4 (Winter 2001), pp. 633–65; P. Baker, 'The Washington National Road Bill and the Struggle to Adopt a Federal System of Internal Improvement', *Journal of the Early Republic* 22:3 (Autumn 2002), pp. 437–64; A. Shankman, *Crucible of American Democracy: the Struggle to Fuse Egalitarianism & Capitalism in Jeffersonian Pennsylvania* (Lawrence, KY: University Press of Kansas, 2004), pp. 225–46; J. R. Van Atta, '"A Lawless Rabble": Henry Clay and the Cultural Politics of Squatters' Rights, 1832–1841', *Journal of the Early Republic* 28:3 (Autumn 2008), pp. 337–78; Howe, *What Hath God Wrought*, pp. 270–84.

16. *Annals of Congress*, 18th Cong., 1st sess. (31 March 1824), pp. 1962–2001; *Register of Debates*, 22nd Cong., 1st sess. (2 February 1832), pp. 256–96.
17. Raymond, *The American System*. For a succinct study of Raymond as an economist, see P. K. Conkin, *Prophets of Prosperity: America's First Political Economists* (Bloomington, IN: Indiana University Press, 1980), pp. 77–107.
18. 'Southern Excitement', *Niles' Weekly Register*, 35 (20 September 1828), pp. 58–68; Raymond, *The Southern Excitement*.
19. Giles, *Mr. Clay's Speech Upon the Tariff*, pp. 93, 108–9.
20. 'Speech of Dr. Cooper', *Niles Weekly Register*, vol. 33 (8 September 1827), p. 32.
21. Ibid., p. 31.
22. *Register of Debates*, 21st Cong., 1st sess. (23 March 1830), p. 647.
23. Bemis, *John Quincy Adams and the Union*, p. 33; Van Deusen, *The Life of Henry Clay*, p. 215; Feller, *The Public Lands in Jacksonian Politics*, p. 59, *The Jacksonian Promise: America, 1815–1840*, pp. 66, 71; Remini, *Henry Clay*, pp. 210–33.
24. H. V. Ames (ed.), *State Documents on Federal Relations: The States and the United States* (Philadelphia, PA: Department of History, University of Pennsylvania, 1911), pp. 140–1.
25. Ibid., pp. 142, 147.
26. Giles, *Mr. Clay's Speech Upon the Tariff*, p. 49.

27. *Register of Debates*, 21st Cong., 1st sess. (23 March 1830), p. 653.
28. 'Veto Messages', 27 May 1830, *Messages and Papers of the Presidents*, ed. Richardson, vol. 2, pp. 1051–2.
29. G. Dangerfield, *The Awakening of American Nationalism 1815–1828* (New York: Harper & Row, Publishers, 1965), p. 221.
30. Baxter, *Henry Clay and the American System*, pp. 16–54; Currie, *The Constitution in Congress*, p. 250.
31. 'National Bank', 13 December 1790, *American State Papers: Finance* 1:67–76.
32. B. Hammond, *Banks and Politics in America from the Revolution to the Civil War* (Princeton, NJ: Princeton University Press, 1957), pp. 116–17.
33. Ibid., p. 117.
34. 'Opinion on the Constitutionality of the Bill for Establishing a National Bank', 15 February 1791, *The Papers of Thomas Jefferson*, ed. J. P. Boyd and R. W. Lester, 35 vols to date (Princeton, NJ: Princeton University Press, 1974), vol. 19, p. 276.
35. 'Opinion on the Constitutionality of an Act to Establish a Bank', 23 February 1791, *The Papers of Alexander Hamilton*, ed. H. C. Syrett and J. E. Cooke, 27 vols (New York: Columbia University Press, 1965), vol. 8, pp. 63–134. The quotations are on pp. 100, 102, 107, 121.
36. For the case of *McCulloch v. Maryland*, see R. E. Ellis, *Aggressive Nationalism: McCulloch v. Maryland and the Foundation of Federal Authority in the Young Republic* (New York: Oxford University Press, 2007).
37. *Annals of Congress*, 18th Cong., 1st sess. (30 January 1824), p. 1315.
38. Raymond, *The American System*, p. 42.
39. 'Bank of the United States', *Niles' Weekly Register*, 35 (27 September 1828), p. 73.
40. R. C. H. Catterall, *The Second Bank of the United States* (Chicago, IL: The University of Chicago Press, 1903), p. 112; W. B. Smith, *Economic Aspects of the Second Bank of the United States* (Westport, CT: Greenwood Press, 1969), p. 44; Hammond, *Banks and Politics in America*, p. 318.
41. Catterall, *The Second Bank of the United States*, pp. 412–14.
42. This was as much a result of circumstances as of choice. The Northeast had its own efficient state banking systems. The West and South did not. Thus the state banks of the West and South could not meet the demand of credit and currency, which was almost insatiable, especially in the new states of Alabama and Mississippi. Therefore the Bank came to dominate the credit demands in the West and South. The Bank also made more profits in these areas. Catterall, *The Second Bank of the United States*, pp. 412, 501; D. R. Dewey, *Financial History of the United States* (New York: Longmans, Green and Co., 1922), pp. 168, 217; Hammond, *Banks and Politics in America*, p. 317; C. S. Sydnor, *The Development of Southern Sectionalism 1819–1848* (Baton Rouge, LA: Louisiana State University Press, 1948), pp. 108–9.
43. Catterall, *The Second Bank of the United States*, p. 422.
44. Ibid., p. 407–12.
45. Ibid., p. 412.
46. *Pennsylvania Gazette* (29 March 1786), cited in R. E. Wright, *The Wealth of Nations Rediscovered: Integration and Expansion in American Financial Market, 1780–1850* (New York: Cambridge University Press, 2002), p. 205.
47. H. Bodenhorn, *A History of Banking in Antebellum America* (New York: Cambridge University Press, 2000), pp. 97–8.

48. 'On the Bill to Renew the Charter of 1791, In Senate', 11 February 1811, *Legislative and Documentary History of the Bank of the United States Including the Original Bank of North America*, ed. M. St C. Clarke and D. A. Hall, 1st repr. (1832; New York: Augustus M. Kelley Publishers, 1967,), p. 314.
49. Bodenhorn, *A History of Banking in Antebellum America*, pp. 107–8.
50. *House Journal*, 18th Cong., 1st sess. (16 April 1824), p. 428–9.
51. Howe, *What Hath God Wrought*, pp. 400–1.
52. Wilson, *Space Time and Freedom*, pp. 49–72; Feller, *The Public Lands in Jacksonian Politics*; Peterson, *The Great Triumvirate*, pp. 68–84; M. F. Holt, *The Rise and Fall of the American Whig Party* (New York: Oxford University Press, 1999), p. 2; Van Atta, 'Western Lands and Henry Clay's'; Baker, 'The Washington National Road Bill and the Struggle to Adopt a Federal System of Internal Improvement', *Journal of the Early Republic* 22:3 (Autumn 2002); Van Atta, '"A Lawless Rabble"'.
53. Wilson, *Space Time and Freedom*, pp. 60–1; Peterson, *The Great Triumvirate*, pp. 83–4; Bemis, *John Quincy Adams and the Union*, p. 78.
54. Van Atta, 'Western Lands and the Political Economy of Henry Clay's American System', p. 656. See also, Van Atta, '"A Lawless Rabble"'. I think Van Atta's distinction between two classes of potential migrants to the West begs the question of how to distinguish between men of 'average means' and 'lower-class' people in the West.
55. 'First Annual Message', 6 December 1825, *Messages and Papers of the Presidents*, ed. Richardson, vol. 2, p. 871. Also see Adams's 'Third Annual Message', 4 December 1827, in ibid., pp. 956–7.
56. 'On Distributing the Proceeds of the Sales of the Public Lands Among the Several States', 16 April 1832, *American State Papers: Public Lands* 6:447.
57. 'State of the Finances', 10 December 1827, *American State Papers: Finance*, 5:638.
58. 'On Distributing the Proceeds of the Sales of the Public Lands Among the Several States', 16 April 1832, *American State Papers: Public Lands* 6:442–3.
59. 'The Public Lands', *Niles' Weekly Register*, 17 (5 February 1820), p. 387.
60. Harrison was instrumental in the passage of the Land Act of 1800, which established a credit system for land sales. This credit feature helped the Western farmers to purchase lands. Senator Williams was the Chairman of the Senate Committee on Public Lands, and prepared the bill that became the Land Act of 1820. The Land Act of 1820 abolished the credit system, because the size of debts owed by the purchasers of public lands to the federal government became uncontrollable. Benton had tirelessly campaigned for his proposal of graduation, the reduction of land prices according to the quality of the lands, from 1824 to 1828. R. M. Robbins, 'Preemption – A Frontier Triumph', *The Mississippi Valley Historical Review* 18:3 (December 1931), pp. 336, 340–1; *Annals of Congress*, 16th Cong., 1st sess., 11 January 1820, p. 78.
61. 'On Distributing the Proceeds of the Sales of the Public Lands Among the Several States', 16 April 1832, *American State Papers: Public Lands* 6:441–51.
62. Larson, *Internal Improvement*, p. 187.
63. 'Speech on Tariff', 30 and 31 March 1824, *The Papers of Henry Clay*, ed. J. F. Hopkins, 11 vols (Lexington, KY: University of Kentucky Press, 1963), vol. 3 p. 686.
64. Ibid., p. 688.
65. Howe, *The Political Culture of the American Whigs*, p. 138.
66. L. A. Peskin, *Manufacturing Revolution: The Intellectual Origins of Early American Industry* (Baltimore, MD: The Johns Hopkins University Press, 2003); C. Sheriff, *The*

Artificial River: The Erie Canal and the Paradox of Progress 1817–1862 (New York: Hill and Wang, 1996), p. 5.
67. M. Schocket, *Founding Corporate Power in Early National Philadelphia* (DeKalb, IL: Northern Illinois University Press, 2007).
68. Bemis, *John Quincy Adams and the Union*, p. 63.
69. Howe, *The Political Culture of the American Whigs*, p. 137; see also D. W. Howe, 'Church, State, and Education in the Young American Republic', *Journal of the Early Republic* 22:1 (Spring 2002), pp. 1–24; *What Hath God Wrought*, pp. 243–84.
70. 'First Annual Message', 6 December 1825, *Messages and Papers of the Presidents*, ed. Richardson, vol. 2, p. 877.
71. Ibid, vol. 2, pp. 877–83.
72. J. L. Brooke, 'Cultures of Nationalism, Movements of Reform, and the Composite-Federal Polity from Revolutionary Settlement to Antebellum Crisis', *Journal of the Early Republic*, 29:1 (Spring 2009), p. 3.

1. Emergence of the American System, 1790–1815

1. 'First Annual Address', 8 January 1790, *Messages and Papers of the Presidents*, ed. Richardson, vol. 1, p. 58.
2. 'Farewell Address', 17 September 1796, ibid., pp. 207–8.
3. Ibid., p. 207.
4. Ibid., p. 208.
5. Ibid.
6. Ibid.
7. Ibid., p. 212.
8. 'Eighth Annual Address', 7 December 1796, ibid., p. 193.
9. Ibid., p. 194; Larson, *Internal Improvement*, p. 49.
10. 'Eighth Annual Address', 7 December 1796, *Messages and Papers of the Presidents*, ed. Richardson, vol. 1, p. 194.
11. Ibid.
12. J. J. Ellis, *His Excellency George Washington* (New York: Vintage Books, 2004).
13. 'Inaugural Address', 4 March 1797, *Messages and Papers of the Presidents*, ed. Richardson, vol. 1, p. 221.
14. 'An Act to Make Further Provision for the Removal and Accommodation of the Government of the United States', 24 April 1800, *Statutes at Large*, 2:56; D. McCullough, *John Adams* (New York: Simon & Schuster, 2001), p. 536.
15. R. Chernow, *Alexander Hamilton* (New York: Penguin Books, 2004), p. 157.
16. Ibid., pp. 157–8, 170, 171, 257.
17. 'Manufactures', 5 December 1791, *American State Papers: Finance* 1:123–44. A different assessment of the report is in J. R. Nelson, Jr, *Liberty and Property: Political Economic and Policymaking in the New Nation, 1789–1812* (Baltimore, MD: The Johns Hopkins University Press, 1987), pp. 37–51, especially pp. 37, 48. Nelson states that Hamilton was 'unquestionably hostile to domestic manufactures' and that his report on manufactures was only intended to benefit the Society for Establishing Useful Manufactures in New Jersey, which Hamilton tried to promote as a project for a large-scale manufacturing society. I think it is more appropriate to say that Hamilton considered the promotion of domestic manufactures more as a long-term policy priority rather than an immediate goal under the financial situation in which the United States found itself after the Revo-

lutionary War. I think that Hamilton possessed a genuine desire to promote domestic manufactures, considering the comprehensiveness and depth of the report. Later supporters of domestic manufactures used every one of the arguments in the report. In addition, one cannot deny the intention just because the expected effects did not materialize.
18. As most historians recognized, it was Trench Coxe who supplied much of the data incorporated in the report. However, Coxe's contribution does not diminish the originality of the report. The crisp and assertive style of writing and the comprehensive and sophisticated logics are uniquely Hamiltonian.
19. 'Manufactures', 5 December 1791, *American State Papers: Finance* 1:123, 1:133.
20. Ibid., 1:125, 1:127.
21. Ibid., 1:134.
22. Ibid., 1:136.
23. Ibid., 1:144.
24. Nelson, *Liberty and Property*, p. 39.
25. Ibid., p. 41.
26. Ibid., p. 48.
27. Ibid., p. 60.
28. 'An Act for Laying a Duty on Goods, Wares, and Merchandises Imported into the United States', 4 July 1789, *Statutes at Large*, 1:24.
29. E. Stanwood, *American Tariff Controversies in the Nineteenth Century*, 2 vols (Boston, MA and New York: Houghton Mifflin Company, 1903), vol. 1, pp. 19–20.
30. See the petitions in 'Manufactures', 11 April 1789, 'Manufactures', 18 April 1789, 'Ship-Builders', 25 May 1789 and 'Ship-Builders and Manufactures', 5 June 1789, *American State Papers: Finance* 1:5–11.
31. A useful glossary on tariff terms is in J. M. Dobson, *Two Centuries of Tariffs: the Background and Emergence of the U.S. Internal Trade Commission* (Washington DC: US Government Printing Office, 1976), pp. 137–8. The glossary defines '*ad valorem* rate' as 'a tariff rate set according to the value of the commodity imported. An *ad valorem* rate is expressed as a percentage of the commodity's value'.
32. Stanwood, *American Tariff Controversies in the Nineteenth Century*, vol. 1, pp. 58–9.
33. H. C. Adams, *Taxation in the United States 1789–1816* (Baltimore, MD: The Johns Hopkins University Press, 1884), p. 36; Baxter, in *Henry Clay and the American System*, p. 18, states that the average rate in the Tariff Act of 1796 was 8 per cent. But an 8 per cent rate is still far below the protection level.
34. Gallatin, in a letter to J. R. Ingersoll stated '[y]et if the average rate of duty which the revenue requires should be from twenty to twenty-five [per] cent, I really think that manufactures which require a larger than that incidental protection must generally be considered as unnatural, forced, hot-house products'. 'Gallatin to Ingersoll', 25 March 1826, *The Writings of Albert Gallatin*, ed. H. Adams, 3 vols (New York: Antiquarian Press Ltd., 1960, original publication 1879), vol. 1, p. 629; H. C. Adams wrote that 25 per cent duty was considered necessary to maintain the domestic manufactures which developed during the Embargo and the War of 1812. Adams, *Taxation in the United States 1789–1816*, p. 77. The rationale for the rates of 20 to 25 per cent was that at least 20 per cent duty was considered necessary to support the federal government. A. Gallatin, 'Memorial of the Committee of the Free Trade Convention', in F. W. Taussig (ed.), *State Papers and Speeches on the Tariff* (New York: Burt Franklin, 1895), p. 117.

35. S. Ratner, *The Tariff in American History* (New York: D. Van Nostrand Company, 1972), p. 12.
36. 'An Act Further to Protect the Commerce and Seamen of the United States Against the Barbary Powers', 26 March 1804, *Statutes at Large*, 2:291–2.
37. Adams, *Taxation in the United States 1789–1816*, pp. 37–8.
38. 'An Act for Imposing Additional Duties Upon All Goods, Wares, and Merchandise Imported from Any Foreign Port or Place, and for Other Purposes', 1 July 1812, *Statutes at Large*, 2:768–9; the declaration of war is in 'Proclamations', 19 June 1812, *Messages and Papers of the Presidents*, ed. Richardson, vol. 1, pp. 497–8; Adams, *Taxation in the United States 1789–1816*, pp. 37–8.
39. D. C. North, *The Economic Growth of the United States, 1789 to 1860* (Mew York: W. W. Norton & Company Inc., 1966), p. 221, Appendix 1, Table B-III.
40. Ibid., p. 229, Appendix 1, Table G-III.
41. Ibid., p. 221, Appendix 1, Table B-III.
42. Ibid., p. 249, Appendix II, Table A-III.
43. Adams, *Taxation in the United States 1789–1816*, p. 70.
44. *The Portable Thomas Jefferson*, ed. M. D. Peterson (New York: The Viking Press, 1975), p. 217.
45. 'First Annual Message', 8 December 1801, *Messages and Papers of the Presidents*, ed. Richardson, vol. 1, p. 318.
46. 'Second Annual Message' 5 December 1802, ibid., p. 346.
47. 'First Annual Message', 4 March 1809, ibid., p. 468.
48. 'Encouragement to Manufactures', 4 February 1803, *American State Papers: Finance* 2:22.
49. 'Encouragement to Manufactures', 9 December 1803, ibid., 2:61. Italics in the original document.
50. 'Encouragement to Manufactures', 30 March 1802, ibid., 1:743.
51. 'Encouragement to Manufactures', 4 February 1803, ibid., 2:22.
52. Encouragement to Manufactures', 22 January 1811, ibid., 2:465.
53. 'Protection to Manufactures', 21 November 1808, 7 June 1809, 31 January 1811, 23 December 1811, 29 January 1812, 3 February 1812, 6 March 1812, 20 March 1812 and 6 February 1813, 'Encouragement to Manufactures', 22 January 1811 and 23 March 1814, 'Encouragement to the Culture of Hemp', 7 December 1811, 'Revision of the Revenue Laws', 9 April 1814, ibid., 2:306, 2:367–8, 2:471, 2:511–12, 2:528, 2:528, 2:553, 2:553, 2:602–3, 2:465–7, 2:832, 2:510–11, 2:834.
54. Jefferson, in his annual message of 8 November 1808, described the relationship between his embargo policy and the growth of domestic manufacture as follows: '[t]he suspension of our foreign commerce, produced by the injustice of the belligerent powers, and the consequent losses and sacrifices of our citizens are subjects of just concern. The situation into which we have thus been forced has impelled us to apply a portion of our industry and capital to internal manufactures and improvements. The extent of this conversion is daily increasing, and little doubt remains that the establishments formed and forming will, under the auspices of cheaper materials and subsistence, the freedom of labour from taxation with us, and of protecting duties and prohibitions, become permanent'. Albert Gallatin, in his Report on Manufacture submitted to the House on 17 April 1810 also stated that 'the injurious violations of the neutral commerce of the United States' had given 'a general impetus, to which must be ascribed the great increase of manufactures during the two last years'. President Madison stated in his fifth annual message of 7

December 1813: '[i]f the war [the War of 1812] has increased the interruptions of our commerce, it has at the same time cherished and multiplied our manufactures so as to make us independent of all other countries for the more essential branches for which we ought to be dependent on none, and is even rapidly giving them an extent which will create additional staples in our future intercourse with foreign markets'. 'Eighth Annual Message', 8 November 1808, *Messages and Papers of the Presidents*, ed. Richardson, vol. 1, p. 443; 'Manufactures', 19 April 1810, *American State Papers: Finance*, 2:430; 'Fifth Annual Message', 7 December 1813, *Message and Papers of the Presidents*, vol. 1, pp. 524–5.

55. T. Coxe, *A Statement of the Arts and Manufactures of the United States, for the Year 1810* (Philadelphia, PA: A. Cornman, 1814); *Supplementary Observations* (September 1814), cited in North, *The Economic Growth of the United States*, p. 56.
56. V. S. Clark, *History of Manufacturers in the United States*, 3 vols (New York: McGraw-Hill, 1929), vol. 1, pp. 266–7.
57. 'To George Washington', 10 May 1789, *The Papers of Thomas Jefferson*, ed. Boyd and Lester, vol. 15, pp. 117.
58. I. Brant, *James Madison: The Nationalist 1780–1787* (Indianapolis, IN: Bobbs-Merrill Company, 1948), pp. 365–8.
59. R. Walters, Jr, *Albert Gallatin: Jeffersonian Financier and Diplomat* (Pittsburgh, PA: University of Pittsburgh Press, 1969, original publication 1957), pp. 1–86.
60. Gallatin's memorandum, quoted in H. Adams, *The Life of Albert Gallatin* (Philadelphia, PA: J.B. Lippincott & Co., 1879), p. 85.
61. 'First Inaugural Address', 4 March 1801, *Messages and Papers of the Presidents*, ed. Richardson, vol. 1., pp. 309–12.
62. Dewey, *Financial History of the United States*, p. 113.
63. 'An Act to Enable the People of the Eastern Division of the Territory Northwest of the River Ohio to Form a Constitution and State Government, and for the Admission of Such State into the Union, on an Equal Footing with the Original States, and for Other Purposes', 30 April 1802, *Statutes at Large* 2:173–5.
64. 'Gallatin to William B. Giles', 13 February 1802, *The Writings of Albert Gallatin*, ed. Adams, vol. 1, pp. 76–9.
65. Ibid., p. 77.
66. *Annals of Congress*, 7th Cong., 1st sess. (30 March 1802), p. 1100.
67. 'Gallatin to Jefferson', 8 November 1809, *The Writings of Albert Gallatin*, ed. Adams, vol. 1, p. 465.
68. 'Second Inaugural Address', 4 March 1805, *Messages and Papers of the Presidents*, ed. Richardson, vol. 1, p. 367.
69. 'Roads and Canals', 6 April 1808, *American State Papers: Miscellaneous* 1:724–921.
70. Ibid., 1:724–5.
71. Ibid., 1:725.
72. Gallatin's proposals, which are the central part of his long report, is in ibid., 1:740.
73. Ibid.
74. 'Cumberland Road', 16 February 1809, *American State Papers: Miscellaneous* 1:947.
75. 'Roads and Canals', 6 April 1808, ibid., 1:741.
76. Ibid.
77. 'Second Inaugural Address', 4 March 1805, *Messages and Papers of the Presidents*, ed. Richardson, vol. 1, p. 367.

78. 'First Inaugural Address', 4 March 1809, ibid., p. 453. Italics added. See also Madison's 'Seventh Annual Message', 5 December 1815, ibid., pp. 552–3.
79. 'Opinion on the Constitutionality of the Bill for Establishing a National Bank', 15 February 1791, *The Papers of Thomas Jefferson*, ed. Boyd and Lester, vol. 19, p. 276.
80. Ibid., p. 279. The italics are by Jefferson himself.
81. 'Debate on the Motion of Mr. Smith, of South Carolina, to Recommit the Bill', 2 February 1791, *Legislative and Documentary History of the Bank of the United States*, p. 43.
82. 'An Act Supplementary to the Act Intituled "An Act to Incorporate the Subscribers to the Bank of the United States"', 23 March 1804, *Statutes at Large* 2:274.
83. The relevant proceedings of the legislation are in *Annals of Congress*, 8th Cong., 1st sess. (29 November 1803, 16, 17 and 19 March 1804), pp. 118–19, 278, 280, 282; See also J. O. Wettereau, 'The Branches of the First Bank of the United States', *Journal of Economic History*, 2, supp. *The Tasks of Economic History* (December 1942), pp. 66–100, pp. 85–7.
84. 'To the Secretary of the Treasury (Albert Gallatin)', 13 December 1803, *The Writings of Thomas Jefferson*, ed. P. L. Ford, 10 vols (New York: G. P. Putnam's Sons, 1892–1899), vol. 8, pp. 284–5.
85. 'An Act to Punish Frauds Committed on the Bank of the United States', 24 February 1807, *Statutes at Large* 2:423–4.
86. 'Bank of the United States', 3 March 1809, *American State Papers: Finance* 2:352. Italicization by Gallatin.
87. 'Bank of the United States', 5 February 1811, ibid., 2:481.
88. See the speech of Senator W. B. Giles in 'On the Bill to Renew the Charter of 1791', 14 February 1811, *Legislative and Documentary History of the Bank of the United States*, pp. 329–52, especially 335 and 347.
89. 'Gallatin to N. Biddle', 14 August 1830, *The Writings of Albert Gallatin*, ed. Adams, vol. 2, p. 435.
90. 'On the Bill to Renew the Charter of 1791', 14 February 1811, *Legislative and Documentary History of the Bank of the United States*, p. 351. For other speeches with same logic, see the speeches of Representatives J. Desha of Kentucky and R. Wright of Maryland in ibid., 12 February 1811, pp. 181–6, 183, and pp. 197–204, 202.
91. 'Report of the Secretary of the Treasury on the Subject of a National Bank, Made to the Senate', 2 March 1809, ibid., p. 116.
92. J. D. Hammond, *History of Political Parties in the State of New York*, 3 vols (Albany, NY: C. Van Benthuysen, 1842–48) vol. 1, p. 578, cited in Hammond, *Banks and Politics in America*, pp. 224–5.
93. 'On the Bill to Renew the Charter of 1791', 22 January 1811, *Legislative and Documentary History of the Bank of the United States*, p. 226.
94. Ibid., 21 January 1811, p. 196.
95. Hammond, *Banks and Politics in Amercia*, p. 145.
96. J. T. Holdsworth and D. R. Dewey, *The First and Second Banks of the United States* (Washington D.C.: Government Printing Office, 1910), pp. 42, 51; Catterall, *The Second Bank of the United States*, pp. 435–8.
97. 'In the General Assembly of the Commonwealth of Pennsylvania', 11 January 1811, found in speech by Senator M. Leib of Pennsylvania in 'On the Bill to Renew the Charter of 1791', 12 February 1811, *Legislative and Documentary History of the Bank of the United States*, pp. 315–17.
98. Ibid.

99. 'On the Bill to Renew the Charter of 1791', 11 February 1811, ibid., p. 310.
100. R. Sylla, J. B. Legler and J. J. Wallis, 'Banks and State Public Finance in the New Republic: The United States, 1790–1860', *The Journal of Economic History*, 47:2 (June 1987), p. 393.
101. Ibid., p. 396.
102. H. Bodenhorn, *State Banking in Early America* (New York: Oxford University Press, 2003), p. 222.
103. Sylla, Legler and Wallis, 'Banks and State Public Finance in the New Republic: The United States, 1790–1860', p. 398.
104. Ibid., p. 399.
105. Remini, *Henry Clay*, pp. 39, 52.
106. 'On the Bill to Renew the Charter of 1791', 15 February 1811, *Legislative and Documentary History of the Bank of the United States*, p. 354.
107. Gallatin wrote, 'I heard many in 1810 deeply regretting that they could not vote for the renewal of the charter of the former bank. With those men the *utility* of the United States Bank in all the fiscal operations of government is not a sufficient argument ... You must prove to them the *necessity* of that institution for carrying into effect some provision of the Constitution'. 'Gallatin to R. Walsh, Jr.', 2 August 1830, *The Writings of Albert Gallatin*, ed. Adams, vol. 2, pp. 430–1.
108. 'On the Bill to Renew the Charter of 1791', 15 February 1811, *Legislative and Documentary History of the Bank of the United States*, p. 357.
109. Ibid., 30 January 1811, p. 301. On this issue, he left a very interesting comment in his later life. In his letter to J. M. Botts, Gallatin stated that '[e]xcept in its character of fiscal agent of the general government, I attach much less importance to a national bank than several of those are in favour of it'. 'Gallatin to John M. Botts, M.C.', 14 June 1841, *The Writings of Albert Gallatin*, ed. Adams, vol. 2, p. 552.
110. 'On the Bill to Renew the Charter of 1791', 2 March 1811, *Legislative and Documentary History of the Bank of the United States*, p. 448.
111. *Senate Journal*, 11th Cong., 3rd sess. (20 February 1811), p. 578; *House Journal*, 11th Cong., 3rd sess. (24 January 1811), pp. 500–1.
112. *Legislative and Documentary History of the Bank of the United States*, 20 February 1811, p. 446.
113. For a lucid and extensive analysis of the causes of the suspension and its results regarding banking and currency, see Gallatin's 'Considerations on the Currency and Banking System of the United States', 1 January 1831, *The Writings of Albert Gallatin*, ed. Adams, vol. 3, pp. 282–90.
114. For a different interpretation of the cause of suspension of specie payment during the War of 1812, see R. H. Timberlake, *Monetary Policy in the United States: An Intellectual and Institutional History* (Chicago, IL: The University of Chicago Press, 1993, original publication 1978), pp. 13–20.
115. See above, Table 1.4.
116. Gallatin, 'Considerations on the Currency and Banking System of the United States', pp. 288, 291.
117. Ibid., p. 363, Statement V.
118. 'State of the Finances', 8 December 1815, *American State Papers: Finance* 3:7, 3:9–10.
119. Ibid., 3:4.
120. For examples, see, J. C. Ballagh, 'Southern Economic History: Tariff and Public Lands', *Annual Report of the American Historical Association for the Year 1898* (Washington DC:

n.p., 1899), p. 238; P. J. Treat, *The National Land System, 1785–1820* (New York: E.B. Treat 1910), p. 389; R. G. Wellington, *The Political and Sectional Influence of the Public Lands* (Cambridge, MA: Riverside Press, 1914), pp. 2–3; B. H. Hibbard, *A History of the Public Land Policies* (Madison, WI: University of Wisconsin Press, 1965), pp. 553–4.

121. 'Plan for Disposing of the Public Lands', 22 July 1790, *American State Papers: Public Lands* 1:4.
122. 'On Distributing the Proceeds of the Sales of the several States', 16 April 1832, ibid., 6:441–51.
123. 'An Act Making Provision for the [Payment of the] Debt of the United States', 4 August 1790, *Statutes at Large*, 1:144. The square brackets in the act's title are from the original text.
124. 'An Act Providing for the Sale of the Lands of the United States in the Territory Northwest of the River Ohio, and Above the Mouth of Kentucky River', 18 May 1796, ibid., 1:464–9. In the 4th Congress, which lasted from 4 March 1795 to 3 March 1797, the political party affiliations were fifty-four from the Federalist Party and fifty-two Democratic-Republicans. M. A. Booker (ed.), *Members of Congress Since 1789*, 3rd edn (Washington: Congressional Quarterly, 1985), p. 183. For Gallatin's leadership in Congress around 1796, see Adams, *Life of Albert Gallatin*, pp. 154–67.
125. *Annals of Congress*, 4th Cong., 1st sess. (17 February 1796), p. 339.
126. Ibid., pp. 339–40.
127. Ibid., p. 340; ibid. (18 February 1796), pp. 348–9.
128. Dewey, *Financial History of the United States*, p. 113.
129. The figure is calculated from Table 1.5.
130. The figure is much smaller than the one in a report of the Secretary of Treasury to the Senate on 24 April 1843. He wrote in the report that the total amount of lands sold before the opening of the Land Offices (1800) was $1,050,085.43. A slightly higher figure was offered by Gallatin. In 1810, Gallatin wrote in his 'Introduction to the Collections of Laws, Treaties, and Other Documents Having Operation and Respect to the Public Lands', that '[n]o more than 121,540 acres had thus been sold prior to the Act of 10th May, 1800, viz.: 72,974 acres at public sale at New York, in the year 1787, for 87,325 dollars, in evidences of the public debt; 43,446 acres at public sale at Pittsburgh, in the year 1796, for 100,427 dollars; and 5120 acres at Philadelphia, in the same year, at two dollars an acre'. The total of Gallatin's figures is $197,992. The difference is due to the difference of fiscal year periods as well as inaccuracies in reports. All three figures are still far short of what Gallatin had originally expected. 'Public Debt', 24 February 1815, *American State Papers: Finance* 2:919; *Senate Document*, No. 246, 27th Cong., 3rd sess., p. 6; 'Introduction to the Collection of Laws, Treaties, and Other Documents Having Operation and Respect to the Public Lands', 1810, *The Writings of Albert Gallatin*, ed. Adams, vol. 3, pp. 221–2.
131. 'Petition to Congress By Citizens of the Territory', 1799, *The Territorial Papers of the United States*, ed. C. E. Carter, 28 vols (Washington: Government Printing Office, 1934), pp. 52–3. Also see the documents 'Application for Lands at Reduced Price', 16 Jan 1798, and 'Applications for Land at Reduced Prices', 19 May 1798, *American State Papers: Public Lands* 1:71, 1:73 for outright demands of sales of public lands at 'reduced price'.
132. 'An Act to Amend the Act Intituled "An Act Providing for the Sale of the Lands of the United States, in the Territory Northwest of the Ohio, and Above the Mouth of Kentucky River"', 10 May 1800, *Statutes at Large* 2:73–8.

133. Not all the lands were for sale at 320 acres. The lands west of Muskinggum River were to be sold by half sections of 320 acres, while the lands lying east of Muskinggum were to be sold by sections of 640 acres.
134. The struggle started with a motion from R. Griswold of Connecticut (Federalist) to strike out the section to sell lands in half sections. Griswold's motion was supported by W. Edmond of Connecticut (Federalist), W. Cooper of New York (Federalist), and S. Lee of Massachusetts (Federalist). On the other hand, Gallatin, Harrison, J. Nicholas of Virginia (Democrat), R. G. Harper of South Carolina (Federalist), and W. Gordon of New Hampshire defended it. The Senate amended the bill to sell the lands lying east of Muskinggum River by sections of 640 acres, not by sections of 320 acres. Harrison informed his constituents that '[t]he bill was adopted by the House of Representatives without any material alteration; but in the Senate, amendments were introduced... that one half of the land (instead of the whole as was provided by the bill from the House of Representatives) should be sold in half sections of 320 acres and the other half in whole sections of 640 acres'. *Annals of Congress*, 6th Cong., 1st sess. (31 March 1800 and 22 April 1800), pp. 651, 165; 'Harrison to His Constituents', 14 May 1800, *Messages and Letters of William Henry Harrison*, ed. Esarey, 2 vols (Indianapolis, IN: Indiana Historical Commission, 1922), vol. 1, p. 13.
135. *Annals of Congress*, 6th Cong., 1st sess. (1 April 1800), p. 652.
136. Caution must be exercised in using the data of land sales in the antebellum period. Some figures are during fiscal years, while some are during calendar years. In addition, the fiscal years were not uniform. That is why the figures in this table are not identical with the figures in the table in P. Gates, *History of Public Land Law Development* (Washington DC, 1968), p. 132. Gates developed his table by compiling data from the Reports of the Secretary of the Treasury in *American State Papers: Finance*, 2. It is difficult to tell which ones are more accurate. On this issue of the reliability of the land sales data, see S. W. Schoene, 'The Economics of U.S. Public Land Policy Prior to 1860', (Unpublished PhD Dissertation, The University of North Carolina, 1981), p. 62. Schoene critically examines land sales data used by historians and presents his own data sets by using manuscript materials compiled by Arthur N. Cole. See chapter 3 of his dissertation for the discussions and new data sets. I chose not to use Schoene's data because it starts from 1806, thus leaving out the period before 1806, which is a very important period for this chapter. Moreover, as Schoene readily acknowledges, the errors in other data sets might not be so serious as long as they are used to argue 'more qualitatively derived conclusions', which is my purpose in using this data.
137. Harrison wrote that 'although the minimum price of land is still fixed at two dollars per acre, the time for making payments has been so extended as to put it in the power of every industrious man to comply with them'. But Gallatin thought differently. Replying to an enquiry of a Committee of the House in 1804, writing that 'it is almost impossible that they should, during the first four years of a new settlement, draw the means of payment from the produce of the land'. 'Harrison to His Constituents', 14 May 1800, *Messages and Letters of William Henry Harrison*, ed. Esarey, vol. 1, p. 13; 'Alteration of the Laws for the Sale of Public Lands', 23 January 1804, *American State Papers: Public Lands* 1:168.
138. *Annals of Congress*, 13th Cong., 3rd sess. (21 September 1814), p. 15.
139. Feller, *The Public Lands in Jacksonian Politics*, p. 30; W. N. Chambers, *Old Bullion Benton: Senator from the New West* (Boston, MA: Little, Brown, 1956), pp. 64–5, 77.

140. 'Petition to Congress By Citizens of the Territory', 20 February 1801, *The Territorial Papers*, ed. Carter, vol. 3, pp. 122–3.
141. *Annals of Congress*, 8th Cong., 1st sess. (22 November 1803), pp. 615–16.
142. The inquiries of the House Committee and Gallatin's reply are in 'Alterations of the Laws for the Sale of Public Lands', 23 January 1804, *American State Papers: Public Lands* 1:166–9.
143. Ibid., 1:167.
144. Ibid.
145. Ibid.
146. Gallatin had always been against pre-emption. He was obviously afraid that the grant of pre-emption rights would reduce the amount of revenue from land sales. But he was also opposed to pre-emption on moral ground as well. While writing to Thomas Worthington, the Register of the Land Office at Chilicothe, on 16 July 1801, Gallatin stated that '[t]he lands are the property of the People of the United States, and Intruders who do not purchase, nor perhaps ever mean to do it, actually attempt to rob every other Individual of the United States of his equal right to the lands'. In other words, Gallatin saw the squatters as thieves of the common property of all American people. 'The Secretary of the Treasury to Thomas Worthington', 16 July 1801, *The Territorial Papers*, ed. Carter, vol. 3, p. 152.
147. Gallatin never veered from this basic position. See 'Gallatin to John W. Eppes, Chairman of Ways and Means', 26 February 1810, *The Writings of Albert Gallatin*, ed. Adams, vol. 1, pp. 470–1.
148. 'Alterations of the Laws for the Sale of Public Lands', 23 January 1804, *American State Papers: Public Lands*, 1:166–7.
149. 'Application of Purchasers of Public Lands for an Extension of Credit', 22 March 1806, *American State Papers: Public Lands* 1:263.
150. As late as 1818, the House instructed a committee to be formed to inquire in the expediency of 'increasing' land prices. The Chairman of the Committee G. Robertson of Kentucky advised the House against the proposal by saying 'the committee feel[s] somewhat apprehensive that the United States, so far from being enabled to increase, will find themselves compelled to lessen the price of the public lands, or to forgo the golden dreams they indulge in, of enormous revenue to arise from their sale'. In a sense, Congress had been mesmerized by the 'golden dreams' of 'enormous revenue' from land sales for too long a period. The reason why the House decided to look into the possibility of raising land prices was the recommendation of President James Monroe in his annual message of 2 December 1817, which Congress considered: 'that such further provision may be made in the sale of the public lands, with a view to the public interest'. In the preceding sentences, Monroe was noting the increase of land value with the settlement of the frontier and was urging the benefits from the competition for lands to operate 'to the advantages of the nation rather than of individuals'. Monroe was obviously urging Congress to look at the possibility of increasing land prices. 'Proposition to Increase the Price of Public Lands', 5 January 1818, *American State Papers: Public Lands* 3:264; 'First Annual Message', 2 December 1817, *Messages and Papers of the Presidents*, ed. Richardson, vol. 1, p. 586.
151. *Massachusetts Senate Documents*, No. 4, p. 13, cited in Hibbard, *A History of the Public Land Policies*, p. 78.
152. 'Relief to Purchasers, Reduction of the Price, and repeal of the Credit System, in the Sale of Public Lands', 19 January 1809, *American State Papers: Public Lands* 1:826.

153. 'Second Inaugural Address', 4 March 1805, *Messages and Papers of the Presidents*, ed. Richardson, vol. 1, p. 367.
154. 'Sixth Annual Message', 2 December 1806, ibid., p. 397.
155. Ibid.
156. Ibid., p. 398.
157. M. D. Peterson, *Thomas Jefferson and the New Nation* (New York: Oxford University Press, 1970), pp. 858–9.
158. 'Second Annual Message', 5 December 1810, *Messages and Papers of the Presidents*, ed. Richardson, vol. 1, p. 470.
159. Peterson, *Thomas Jefferson and the New Nation*, p. 859.
160. 'Seventh Annual Message', 5 December 1815, *Messages and Papers of the Presidents*, ed. Richardson, vol. 1, p. 553.
161. 'Eighth Annual Message', 3 December 1816, ibid., p. 561.

2. The Growth of the American System and Its Challenges, 1815–1824

1. 'Gallatin to Matthew Lyon', 7 May 1816, *The Writings of Albert Gallatin*, ed. Adams, vol. 1, p. 700.
2. 'Seventh Annual Message', 5 December 1815, *Messages and Papers of the Presidents*, ed. Richardson, vol. 1, p. 553.
3. Ibid., pp. 550–2.
4. Ibid., p. 553.
5. Howe, *What Hath God Wrought*, p. 80.
6. 'Seventh Annual Message', 5 December 1815, *Messages and Papers of the Presidents*, ed. Richardson, vol. 1, p. 553.
7. Taussig (ed.), *State Papers and Speeches on the Tariff*, p. 12.
8. North, *The Economic Growth of the United States*, Tables E-III on p. 228 and C-VIII on p. 234.
9. 'Protection to Manufacturers', 22 December 1815, *American State Papers: Finance*, 3:54.
10. The proposed bill is 'Tariff of Duties on Imports', 13 February 1816, *American State Papers: Finance* 3:85–99.
11. 'State of the Finances', 8 December 1815, *American State Papers: Finance 3:15–16*. The national debt stood at more than $120 million on 1 January 1816. A. Gallatin, 'Memorial of the Committee of the Free Trade Convention, 1831', in Taussig (ed.), *State Papers and Speeches on the Tariff*, p. 110.
12. 'State of the Finances', 8 December 1815, *American State Papers: Finance* 3:15.
13. Ibid.
14. *Annals of Congress*, 14th Cong., 1st sess. (20 March 1816), p. 1234.
15. Ibid., p. 1240.
16. Adams, *Taxation in the United States, 1789–1816*, p. 19.
17. Calhoun's speech is in *Annals of Congress*, 14th Cong., 1st sess. (4 April 1816), pp. 1329–36. The quote is on p. 1330.
18. Ibid., p. 1331.
19. Ibid., p. 1335.

20. D. Webster wrote to S. A. Bradley: '[t]he manufacturing interest has become a *strong distinct political party*'. 'To Samuel Ayer Bradley', 21 April 1816, *The Papers of Daniel Webster: Correspondence 1798–1824*, ed. C. M. Wiltse, 6 vols (Hanover, NH: University Press of New England, 1974), vol. 1, p. 197.
21. N. W. Preyer, 'Southern Support of the Tariff of 1816 – A Reappraisal', *Journal of Southern History* 25:3 (August 1959), pp. 306–22.
22. North, *Economic Growth of the United States*, see tables B-III on p. 221 and A-VIII on p. 233.
23. 'To Benjamin Austin', 9 January 1816, *The Writings of Thomas Jefferson*, ed. Ford, vol. 10, p. 10.
24. Ibid.
25. Gallatin said that '[t]he establishment of the [Second] Bank of the United States was recommended by the Treasury, and that institution was incorporated by Congress, for the express and avowed purpose of removing an evil which the difference in the rate of depreciation between the paper currencies of the several States, and even those of different places in the same State, had rendered altogether intolerable', in 'Considerations on the Currency and Banking System of the United States', p. 236.
26. 'An Act to Incorporate the Subscribers to the Bank of the United States', 10 April 1816, *Statutes at Large* 3:266–77.
27. 'Seventh Annual Message', 5 December 1815, *Messages and Papers of the Presidents*, ed. Richardson, vol. 1, pp. 550–1.
28. 'The State of the Finances', 8 December 1815, *American State Papers: Finance* 3:19.
29. Ibid.
30. J. T. Holdsworth and Dewey, *The First and Second Banks of the United States*, pp. 42, 51; Catterall, *The Second Bank of the United States*, pp. 435–8.
31. 'National Bank', 8 January 1816, *American State Papers: Finance* 3:57–61.
32. 'On the Grant of the Charter of 1816: A Bill to Incorporate the Subscribers to the Bank of the United States', 8 January 1816, *Legislative and Documentary History of the Bank of the United States*, pp. 621–30.
33. 'On the Grant of the Charter of 1816', 26 February 1816, *Legislative and Documentary History of the Bank of the United States*, p. 631.
34. Ibid., pp. 632, 633.
35. Ibid., 9 March 1816, p. 670.
36. Ibid., 27 February 1816, p. 641.
37. For example, see Senator J. Barbour's speech in ibid., 2 March 1816, p. 687.
38. *Annals of Congress*, 14th Cong., 1st sess. (29 January 1816), pp. 787, 792.
39. Ibid. (31 January 1816), pp. 832–3.
40. Ibid., p. 836.
41. *Annals of Congress*, 14th Cong., 2nd sess. (16 December 1816), p. 296.
42. Ibid. (23 December 1816), p. 361.
43. Ibid. (11 January 1817), p. 466
44. Ibid. (4 February 1817), pp. 851–4.
45. Ibid., p. 855. See also Clay's able speech in defense of the bill, ibid. (14 February 1817), pp. 866–8; also the speech by T. R. Gold of New York, ibid. (16 February 1817), pp. 878–80; T. Wilson of Pennsylvania, ibid. (6 February 1817), pp. 899–910.
46. Ibid. (16 February 1817), pp. 893–4.
47. Ibid., pp. 894, 895.

48. Senators D. Daggett of Connecticut and E. P. Ashmun of Massachusetts, and N. Macon of North Carolina also attacked the bill by arguing it to be unconstitutional. ibid. (26 February 1817), pp. 165–77, 179–80, 177–9.
49. 'Veto Message', 3 March 1817, *Messages and Papers of the Presidents*, ed. Richardson, vol. 1, pp. 569–70.
50. In this context, it is significant to note that historian Herman V. Ames assessed that it was not until 1827 that protective tariffs became a more serious target of attacks against the American System than internal improvements. Ames (ed.), *State Documents on Federal Relations*, p. 133.
51. *Annals of Congress*, 15th Cong., 1st sess. (30 March 1818 and 14 April 1818), pp. 1649–50, 1678–9; 'Roads and Canals', 7 January 1819, *American State Papers: Miscellaneous* 2:533–7.
52. 'Roads and Canals', 7 January 1819, *American State Papers: Miscellaneous* 2:534–6.
53. Ibid.
54. Ibid., p. 536, Italicization by Calhoun.
55. Ibid.
56. 'Roads and Canals', 6 April 1808, ibid., 1:741.
57. J. S. Young, *A Political and Constitutional History of the Cumberland Road* (Chicago, IL: University of Chicago Press, 1904), p. 64.
58. Dewey, *Financial History of the United States*, p. 170.
59. Ibid.; Howe, *What Hath God Wrought*, p. 149; Sellers, *The Market Revolution*, pp. 126–7.
60. Howe, *What Hath God Wrought*, p. 149.
61. W. W. Freehling, *The Road to Disunion: Secessionists at Bay, 1776–1854* (New York: Oxford University Press, 1990), pp. 153–4; R. P. Forbes, *The Missouri Compromise and Its Aftermath: Slavery and the Meaning of America* (Chapel Hill, NC: The University of North Carolina Press, 2007), pp. 45–6.
62. Howe, *What Hath God Wrought*, pp. 152, 154.
63. Ibid., p. 150; *House Journal*, 15th Cong., 2nd sess. (16 February 1819), p. 273; *Senate Journal*, 15th Cong., 2nd sess. (27 February 1819), p. 322.
64. Howe, *What Hath God Wrought*, p. 156.
65. R. H. Brown, 'The Missouri Crisis, Slavery, and the Politics of Jacksonianism' *The South Atlantic Quarterly*, 65:1 (Winter 1966), p. 61.
66. 'Jefferson to Gallatin', 26 December 1820, *The Writings of Albert Gallatin*, ed. Adams, vol. 2, p. 176–7.
67. Sellers, *The Market Revolution*, pp. 138, 162–3; C. Sellers, 'Banking and Politics in Jackson's Tennessee, 1817–1827', *The Mississippi Valley Historical Review*, 41:1 (June, 1954), pp. 61–84.
68. 'Mr. Trimble's Resolution', 19 January 1819 and 'Mr. Johnson's Resolution for a Repeal of the Charter', 9 February 1819, *Legislative and Documentary History of the Bank of the United States*, pp. 732, 734.
69. Ibid., p. 734.
70. 'An Act Providing for the Division of Certain Quarter Sections, in Future Sales of the Public Lands', 22 February 1817, *Statutes at Large*, 3:346. The act had only this one clause.
71. 'An Act Making Further Provision for the Sale of Public Lands', 24 April 1820, ibid., 3:566.
72. 'Public Lands', *Niles's Weekly Register*, vol. 17 (5 February 1820), p. 386.

73. Treat, *The National Land System*, pp. 129, 143, 161.
74. 'Alterations of the Laws for the Sale of Public Lands', 23 January 1804, 'Credit on Public Lands', 5 April 1806, 'Relief to Purchase, Reduction of Price, and Repeal of the Credit System', 19 January 1809, *American State Papers: Public Lands* 1:166–7, 1:265–7, 1:825–6.
75. North, *Economic Growth of the United States*, pp. 128–9.
76. 'Plan to Prevent Fraudulent Combinations at the Resale of Relinquished Lands, and to Authorize Their Entry At Fixed Prices', 17 January 1828, *American State Papers: Public Lands* 5:377; C. F. Emerick, *The Credit System and the Public Domain* (Nashville, TN: Cumberland Presbyterian Publishing House, 1899), p. 7; A. H. Cole, 'Cyclical and Sectional Variations in the Sale of Public Lands, 1816–1860', in V. Carstensen (ed.), *The Public Lands: Studies in the History of the Public Domain* (Madison, WI: University of Wisconsin Press, 1963), pp. 229–52, 248.
77. See the account of lands purchased by J. Brahan from the United States, from 1 January 1817 to 10 April 1819, which is in *American States Papers: Public Lands*, 3:488–91.
78. *Annals of Congress*, 16th Cong., 1st sess. (24 February 1820), p. 446.
79. The balance for the States of Ohio, Indiana, Illinois, Missouri and the Territory of Michigan was $9,646,516.35, and the balance for the States of Mississippi and Alabama was $12,153,046.47. 'State of the Finances', 5 December 1820, *American State Papers: Finance*, 3:560, 3:562.
80. Senator Walker also attributed the speculation fever to the paper money of the newly created banks of Kentucky and Tennessee, which was 'profusely scattered over the country' and the high price of cotton. Ibid., 3:551; *Annals of Congress*, 16th Cong., 1st sess. (24 February 1820), p. 446.
81. *Kentucky Reporter* article cited in 'Public Lands', *Niles' Weekly Register*, vol. 17 (4 September 1819), p. 10.
82. 'Banks in which the Receipts from the Public Lands are Deposited', 15 February 1822, *American State Papers: Finance*, 3:718.
83. *St Louis Enquirer* (1 September 1819), cited in M. J. Rohrbough, *The Land Office Business: The Settlement and Administration of American Public Lands, 1789–1837* (New York: Oxford University Press, 1968), p. 142.
84. Edward Tiffin to Josiah Meigs, National Archive, General Land Office, Letters and Records, SG, NW, 5: October, 31, 1819, cited in ibid., p. 142.
85. 'State of the Finances', 5 December 1820, *American State Papers: Finance* 3:551.
86. S. Sato, *History of the Land Question in the United States* (Baltimore, MD: The Johns Hopkins University, 1886), p. 150.
87. It should be remembered that the Land Act of 1817 authorized the sale of public lands at the minimum size of half quarter sections (eighty acres) for only six of the thirty-six sections of a township. Ibid., p. 143; 'An Act Providing for the Division of Certain Quarter Sections in Future Sales of the Public Lands', 22 February 1817, *Statutes at Large* 3:346.
88. *Annals of Congress*, 16th Cong. 1st sess. (20 December 1819), p. 27.
89. Ibid. (11 January 1820), p. 78.
90. The Senators who spoke in favor of the bill in one form or another were R. King of New York (Federalist), H. G. Otis of Massachusetts (Federalist), B. Ruggles of Ohio (Republican), W. A. Trimble of Ohio, N. Macon of North Carolina (Republican), and those who opposed the cash bill in various ways were J. W. Walker of Alabama (Republican), N. Edwards of Illinois (Republican), H. Johnson of Louisiana (Republican), R. M. Johnson of Kentucky (Republican), J. Noble of Indiana (Republican), and W. Smith of

South Carolina (Republican). See *Annals of Congress*, 16th Cong., 1st sess. (16 December 1819, 21 December 1819, 11 January 1820, 12 January 1820, 16 February 1820, 17 February 1820, 22 February 1820, 24 February 1820, 28 February 1820, 1 March 1820, 6 March 1820, 8 March 1820 and 9 March 1820), pp. 26–7, 32, 78, 81, 417, 426, 437–8, 444–52, 458, 463–6, 476–7, 481–7, 489.

91. Ibid. (9 March 1820), p. 489.
92. T. Fuller of Massachusetts (Republican), H. R. Storrs of New York (Federalist), R. C. Anderson, Jr. and G. Robertson of Kentucky (Republicans), H. Brush and J. Sloane of Ohio (Republicans), P. P. Barbour of Virginia (Republican) supported the bill, while D. P. Cook of Illinois (Republican), W. Hendricks of Indiana (Republican), F. Jones of Tennessee (Republican), W. Brown, H. Clay and A. McLean all from Kentucky (Republicans), J. Crowell of Alabama (Republican) and T. Butler of Louisiana (Republican) opposed the bill. Ibid. (17 April 1820 and 19 April 1820), pp. 1862–3, 1889.
93. Ibid. (20 April 1820), p. 1901.
94. Congress lived up to its tacit promise to the West. In 1821, Congress passed an act allowing farmers to revert parts of their lands, purchased from the United States government, towards the payment on the rest. Eventually, Congress passed eleven relief acts before completing liquidation of land debts: 'An Act for the Relief of the Purchasers of Public Lands Prior to the First Day of July, Eighteen Hundred and Twenty', 2 March 1821, 'An Act Supplementary to the Act, Entitled "An Act for the Relief of the Purchasers of Public Lands Prior to the First Day of July, Eighteen Hundred and Twenty"', 20 April 1822, 'An Act Further to Extend the Provisions of the Act Entitled "An Act Supplementary to the Act, Entitled 'An Act for the Relief of the Purchasers of Public Lands Prior to the First Day of July, Eighteen Hundred and Twenty'"', 3 March 1823, 'An Act to Provide for the Extinguishment of the Debt due to the United States, by the Purchase of Public Lands', 18 May 1824, 'An Act Explanatory of An Act, entitled "An Act to Provide for the Extinguishment of the Debt due to the United States, by the Purchase of Public Lands", approved on the Eighteenth Day of May, One Thousand Eight Hundred and Twenty Four, 26 May 1824, 'An Act Making Further Provision for the Extinguishment of the Debt Due to the United States, By the Purchasers of Public Lands', 4 May 1826, 'An Act to Revive and Continue in Force the Several Acts Making Provision for the Extinguishment of the Debt Due to the United States by the Purchasers of the Public Lands', 21 March 1828, 'An Act for the Relief of Purchasers of the Public Lands That Have Reverted for Non-Payment of the Purchase Money', 23 May 1828, 'An Act for the Relief of the Purchasers of Public Lands, and for the Suppression of Fraudulent Practices at the Public Sales of the United States', 31 March 1830, 'An Act Supplemental to an Act Passed on the Thirty-First March, One Hundred Thousand Eight Hundred And Thirty, Entitled "An Act for the Relief of the Purchasers of Public Lands, and for the Suppression of Fraudulent Practices at the Public Sales of the United States"', 25 February 1831 and 'An Act to Amend An Act Entitled "An Act for the Relief of Purchasers of the Public Lands That Have Reverted for Non-Payment of the Purchase Money", Passed Twenty-Third Day of May, One thousand Eight Hundred And Twenty-Eight', 9 July 1832, *Statutes at Large*, 3:612–14, 3:665–6, 3:781, 4:24–5, 4:60, 4:158–9, 4:259–60, 4:286–8, 4:390–2, 4:445–6, 4:567–8. The specifics of each act are in Treat, *The National Land System*, p. 161. By 30 September 1821, the debt was reduced to $11,957,430, close to 50 per cent of the amount of debts in 1820. On 30 June 1825, the debt stood at $6,322,765.64 ½. The final relief act was passed in 1832. Emerick summarizes the way the debts were liquidated as following: '[t]o sum up: 4,602,573 acres were relinquished;

70 per cent of the debt was liquidated in this way; fifteen and two-tenths per cent by cash and discounts; six and four-tenths per cent by abatement; and the remainder in one or another of the following ways: (1) cancellation of indebtedness on land upon which certificates for forfeitures were issued; (2) cash incidental to abatement; (3) cash without discount on installments; (4) reversions'. 'Relinquished Lands', 27 January 1826, 'Operations of the Land System, and the Number of Military Bounty Land Warrants Issued During the Last Year', 5 December 1826, *American State Papers: Public Lands* 4:482, 4:790–5; Emerick, *The Credit System and the Public Domain*, pp. 12, 14.

95. 'An Act to Regulate the Duties on Imports and Tonnage', 27 April 1816, *Statutes at Large* 3:310–15.
96. *Annals of Congress*, 16th Cong., 1st sess. (21 April 1820), p. 1921. E. C. Gross of New York (Republican) also called the Tariff Act of 1816 a 'revenue act'. *Annals of Congress*, 16th Cong., 1st sess. (24 April 1820), p. 1966.
97. 'Eighth Annual Message', 3 December 1816, *Messages and Papers of the Presidents*, ed. Richardson, vol. 1, p. 559.
98. M. R. Eiselen, *The Rise of Pennsylvania Protectionism* (New York: Garland Publishing, Inc., 1974), p. 42.
99. 'First Inaugural Address', 4 March 1817, *Messages and Papers of the Presidents*, ed. Richardson, vol. 2, p. 577.
100. Ibid., pp. 577–8.
101. Eiselen, *The Rise of Pennsylvania Protectionism*, p. 44, fn. 32.
102. Ibid., p. 45.
103. Ibid., p. 14.
104. *Annals of Congress*, 16th Cong., 1st sess. (8 December 1819), p. 710.
105. Stanwood, *American Tariff Controversies in the Nineteenth Century*, vol. 1, p. 180.
106. The comparative tariff schedules of the old tariff act and the new tariff bill is in *Annals of Congress*, 16th Cong., 1st sess. (21 April 1820), pp. 1913–16.
107. N. K. Risjord, *The Old Republicans: Southern Conservatism in the Age of Jefferson* (New York: Columbia University Press, 1965), p. 211.
108. See Baldwin's and Clay's speeches, *Annals of Congress*, 16th Cong., 1st sess. (21 April 1820), p. 1917; (26 April 1820), p. 2036.
109. The address can be found in ibid. (24 April 1820), pp. 1952–63.
110. From Adams's diary entry on, 8 January 1820, *Memoirs of John Quincy Adams*, ed. Adams, vol. 4, p. 497.
111. Preyer, 'Southern Support of the Tariff of 1816 – A Reappraisal', pp. 320–1.
112. Risjord, *The Old Republicans*, p. 213.
113. Young, *A Political and Constitutional Study of the Cumberland Road*, pp. 64–5.
114. *Annals of Congress*, 17th Cong., 1st sess. (3 May 1822 and 29 April 1822), pp. 444, 1734.
115. 'Veto Message', 4 May 1822, *Messages and Papers of the Presidents*, ed. Richardson, vol. 1, pp. 711–12, and also see the longer message Monroe submitted to the House of Representatives along with the veto message: 'Veto Message: Views of the President of The United States on the Subject of Internal Improvements', 4 May 1822, ibid., pp. 713–52.
116. Ibid., p. 711.
117. Ibid., pp. 711–12.

118. According to John Quincy Adams, Monroe wrote the thesis in the winter of 1818–19. See Adams's diary entry on, 3 December 1819, *Memoirs of John Quincy Adams*, ed. Adams, vol. 4, p. 462.
119. The 'Veto Message: Views of the President' is forty pages of small font in Richardson's *Messages and Papers of the Presidents*. The expediency aspect of the issue spans only four pages, pp. 743–6.
120. 'Madison to Monroe', 27 December 1817, *Writings of James Madison*, vol. 8, p. 403, cited in J. H. Harrison, 'The Internal Improvement Issue in the Politics of the Union, 1783–1825' (PhD dissertation, University of Virginia, 1954), part 2, p. 404.
121. 'Seventh Annual Message', 2 December 1823, *Messages and Papers of the Presidents*, ed. Richardson, vol. 2, pp. 785–6.
122. *Annals of Congress*, 18th Cong., 1st sess. (15 December 1823), pp. 829–30.
123. Ibid. (12 January 1824), p. 994.
124. Ibid, p. 999.
125. Ibid., pp. 999–1000.
126. Ibid. (13 January 1824), p. 1006.
127. Ibid., p. 1007.
128. Ibid., pp. 1011–12.
129. Ibid. (14 January 1824), pp. 1022–41.
130. Ibid. (30 January 1824), pp. 1307–8.
131. 'Macon to Bartlett Yancey', 15 April 1818, cited in W. E. Dodd, *The Life of Nathaniel Macon* (Raleigh, NC: Edwards & Broughton, Printers and Binders, 1903), p. 310.
132. *Annals of Congress*, 18th Cong., 1st sess. (30 January 1824), p. 1315.
133. For the record, W. H. Crawford of Georgia used this logic for the first time. During his passionate defense of the rechartering of the First Bank of the United States on 11 February 1811 in the Senate, Crawford spoke of: '[t]he original powers granted to the Government by the constitution, [which] can never change with the varying circumstances of the country; but the means by which those powers are to be carried into effect, must necessarily vary with the varying state and circumstances of the nation'. At that time, Clay rejected this doctrine. 'On the Bill to Renew the Charter of 1791', 11 February 1811, *Legislative and Documentary History of the Bank of the United States*, p. 309.
134. J. S. Barbour of Virginia, R. A. Buckner of Kentucky, G. McDuffie of South Carolina, J. B. Reynolds of Tennessee, J. W. Gazlay of Ohio, R. Neale of Maryland, and E. Livingston of Louisiana supported the bill, while G. Tucker, W. C. Rives, A. Smyth of Virginia, R. D. Spaight of North Carolina, and S. A. Foote of Connecticut rose to oppose the bill. Their speeches are in *Annals of Congress*, 18th Cong., 1st sess. (3 February 1824 and 9–11 February 1824), pp. 1324–7, 1430–69.
135. Ibid. (10–11 February 1824), pp. 1468–71.
136. For examples, see the speeches of Richard M. Johnson of Kentucky, John Holmes of Maine, John Taylor of Virginia, and Nathan Macon of North Carolina, ibid. (21 April to 23 April 182), pp. 541–65, 568.
137. Ibid. (24 April 1824), pp. 570–1.
138. Feller, *The Public Lands in Jacksonian Politics*, p. 61.
139. 'Calhoun to Robert S. Garnett', 3 July 1824, *The Papers of John C. Calhoun*, eds. W. E. Hemphill, C. N Wilson, S. B. Cook and A. Moore, 28 vols (Columbia, SC: University of South Carolina Press, 1976), vol. 9, pp. 198–202.
140. See Adams's diary entry on, 1 October 1822, *Memoirs of John Quincy Adams*, ed. Adams, vol. 6, p. 75.

141. Ibid., p. 76.
142. 'Sixth Annual Message', 3 December 1822, 'Seventh Annual Message', 2 December 1823, *Messages and Papers of the Presidents*, ed. Richardson, vol. 1 and 2, pp. 759–61, 785–6.
143. Stanwood, *American Tariff Controversies in the Nineteenth Century*, vol. 1, p. 198.
144. 'Protection to Agriculture', 19 March 1824, *American State Papers: Finance* 4:494.
145. Ibid.
146. *Annals of Congress*, 18th Cong., 1st sess. (9 January 1824), pp. 960–5.
147. In 1822 receipts were $20,232,000 in total, while the total expenses were $14,999,000. In 1823, the receipts were $20,540,000, while the expenses were $14,706,000. Dewey, *Financial History of the United States*, pp. 169–70.
148. *Annals of Congress*, 18th Cong., 1st sess. (11 February 1824), p. 1478.
149. D. Webster of Massachusetts stated in the House that: '[b]eing intrusted [*sic*] with the interests of a district highly commercial, and deeply interested in manufactures', ibid. (2 April 1824), p. 2027.
150. Ibid. (27 February 1824), pp. 1695, 1699–700, 1701; (19 March 1824), pp. 1867, 1869; (23 March 1824), p. 1888; (24 March 1824), p. 1904; (2 April 1824), pp. 2026–68.
151. For the speeches of Hamilton and McDuffie, see ibid. (13 February 1824), pp. 1518–19; (17 February 1824), 1552–5.
152. Ibid. (26 March 1824), p. 1918.
153. Van Deusen, *The Life of Henry Clay*, p. 57.
154. Baxter, *Henry Clay and the American System*, p. 5.
155. Van Deusen, *The Life of Henry Clay*, p. 57.
156. 'Encouragement to Manufactures', 22 January 1811, *American State Papers: Finance* 2:465–7.
157. Baxter, *Henry Clay and the American System*, p. 3.
158. Van Deusen, a perceptive though not overly sympathetic biographer of Clay, entitled his chapter on Clay's activities during the 18th Congress (1823–5) 'The Lure of the President's Palace'. R. V. Remini, probably the best authority on the political history of this period, called the presidential ambition of Clay during this time 'lust' in his biography of Clay. Van Deusen, *The Life of Henry Clay*, pp. 160–78; Remini, *Henry Clay*, p. 218.
159. Clay gave his speech for two days on the 30th and 31st of March 1824. The full speech is in *Annals of Congress*, 18th Cong., 1st sess. (30 to 31 March 1824), pp. 1961–2001.
160. Ibid., p. 1994.
161. Ibid., p. 1978.
162. Ibid., p. 1966.
163. N. E. Cunningham, Jr, *The Presidency of James Monroe* (Lawrence, KS: University Press of Kansas, 1996), p. 8.
164. Ibid.
165. I. Brant, *James Madison*, 6 vols (New York: The Bobbs-Merrill Company, inc., 1961), vol. 6, p. 450.
166. 'To William T. Barry', 4 August 1822, R. Ketcham (ed.), *Selected Writings of James Madison* (Indianapolis, IN: Hackett Publishing Company, inc., 2006), pp. 309–10.
167. 'First Annual Message', 2 December 1817, *Messages and Letters of the Presidents*, ed. Richardson, vol. 1, p. 587.
168. Ibid.
169. D. W. Howe, 'Church, State, and Education in the Young American Republic', *Journal of the Early American Republic*, 22:1 (Spring 2002), p. 3.

3. The Reform Mentalities and the Implementation of the American System, 1825–1828

1. Howe, *What Hath God Wrought*, pp. 247–8.
2. Ibid., pp. 108–9.
3. Ibid., pp. 111–15.
4. R. G. Walters, *American Reformers 1815–1860*, revised edn (New York: Hill and Wang, 1997, original publication 1978).
5. L. P. Masur, *1831: Year of Eclipse* (New York: Hill and Wang, 2001), p. 65.
6. Ibid., pp. 65–7.
7. W. G. McLoughlin, *Revivals, Awakenings and Reform* (Chicago, IL: University of Chicago Press, 1980), p. 114.
8. Walters, *American Reformers*, pp. 21–37.
9. M. Raja, *Evangelizing the South* (New York, Oxford University Press, 2008). Quotes are on p. 4.
10. Masur, *1831: Year of Eclipse*, p. 68.
11. Howe, *What Hath God Wrought*, p. 175.
12. J. Claiborne, *Life and Correspondence of John A. Quitman* (New York, 1860), p. 109, cited in Masur, *1831: Year of Eclipse*, p. 73.
13. Walters, *American Reformers*.
14. J. L. Thomas, 'Romantic Reform in America, 1815–1865', *American Quarterly* 17:4 (Winter, 1965), p. 659.
15. K. Barry, *Susan B. Anthony: A Biography of a Singular Feminist* (New York: New York University Press, 1988), p. 38.
16. Brooke, 'Cultures of Nationalism, Movements of Reform, and the Composite-Federal Polity', p. 15.
17. Ibid., p. 20.
18. Ibid., p. 18.
19. 'Macon to Bartlett Yancey', 8 March 1818, cited in W. E. Dodd, *The Life of Nathaniel Macon* (Raleigh, NC: Edwards & Broughton, Printers and Binders, 1903), p. 313.
20. Howe, *The Political Culture of the American Whigs*, p. 153.
21. 'First Annual Message', 6 December 1825, *Messages and Papers of the Presidents*, ed. Richardson, vol. 2, p. 877.
22. *Daily National Intelligencer* (7 July 1828).
23. Bemis, *John Quincy Adams and the Union*, p. 103.
24. From Adams's diary entry on 26 November 1825, *Memoirs of John Quincy Adams*, ed. Adams, vol. 7, p. 62.
25. Ibid., p. 63.
26. 'To Charles Hammond', 27 May 1829, *The Papers of Henry Clay*, ed. R. Seager II and M. P. Hay, 11 vols (Lexington, KY: The University Press of Kentucky, 1984), vol. 8, p. 59.
27. *Register of Debates*, 22nd Cong., 1st sess. (20 June 1832), p. 1118.
28. Howe, *The Political Culture of the American Whigs*, pp. 125–32.
29. 'To James Barbour', 21 November 1829, *The Papers of Henry Clay*, ed. Seager and Hay, vol. 8, p. 127; Holt, *The Rise and Fall of the American Whig Party*, p. 10.
30. Holt, *The Rise and Fall of the American Whig Party*, p. 14.
31. T. H. Benton, *Thirty Years' View: A History of the Working of the American Government for Thirty Years, From 1820–1850*, 2 vols (New York: D. Appleton and Company, 1864), vol. 1, p. 102.

32. Chambers, *Old Bullion Benton*, pp. 3, 61, 64–5, 77, 89–90; A. S. Weiner, 'John Scott, Thomas Hart Benton, David Barton, and the Presidential Election of 1824', *Missouri Historical Review*, 60:4 (July 1966), pp. 460–94, p. 464.
33. Benton, *Thirty Years' View*, vol. 1, p. 102.
34. Fayette *Missouri Intelligencer* (2 August 1826), cited in Weiner, 'John Scott, Thomas Hart Benton, David Barton, and the Presidential Election of 1824', p. 478.
35. 'Senate Chamber February 8, 1825', *Niles' Weekly Register*, vol. 28 (26 March 1825), p. 51.
36. 'Application of Illinois for the Reduction in the Price of Certain Lands', 3 February 1825, 'Application of Indiana for the Relief of Purchasers and for Reduction in Price of Public Lands', 14 December 1825, 'Application of Alabama for Relief of Purchasers, for Reduction of Prices, Change in Mode of Selling, and Cession of Certain Public Lands to that State', 8 February 1826, *American States Papers: Public Lands* 4:148, 4:429–30, 4:528–9.
37. *Annals of Congress*, 18th Cong., 1st sess. (28 April 1824), pp. 582–3.
38. Ibid. (3 May 1824), p. 656.
39. Ibid. (21 May 1824), p. 769.
40. Chambers, *Old Bullion Benton*, p. 70.
41. At one point, Scott wrote Barton '[f]or God's sake, exert yourself for Benton ... Can you not make [Governor Alexander] McNair act right in regard to Benton? ... We must act so as to save our friends'. 'Scott to Barton', 19 September 1820, in the St. Louis *Missouri Republican*, 21 August 1822, cited in Weiner, 'John Scott, Thomas Hart Benton, David Barton, and the Presidential Election of 1824', pp. 467–8.
42. Ibid., p. 468; Chambers, *Old Bullion Benton*, p. 100.
43. 'Late Presidential Election', *Niles' Weekly Register*, vol. 29 (19 November 1825), p. 187.
44. Weiner, 'John Scott, Thomas Hart Benton, David Barton, and the Presidential Election of 1824'.
45. 'Application of Illinois for the Reduction in the Price of Certain Lands', 3 February 1825, 'Application of Missouri for a Reduction in the Price of Public Lands and a Donation to Actual Settlers', 27 December 1827, *American State Papers: Public Lands* 4:148, 5:36.
46. *Register of Debates.*, 19th Cong., 1st sess. (16 May 1826), pp. 720–49.
47. The bill is in *Register of Debates*, 19th Cong., 2nd sess. (12 January 1826), pp. 39–40.
48. *Register of Debates*, 19th Cong., 1st sess. (16 May 1826), pp. 720–6.
49. Ibid., p. 727.
50. Ibid.
51. Ibid., pp. 727, 742.
52. Barton's speech is in ibid., pp. 749–53.
53. *Register of Debates*, 19th Cong., 2nd sess. (9 January 1827), pp. 39–48.
54. On the political rivalry between Benton and Barton, and the final results of their conflict, see Weiner, 'John Scott, Thomas Hart Benton, David Barton and the Presidential Election of 1824'.
55. *Register of Debates*, 19th Cong., 2nd sess. (9 January 1827), pp. 45–6.
56. Ibid., p. 42.
57. Hibbard, *A History of the Public Land Policies*, pp. 45–53; Rohrbough, *The Land Office Business*, p. 17.
58. *Register of Debates*, 19th Cong., 2nd sess. (19 January 1827), p. 43.

59. D. Barton of Missouri, W. Hendricks of Indiana, R. M. Johnson of Kentucky, J. McKinley of Alabama, J. H. Eaton of Tennessee, E. K. Kane of Illinois, J. Noble of Indiana, J. S. Johnston of Louisiana and M. Van Buren of New York spoke on the bill. *Register of Debates*, 19th Cong., 2nd sess. (9 January 1827 and 14 February 1827), pp. 39–52, 346–7.
60. Ibid. (14 February 1827), pp. 346–7.
61. 1 December 1826, *Memoirs of John Quincy Adams*, ed. Adams, vol. 7, p. 194; 'Second Annual Message', 5 December 1826, *Messages and Papers of the Presidents*, ed. Richardson, vol. 2, pp. 916–30.
62. 1 December 1826, *Memoirs of John Quincy Adams*, ed. Adams, vol. 7, p. 194.
63. 10 November 1826 and 1 December 1826, ibid., pp. 173, 194.
64. 'Application of Missouri for a Reduction in the Price of Public Lands and a Donation to Actual Settlers', 27 December 1827, 'Application of Arkansas for a Graduation of the Price of the Public Land and an Exchange of School Lands', 31 December 1827, 'Plan for the Disposition of the Public Lands in Louisiana', 16 December 1828, *American State Papers: Public Lands* 5:36, 5:37, 5:582–3.
65. 'Twentieth Congress – 1st Session. Senate', *Niles' Weekly Register*, vol. 33 (5 January 1828), p. 290.
66. *Register of Debates*, 20th Cong., 1st sess. (24 December 1827), pp. 23–8.
67. During the ensuing debates after Benton's speech, Barton correctly pointed out this inconsistency of Benton's position. Ibid. (25 March 1828), pp. 490–1.
68. Duncan's report is in 'Reduction and Graduation of the Price of the Public Lands', 5 February 1828, *American State Papers: Public Lands* 5:447–50.
69. *Register of Debates.*, 20th Cong., 1st sess. (24 December 1827 and 25 March 1828), pp. 28–9, 483–97.
70. Feller, *The Public Lands in Jacksonian Politics*, pp. 30–1; also see, P. W. Gates, 'The Role of the Land Speculator in Western Development', in *The Jeffersonian Dream: Studies in the History of American Land Policy and Development* (Albuquerque, NM: University of New Mexico Press, 1996), especially pp. 6–8, original publication in *Pennsylvania Magazine of History and Biography* 66 (July 1942), pp. 314–33.
71. *Register of Debates.*, 20th Cong., 1st sess. (25 March 1828), pp. 484–5.
72. Ibid. (28 March 1828), p. 486.
73. Ibid. (25 March 1828), p. 497.
74. It seems that a five-year residency was considered the barometer of permanent settlement. The Homestead Act of 1862 required settlers to meet the five-year residency requirement before they received the titles to their homesteads. Hibbard, *A History of the Public Land Policies*, p. 85.
75. In addition to Benton's speech, see the speech of E. K. Kane of Illinois, *Register of Debates*, 20th Cong., 1st sess. (25 March 1828), pp. 499–500.
76. For example, see the speech of John McKinley of Alabama in ibid (26 March 1828), p. 518.
77. 'Third Annual Message', 4 December 1827, *Messages and Papers of the Presidents*, ed. Richardson, vol. 2, p. 957.
78. 'The maxim is held to be a sound one, that the ratio of capital to population should, if possible, be kept on the increase ... It is a proposition too plain to require elucidation, that the creation of capital is retarded, rather than accelerated, by the diffusion of a thin population over a great surface of soil. Anything that may serve to hold back this tendency to diffusion from running too far and too long into an extreme can scarcely

prove otherwise than salutary ... If the population of these States, not yet redundant in fact, though appearing to be so, under this legislative incitement to emigrate, remained fixed in more instances, as it probably would by extending the motives to manufacturing labour, it is believed that the nation at large would gain in two ways: 1st, by the more rapid accumulation of capital; and next, by the gradual reduction of the excess of its agricultural population over that engaged in other vocations'. 'State of the Finances', 10 December 1827, *American State Papers: Finance* 5:638.

79. *Register of Debates*, 20th Cong., 1st sess. (14 April 1828), p. 656.
80. Ibid. (22 April 1828), p. 677.
81. Ibid. (15 April 1828), pp. 657–60.
82. 'To Charles Hammond', 27 May 1829, *The Papers of Henry Clay*, ed. Seager and Hay, vol. 8, pp. 59–60.
83. 'Twentieth Congress – 2nd Session. Senate', *Niles' Weekly Register*, vol. 35 (27 December 1828), p. 293.
84. Wellington, *The Political and Sectional Influence of the Public Lands*, p. 10.
85. The Westerners were eventually satisfied in their demands with the passages of the Pre-emption Acts of 1830, 1841 and the Homestead Act of 1862. The pre-emption acts granted squatters, unauthorized settlers on public lands, the right to occupy and cultivate 160 acres of public lands and to purchase them later at the minimum price without competitive bids. The Homestead Act granted 160 acres of lands to settlers free of charge, except some minor fees for filing the claims. Hibbard, *A History of the Public Land Policies*, pp. 153, 158, 385.
86. 'Inaugural Address', 4 March 1825, *Messages and Papers of the Presidents*, ed. Richardson, vol. 2, p. 864.
87. Ibid., p. 865.
88. 'First Annual Message', 6 December 1825, ibid., pp. 879–80. One of Adams's memorable statements was that 'the spirit of internal improvement is catholic and liberal', *Daily National Intelligencer* (7 July 1828).
89. 'First Annual Message', 6 December 1825, *Messages and Papers of the Presidents*, ed. Richardson, vol. 2, p. 877.
90. Ibid., pp. 877–8.
91. Ibid., p. 882.
92. 'Farewell Address', 17 September 1796, ibid., vol. 1, p. 208.
93. 'First Annual Message', 6 December 1825, ibid., vol. 2, p. 882.
94. 'Gallatin to Jefferson', 16 November 1806, *The Writings of Albert Gallatin*, ed. Adams, vol. 1, p. 319.
95. Adams wrote of Clay's response: 'Clay approved of the general principles, but scrupled great part[s] of the details'. This must have been Clay's shrewd way of indicating his complete disapproval of the message itself, considering the level of Clay's understanding of the importance of 'details' over 'principles' in policy. Adams's Secretary of War, James Barbour of Virginia also initially opposed the message, but eventually 'very reluctantly withdrew his objection to the whole topic [of internal improvement]'. These seasoned politicians knew better. See Adams's diary entry on, 26 November 1825, *Memoirs of John Quincy Adams*, ed. Adams, vol. 7, pp. 62–3.
96. 'First Annual Message, 6 December 1825, *Messages and Papers of the Presidents*, ed. Richardson, vol. 2, p. 883.
97. 26 November 1825, *Memoirs of John Quincy Adams*, ed. Adams, vol. 7, p. 63.

98. Bemis, *John Quincy Adams and the Union*, pp. 103–4; *Daily National Intelligencer* (7 July 1828).
99. 'Crawford to Clay', 4 February 1828, Clay's *Works*, IV, p. 192, cited in C. M. Wiltse, *John C. Calhoun: Nationalist, 1782–1828* (Indianapolis, IN: Bobbs-Merrill Co., 1944), p. 321.
100. 'Macon to Bartlett Yancey', 8 December 1825, Bartlett Yancey Papers, University of North Carolina, cited in S. J. Barry, 'Nathaniel Macon: The Prophet of Pure Republicanism, 1758–1837' (PhD dissertation, State University of New York at Buffalo, 1996), p. 257.
101. 'To William B. Giles', 26 December 1825, *The Writings of Thomas Jefferson*, ed. A. E. Bergh, R. H. Johnson and A. A. Lipscomb, 20 vols (Washington DC: The Thomas Jefferson Memorial Association, 1903), vol. 16, pp. 149–50.
102. M. Van Buren, *Autobiography of Martin Van Buren*, ed. J. C. Fitzpatrick, 2 vols (1920; New York: A.M. Kelley, 1969), vol. 2 p. 195.
103. The Virginia General Assembly passed similar resolutions on 6 March 1827 too. Ames (ed.), *State Documents on Federal Relations*, pp. 142–3.
104. Ibid., p. 147. Italics in the original document.
105. Ibid., p. 139.
106. A. G. Smith, Jr, *Economic Readjustment of an Old Cotton State: South Carolina, 1820–1860* (Columbia, SC: University of South Carolina Press, 1958), pp. 1–18.
107. M. W. M. Hargreaves, *The Presidency of John Quincy Adams* (Lawrence, KS: University Press of Kansas 1985), p. 167.
108. Diary entry on 26 August 1826, *Memoirs of John Quincy Adams*, ed. Adams, vol. 7, pp. 145–6.
109. Hargreaves, *The Presidency of John Quincy Adams*, pp. 167–72.
110. The first subscription to a company for a project of internal improvement occurred on 3 March 1825, the last day of Monroe's administration. Congress authorized the Secretary of the Treasury to subscribe for 1,500 shares ($300,000) of stock in the Chesapeake and Delaware Company. 'An Act Authorizing the Subscription of Stock in the Chesapeake and Delaware Canal Company', 3 March 1825, *Statutes at Large* 4:124.
111. The percentage is calculated from Table 3.2 and 3.3.
112. *Senate Journal*, 20th Cong., 1st sess. (21 May 1828), pp. 448–9; *House Journal*, 20th Cong., 1st sess. (9 May 1828), pp. 716–18
113. For reckless banking during the administration of W. Jones see Catterall, *The Second Bank of the United States*, pp. 22–67.
114. Catterall, *The Second Bank of the United* States, pp. 68–92.
115. Ibid., pp. 93–163.
116. R. A. Bayley, *History of the National Loans of the United States from July 4, 1776, to June 30, 1880*, 2nd edn (Washington, 1882), pp. 355–60.
117. The yearly expenditures of the general government are from Dewey, *Financial History of the United States*, p. 169. The figures are derived by adding up government expenditures between 1816 and 1830 and dividing the sum by the number of years.
118. 'Public Debt', 14 April 1808, *American State Papers: Finance*, 2:288–9.
119. The total amount of debts during the Federalist administrations did not decrease but rather increased from $75,463,000 in 1791 to $82,976,000 in 1800. After the Jeffersonians came to power, the amount decreased gradually until it reached $45,210,000 in 1812. Because of the cost of the War of 1812, however, the total amount of public debt shot up to $123,492,000 in 1817, from where it decreased again until it was all paid off in 1835. The statistics of the

amount of national debts between 1791 and 1835 are from '*Historical Statistics of the United States*', House Document: No. 33, 86th Cong., 1st sess, p. 721.
120. Smith, *Economic Aspects of the Second Bank of the United States*, p. 56.
121. Gallatin, 'Considerations on the Currency and Banking System of the United States', 1 January 1831, *The Writings of Albert Gallatin*, ed. Adams, vol. 3, p. 281.
122. Section fourteen of the incorporation of the 2BUS in 'An Act to Incorporate the Subscribers to the Bank of the United States', 10 April 1816, Statutes at Large 3:274.
123. Article eight of section eleven of the incorporation act of the 2BUS in ibid., 3:272.
124. Section seventeen of the incorporation act in ibid., 3:274–5.
125. Smith, *Economic Aspects of the Second Bank of the United States*, pp. 47–8.
126. Catterall, *The Second Bank of the United States*, p. 502.
127. J. T. Holdsworth and Dewey, *The First and Second Banks of the United States*, pp. 42, 51; Catterall, *The Second Bank of the United States*, pp. 435–8.
128. Ratner, *The Tariff in American History*, p. 15.
129. 'Pennsylvania', *Niles' Register*, 30 (3 June 1826), p. 239.
130. Taussig (ed.), *State Papers and Speeches on the Tariff*, p. 190; 'Woollen Manufactures', *Niles' Register*, vol. 31 (11 November 1826), pp. 185–6.
131. *Register of Debates*, 19th Cong., 2nd sess., 10 and 28 February 1827, pp. 1099, 496.
132. Howe, *What Hath God Wrought*, p. 273.
133. Risjord, *The Old Republicans*, p. 263–64; Wiltse, *John C. Calhoun: Nationalist*, pp. 343, 351, 353; Holt, *The Rise and Fall of the American Whig Party*, pp. 11–12.
134. Ratner, *The Tariff History in American History*, p. 15.
135. For an example of an expression of Rush's protective sentiment, see 'State of the Finances', 12 December 1826, *American State Papers: Finance*, 5:526.
136. Feller, *The Public Lands in Jacksonian Politics*, p. 121; R. N. Current, *Daniel Webster and the Rise of National Conservatism* (Boston, MA: Little, Brown and Company, 1955), p. 40.
137. For an example of the economic complaints of the South against protective tariffs, see Thomas Cooper's speech in 'Speech of Dr. Cooper', *Niles' Weekly Register*, vol. 33 (8 September 1827), pp. 28–32. A clear analysis of such a view is in W. W. Freehling, *Prelude to Civil War* (New York: Harper & Row, Publishers, 1965), pp. 106–7
138. W. W. Freehling (ed.), *The Nullification Era: A Documentary Record* (New York: Harper & Row, Publishers, 1967), pp. 33–4.
139. Ibid., p. 37.
140. 'Speech of Dr. Cooper', *Niles' Weekly Register*, vol. 33 (8 September 1827), p. 28.
141. Ibid., p. 32.
142. In the election of 1824, Ohio, Missouri and Kentucky voted for Clay. R. V. Remini, 'Martin Van Buren and the Tariff of Abominations', *American Historical Review*, 63:4 (July 1958), p. 904.
143. Eiselen, *The Rise of Pennsylvania Protectionism*, pp. 82–5.
144. Wiltse, *John C. Calhoun: Nationalist*, p. 369.

4. Decline of the American System, 1829–1837

1. *Senate Journal*, 18th Cong., 1st sess. (23 January 1824, 20 February 1824, 22 April 1824, 24 April 1824 and 19 May 1824), pp. 126–7, 184, 313–18, 321–2, 441; *Senate Journal*, 18th Cong., 2nd sess. (26 January 1825, 23 February 1825 and 24 February 1825), pp. 111, 189, 194–5.

2. Sellers, *The Market Revolution*, p. 193.
3. A. Jackson, 'Gen. Jackson on the Tariff', in *Andrew Jackson and Early Tennessee History, Illustrated*, ed. S. G. Heiskell, 3 vols (Nashville, TN: Ambrose Printing Company, 1921), vol. 3, pp. 69–71, 71.
4. R. V. Remini, *The Life of Andrew Jackson* (New York: Harper & Row, 1988), This section relies heavily on Remini's book.
5. Ibid., pp. 7–11.
6. Wilentz, *The Rise of American Democracy*, p. 169.
7. Remini, *The Life of Andrew Jackson*, p. 12.
8. Freehling, *The Road to Disunion*, p. 263.
9. Remini, *The Life of Andrew Jackson*, pp. 17, 24–6.
10. Ibid, pp. 33–4.
11. Wilentz, *The Rise of American Democracy*, p. 172.
12. R. V. Remini, *Andrew Jackson and His Indian Wars* (New York: Penguin Books, 2001), p. 142.
13. Remini, *The Life of Andrew Jackson*, p. 128.
14. Hargreaves, *The Presidency of John Quincy Adams*, pp. 20–1, 26–7, 37–8; Howe, *What Hath God Wrought*, p. 209.
15. Remini, *The Life of Andrew Jackson*, p. 155; Howe, *What Hath God Wrought*, p. 211.
16. Remini, *The Life of Andrew Jackson*, pp. 176–7.
17. 'Inaugural Address', 4 March 1829, *Messages and Papers of the Presidents*, ed. Richardson, p. 1000.
18. Howe, *What Hath God Wrought*, pp. 356–7.
19. D. S. Heidler and J. T. Heidler, *Indian Removal* (New York: W.W. Norton & Company, 2007), p. 83; Remini, *The Life of Andrew Jackson*, pp. 19–21, 23, 28–30.
20. Howe, *What Hath God Wrought*, p. 342.
21. R. N. Satz, *American Indian Policy in the Jacksonian Era* (Norman, OK; University of Oklahoma Press, 2002), p. 12; Howe, *What Hath God Wrought*, p. 346.
22. *A Digest of the Laws of the State of Georgia* (Athens, GA: State of Georgia, 1837), p. 285.
23. A. F. C. Wallace, *The Long Bitter Trail: Andrew Jackson and the Indians* (New York: Hill and Wang, 1993), p. 4.
24. D. Williams, *Georgia Gold Rush: Twenty-Niners, Cherokees and Gold Fever* (Columbia, SC: University of South Carolina Press, 1993), p.12.
25. J. Mooney, *History, Myths and Sacred Formulas of the Cherokee* (Fairview, NC: Bright Mountain Books, Inc., 1992), p. 116.
26. J. Meacham, *American Lion: Andrew Jackson in the White House* (New York: Random House, 2008), p. 92.
27. Howe, *What Hath God Wrought*, p. 342; P. S. Onuf, *Statehood and Union: A History of the Northwest Ordinance* (Bloomington, IN: Indiana University Press, 1987), p. 10.
28. 'Inaugural Address', 4 March 1829, *Messages and Papers of the Presidents*, ed. Richardson, vol. 2, p. 1001.
29. 'First Annual Address', 8 December 1829, ibid., p. 1021.
30. 'Indian Removal Act', in F. P. Prucha (ed.), *Documents of United States Indian Policy* (Lincoln: University of Nebraska Press, 1975), pp. 52–53. See Also; Appendix B, "Text of the Removal Act," in Wallace, *The Long Bitter Trail*, pp. 125–8.
31. *Senate Journal*, 21st Cong., 1st sess. (24 April 1830), p. 268; *House Journal*, 21st Cong., 1st sess. (26 May 1830), pp. 729–30.

32. Satz, *American Indian Policy*, pp. 64–9; Remini, *The Life of Andrew Jackson*, pp. 215–16.
33. Satz, *American Indian Policy*, pp. 75–9.
34. Ibid., pp. 81–2.
35. Ibid., pp. 100–1.
36. Ibid., 112.
37. R. Sutch and S. B. Carter (eds), *Historical Statistics of the United States: Earliest Times to the Present, Millennial Edition*, 5 vols (New York: Cambridge University Press, 2006), 1:180–1:359.
38. P. Kolchin, *American Slavery, 1619–1877* (1993; New York: Hill & Wang, 2003), p. 95; W. Johnson, *Soul by Soul: Life Inside the Antebellum Slave Market* (Cambridge, MA: Harvard University Press, 1999), pp. 5, 48–9.
39. Kolchin, *American Slavery*, p. 95.
40. A. Fishlow, 'Antebellum Interregional Trade Reconsidered', *American Economic Review*, 54:3 (May, 1964), pp., 32–64, pp. 353–5.
41. Ibid., p. 362.
42. Ibid., see table 3 on p. 360.
43. Ibid, pp. 353–5, 360–2.
44. North, *The Economic Growth of the United States*, p. 130.
45. G. R. Taylor, *The Transportation Revolution, 1815–1860* (New York: Rinehart & Company, 1957), p. 133.
46. Ibid., p. 135.
47. Ibid., p. 136.
48. Ibid., p. 137.
49. Ibid., p. 139.
50. Ibid., p. 143.
51. Ibid., p. 136.
52. North, *The Economic Growth of the United States*, pp. 35, 51, 103–5, 154.
53. Ibid., pp. 140–1.
54. Ibid., pp. 192, 196–7, p. 197 n. 18.
55. Ibid., pp. 130–1, 258 Table C-X.
56. Baxter, *Henry Clay and the American System*, pp. 111–12; the full name of the company is *Maysville, Washington, Paris, and Lexington Turnpike Road Company*.
57. Feller, *The Public Lands in Jacksonian Politics*, p. 137; for the national road extending to New Orleans see Baxter, *Henry Clay and the American System*, p. 113.
58. *Senate Journal*, 18th Cong., 1st sess. (24 April 1824), pp. 321–2.
59. 'First Annual Message', 8 December 1829, *Messages and Papers of the Presidents*, ed. Richardson, vol. 2, pp. 1014–15.
60. *Senate Journal*, 21st Cong., 1st sess. (31 May 1830), p. 368.
61. Ibid., p. 364
62. Ibid.
63. 25 June 1830, *Memoirs of John Quincy Adams*, ed. Adams, vol. 8, p. 233.
64. Van Buren, *The Autobiography of Martin Van Buren*, ed. Fitzpatrick, vol. 2, p. 337.
65. 'Second Annual Message', 6 December 1830, *Messages and Papers of the Presidents*, ed. Richardson, vol. 2, p. 1073.
66. Ibid.
67. See the discussion on this matter in fn. 72, in Feller, *The Public Lands in Jacksonian Politics*, pp. 233–4. For a different interpretation of the importance of the veto message, see

'Speech of Mr. J. A. Rockwell', 11 January 1848, *Congressional Globe*, 30th Cong., 1st sess. (11 January 1848), Appendix p. 106–7.
68. Feller, *The Public Lands in Jacksonian Politics*, p. 148.
69. 'On Distributing the Proceeds of the Sales of the Public Lands Among the Several States', 16 April 1832, *American State Papers: Public Lands* 6:441–51; *Senate Journal*, 22nd Cong., 2nd sess. (25 January 1833) p. 138; *House Journal*, 22nd Cong., 2nd sess. (1 March 1833), p. 460.
70. Baxter, *Henry Clay and the American System*, p. 116; Van Atta, 'Western Lands and the Political Economy of Henry Clay's American System, 1819–1832'; Van Atta, '"A Lawless Rabble"'.
71. Baxter, *Henry Clay and the American System*, p. 114.
72. 'Third Annual Message', 6 December 1831, *Messages and Papers of the Presidents*, ed. Richardson, vol. 2, p. 1119.
73. 'To Francis T. Brooke', 4 October 1831, *The Papers of Henry Clay*, ed. Seager and Hay, 11 vols (Lexington, KY: University of Kentucky Press, 1963), vol. 8, p. 413
74. Feller, *The Public Lands in Jacksonian Politics*, pp. 153–4.
75. Ibid., pp. 154–5.
76. Holt, *The Rise and Fall of the American Whig Party*, p. 17.
77. Remini, *Henry Clay*, pp. 378–411.
78. Feller, *The Public Lands in Jacksonian Politics*, p. 158.
79. *Senate Journal*, 22nd Cong., 2nd sess. (25 January 1833), p. 138; *House Journal*, 22nd Cong., 2nd sess. (1 March 1833), p. 460.
80. Feller, *The Public Lands in Jacksonian Politics*, pp. 163–4, especially look at Table 6.2 on p. 164.
81. Ibid., pp. 153–5, especially look at Table 6.1 on p. 154.
82. Freehling, *Prelude to Civil War*, pp. 7–24.
83. Ibid., pp. 361–2, Appendix A, Table 1.
84. Ibid., pp. 361–2, Appendix A, Table 1.
85. Ibid., pp. 27, 47.
86. Freehling, *The Road to Disunion*, pp. 254–7
87. Freehling,, *Prelude to Civil War*, pp. 107, 117.
88. Freehling (ed.), *The Nullification Era*, p. 27.
89. *Niles' Weekly Register*, 33 (8 September 1827), p. 31.
90. This is the chapter title used by Sydnor, *The Development of Southern Sectionalism 1819–1848*, pp. 157–76.
91. Ibid.
92. 17 February 1832, *Memoirs of John Quincy Adams*, ed. Adams, vol. 8, p. 474.
93. 'Jackson's Denunciation of Nullification: the Nullification Proclamation', 10 December 1832, in *Andrew Jackson, Nullification, and the State-Rights Tradition*, ed. C. Sellers (Chicago, IL: Rand McNally & Company, 1963) pp. 7–15; Wilentz, *The Rise of American Democracy*, pp. 380, 382.
94. M. Wiltse, *John C. Calhoun: Nullifier, 1829–1839* (New York: Russell & Russell, 1968), pp. 184–5; M. D. Peterson, *Olive Branch and Sword – The Compromise of 1833* (Baton Rouge, LA: Louisiana State University Press, 1982), p. 53.
95. T. P. Govan, *Nichols Biddle: Nationalist and Public Banker, 1786–1844* (Chicago, IL: The University of Chicago Press, 1959), pp. 22–3.

96. Ibid., pp. 59, 80; R. H. Timberlake, *The Origins of Central Banking in the United States* (Cambridge, MA: Harvard University Press, 1978), pp. 31–3; Catterall, *The Second Bank of the United States*, pp. 440–1.
97. P. Temin, *The Jacksonian Economy* (New York: W. W. Norton & Company Inc, 1969), pp. 49–50.
98. Ibid., pp. 50–1.
99. 'First Annual Message', 8 December 1829, *Messages and Papers of the Presidents*, ed. Richardson, vol. 2, pp. 1014, 1025.
100. 'Second Annual Message', 6 December 1830, ibid., p. 1092.
101. 'Third Annual Message', 6 December 1831, ibid., p. 1121.
102. Baxter, *Henry Clay and the American System*, pp. 89; Howe, *What Hath God Wrought*, p. 378; After the veto 'the blindness of the bank's supporters ... said the bank's life depended "on getting the veto *now* – so that the nation may be roused before the autumnal elections"', Catterall, *The Second Bank of the United States*, p. 240. Italics from the original text.
103. Catterall, *The Second Bank of the United States*, p. 223.
104. Remini, *The Life of Andrew Jackson*, p. 227.
105. Biddle to Cadwalader, 3 July 1832, Biddle papers, Library of Congress, cited in Remini, *The Life of Andrew Jackson*, p. 227.
106. Remini, *The Life of Andrew Jackson*, p. 227.
107. *Senate Journal*, 21st Cong., 1st sess. (31 May 1830), p. 360–9; R. V. Remini, *Andrew Jackson and the Bank War* (New York: W. W. Norton & Company, 1967), pp. 84–5; Hammond, *Banks and Politics in America*, pp. 405–11; Temin breaks down the economic inconsistencies of the veto that conflicted with the reality of the banking situation in *The Jacksonian Economy*, pp. 28–58.
108. Baxter, *Henry Clay and the American System*, p. 95; Gavon, *Nichols Biddle*, p. 203.
109. Howe, *What Hath God Wrought*, pp. 382, 393; for Democrat banking needs in the Northeast and their support for State and independent banks to replace the BUS before and after the veto see W. G. Shade, *Banks or No Banks The Money Issue in Western Politics* (Detroit: Wayne State University Press, 1972), pp. 20–39.
110. Catterall, *The Second Bank of the United States*, pp. 289–90; Howe, *What Hath God Wrought*, p. 387.
111. Catterall, *The Second Bank of the United States*, pp. 287, 296–7.
112. Remini, *Andrew Jackson and the Bank War*, pp. 126, 136–7, 141–2; Howe, *What Hath God Wrought*, p. 389. Following the dismissal of the two Secretaries of Treasury, Clay led Congress in passing a censure against Jackson. Characteristically of Jackson, his first response to the censure was to threaten to challenge Clay to a duel for instigating the censure in the Senate but he refrained in the end, simply scolding Congress for interfering in his 'presidential prerogatives' over cabinet officers.
113. Howe, *What Hath God Wrought*, pp. 391–2.
114. Remini, *Andrew Jackson and the Bank War*, p. 125
115. P. W. Gates, *History of Public Land Law Development* (Washington: US Government Printing Office, 1968), p. 166.
116. Remini, *Andrew Jackson and the Bank War*, p. 173
117. J. W. Markham, *Financial History of the United States: From Christopher Columbus to the Robber Barons 1492–1900*, 3 vols (New York: M. E. Sharpe, 2001), vol. 1, p. 148.
118. R. C. McGrane, *The Panic of 1837: Some Financial Problems of the Jacksonian Era* (Chicago, IL: The University of Chicago Press, 1924), p. 93.

119. P. L. Rousseau, 'Jacksonian Monetary Policy, Specie Flows, and the Panic of 1837', *The Journal of Economic History*, 62:2 (June 2002), p. 457.
120. McGrane, *The Panic of 1837*, p. 98.
121. S. Rezneck. 'The Social History of an American Depression, 1837–1843', *The American Historical Review* 40 (July 1935), p. 664.
122. McGrane, *The Panic of 1837*, p. 99.
123. Ibid., p. 100.
124. Howe, *What Hath God Wrought*, p. 505.
125. 'To Francis T. Brooke', 9 October 1838, *The Papers of Henry Clay*, ed. Seager and Hay, vol. 9, p. 239.
126. 'Clay to Tucker', 10 October 1838, *The Letters and Times of the Tylers*, ed. L. G. Tyler, 2 vols (Richmond: Whitter & Shepperson, 1884), vol. 1, pp. 601–2; Holt, *The Rise and Fall of the American Whig Party*, p. 94.
127. 'Inaugural Address', 4 March 1829, *Messages and Papers of the Presidents*, ed. Richardson, vol. 2, p. 1000.
128. 'First Annual Message', 8 December 1829, ibid., p. 1014

Conclusion: The American System and American Society and Economy, 1790–1837

1. See D. Webster's speech to the Senate in *Register of Debates*, 21st Cong., 1st ses. (26 and 27 January 1830), pp. 58–73.
2. Benton, *Thirty Years' View*, vol. 1, p. 73.
3. For an analysis on the struggle between minority interests and majority rule in the Jacksonian era, see R. E. Ellis, *The Union at Risk: Jacksonian Democracy, States' Rights, and the Nullification Crisis* (New York: Oxford University Press, 1987).
4. T. Brown, *Politics and Statesmanship: Essays on the American Whig Party* (New York: Columbia University Press, 1985), p. 126.
5. Howe, *What Hath God Wrought*, p. 283.
6. W. Licht, *Industrializing America: The Nineteenth Century* (Baltimore, MD: The Johns Hopkins University Press, 1995), p. 86.
7. Van Buren, *The Autobiography of Martin Van Buren*, ed. Fitzpatrick, vol. 2, p. 338.
8. Fishlow, 'Antebellum Interregional Trade Reconsidered'; D. Lindstrom, *Economic Development in the Philadelphia Region, 1810–1850* (New York: Columbia University Press, 1978).
9. Lindstrom, *Economic Development*, pp. 5–7.
10. D. R. Meyer, *The Roots of American Industrialization* (Baltimore, MD: The Johns Hopkins University Press, 2003), p. 2.
11. Howe, *What Hath God Wrought*, pp. 605, 851–2; D. M. Henkin, *The Postal Age: The Emergence of Modern Communications in Nineteenth-Century America* (Chicago, IL: University of Chicago Press, 2007).
12. See Feller, *The Jacksonian Promise*; also see D. W. Howe's book review, 'Jacksonianism and the Promise of Improvement', *Reviews in American History*, 25 (1997), pp. 58–62.
13. H. C. Richardson, *The Greatest Nation of the Earth: Republican Economic Policies During the Civil War* (Cambridge, MA: Harvard University Press, 1997), pp. 105–8; J. R. Hummel, 'The Civil War and Reconstruction', in *Government and the American Economy: A New History* (Chicago and London: The University of Chicago Press, 2007), pp. 188–231, 206.

14. Richardson, *The Greatest Nation of the Earth*, p. 86.
15. Ibid., pp. 87–8.
16. Ibid., p. 195.
17. Ibid., pp. 155–60; L. A. Cremin, *American Education: The National Experience 1783–1876* (New York: Harper & Row, Publishers, 1980), pp. 149, 341, 364, 406, 516, 583.

WORKS CITED

Government Documents

10th Census Reports (Washington, 1884).

American State Papers: Indian Affairs, vol. 2; *Finances*, vol. 1–5; *Public Lands*, vol. 1–6; *Miscellaneous*, vol. 1–2.

Annals of Congress: 4th Cong., 1st sess.; 6th Cong., 1st sess.; 7th Cong., 1st sess.; 8th Cong., 1st sess.; 13th Cong., 3rd sess.; 14th Cong., 1st and 2nd sess.; 15th Cong., 1st sess.; 16th Cong., 1st sess.; 17th Cong, 1st sess.; and 18th Cong., 1st sess.

Biographical Directory of the American Congress 1774–1961 (Washington DC: United States Government Printing Office, 1961).

Congressional Globe: 30th Cong., 1st sess.

A Digest of the Laws of the State of Georgia (Athens, GA: State of Georgia, 1837).

House Documents: No. 172, 26th Cong., 1st sess.; No. 33, 86th Cong., 1st sess.

House Journal: 11th Cong., 3rd sess.; 14th Cong., 1st sess.; 16th Cong., 1st sess.; 18th Cong., 1st sess.; 20th Cong., 1st and 2nd sess.; 21st Cong., 1st sess.; 22nd Cong., 1st and 2nd sess.

Register of Debates: 19th Cong., 1st and 2nd sess.; 20th Cong., 1st sess.; 21st Cong., 1st sess.; 22nd Cong., 1st sess.

Senate Documents, No. 246, 27th Cong., 3rd sess.

Senate Journal: 11th Cong., 3rd sess.; 14th Cong., 1st sess.; 16th Cong., 1st sess.; 18th Cong., 1st and 2nd sess.; 20th Cong., 1st and 2nd sess.; 21st Cong., 1st sess.; 22nd Cong., 2nd sess.

Statutes at Large: vol. 1–5, 12.

Booker, M. A. (ed.), *Members of Congress Since 1789*, 3rd edn (Washington: Congressional Quarterly, 1985).

The Territorial Papers of the United States, ed. C. E. Carter, 28 vols (Washington: Government Printing Office, 1934).

Legislative and Documentary History of the Bank of the United States Including the Original Bank of North America, eds. M. St C. Clarke and D. A. Hall, 1st repr. (1832; New York: Augustus M. Kelley Publishers, 1967).

A Compilation of the Messages and Papers of the Presidents, ed. J. D. Richardson, 11 vols (New York: Bureau of National Literature, 1911), vol. 1–2.

Sutch, R., and S. B. Carter (eds), *Historical Statistics of the United States: Earliest Times to the Present, Millennial Edition*, 5 vols (New York: Cambridge University Press, 2006), vol. 1–2.

Newspapers, Periodicals, and Websites

Daily National Intelligencer.

Niles' Weekly Register.

United States Census Bureau, http://www.census.gov/ (accessed 27 March 2009).

Harvard Buisness School, *Sunk In Lucre's Sordid Charms: South Sea Bubble Resources in the Kress Collection at Baker Library*, ed. Karen Bailey, September 2005, http://www.library.hbs.edu/hc/ssb/index.html (accessed 12 March 2009).

Published Correspondences, Diaries, Memoirs, and Autobiographies

Memoirs of John Quincy Adams (1874–7), ed. C. F. Adams, 12 vols (Freeport, NY: Books For Libraries Press, 1969).

The Papers of John C. Calhoun, ed. W. E. Hemphill, C. N Wilson, S. B. Cook and A. Moore, 28 vols (Columbia, SC: University of South Carolina Press, 1976).

The Papers of Henry Clay, ed. J. F. Hopkins, R. Seager II, and M. P. Hay, 11 vols (Lexington, KY: University of Kentucky Press, 1963).

The Writings of Albert Gallatin, ed. H. Adams, 3 vols (New York: Antiquarian Press Ltd., 1960, original publication 1879).

The Papers of Alexander Hamilton, eds. H. C. Syrett and J. E. Cooke, 27 vols (New York: Columbia University Press, 1965).

Messages and Letters of William Henry Harrison, ed. L. Esarey, 2 vols (Indianapolis, IN: Indiana Historical Commission, 1922).

The Writings of Thomas Jefferson, ed. P. L. Ford, 10 vols (New York: G. P. Putnam's Sons, 1892–1899).

The Writings of Thomas Jefferson, ed. A. E. Bergh, R. H. Johnson and A. A. Lipscomb, 20 vols (Washington DC: The Thomas Jefferson Memorial Association, 1903).

The Papers of Thomas Jefferson, eds. J. P. Boyd and B. B. Oberg, 35 vols to date (Princeton, NJ: Princeton University Press, 1974).

Robertson, G., *An Outline of the Life of George Robertson* (Lexington, KY, 1876).

Life and Letters of Joseph Story, ed. W. W. Story, 2 vols (New York: Books for Libraries Press, 1971, original publication 1851).

The Letters and Times of the Tylers, ed. L. G. Tyler, 2 vols (Richmond, Whitter & Shepperson, 1884).

Van Buren, M., *Autobiography of Martin Van Buren*, ed. J. C. Fitzpatrick, 2 vols (1920; New York: A. M. Kelley, 1969).

The Papers of Daniel Webster: Correspondence 1798–1824, ed. C. M. Wiltse, 6 vols (Hanover, NH: University Press of New England, 1974).

Books and Articles

Adams, H. C., *The Life of Albert Gallatin* (Philadelphia, PA: J. B. Lippincott & Co., 1879).

—, *Taxation in the United States 1789–1816* (Baltimore, MD: Johns Hopkins University Press, 1884).

Ames, H. V. (ed.), *State Documents on Federal Relations: The States and the United States* (Philadelphia, PA: Department of History, University of Pennsylvania, 1911).

Baker, P., 'The Washington National Road Bill and the Struggle to Adopt a Federal System of Internal Improvement', *Journal of the Early Republic* 22:3 (Autumn 2002), pp. 437–64.

Ballagh, J. C., 'Southern Economic History: Tariff and Public Lands', *Annual Report of the American Historical Association for the Year 1898* (Washington DC: n.p., 1899).

Barry, K., *Susan B. Anthony: A Biography of a Singular Feminist* (New York: New York University Press, 1988).

Barry, S. J., 'Nathaniel Macon: The Prophet of Pure Republicanism, 1758–1837' (PhD dissertation, State University of New York at Buffalo, 1996).

Baxter, M. G., *Henry Clay and the American System* (Lexington, KY: The University Press of Kentucky, 1995).

Bayley, R. A., *History of the National Loans of the United States from July 4, 1776, to June 30, 1880*, 2nd edn (Washington, 1882).

Bemis, S. F., *John Quincy Adams and the Union* (New York: Knopf, 1956).

Benton, T. H., *Thirty Years' View: A History of the Working of the American Government for Thirty Years, From 1820–1850*, 2 vols (New York: D. Appleton and Company, 1864).

Bodenhorn, H., *A History of Banking in Antebellum America* (New York: Cambridge University Press, 2000).

—, *State Banking in Early America* (New York: Oxford University Press, 2003).

Brant, I., *James Madison: The Nationalist 1780–1787* (Indianapolis, IN: Bobbs-Merrill Company, 1948).

—, *James Madison*, 6 vols (New York: The Bobbs-Merrill Company, inc., 1961).

Brooke, J. L., 'Cultures of Nationalism, Movements of Reform, and the Composite-Federal Polity from Revolutionary Settlement to Antebellum Crisis', *Journal of the early Republic* 29:1 (Spring 2009), pp. 1–33.

Brown, R. H., 'The Missouri Crisis, Slavery, and the Politics of Jacksonianism', *South Atlantic Quarterly* 65:1 (Winter 1966), pp. 55–72.

Brown, T., *Politics and Statesmanship: Essays on the American Whig Party* (New York: Columbia University Press, 1985).

Calhoun, J. C., 'Calhoun's Argument for Nullification: the Fort Hill Address', 26 July 1831, *Andrew Jackson, Nullification, and the State-Rights Tradition*, ed. C. Sellers (Chicago, IL: Rand McNally & Company, 1963), pp. 3–7.

Catterall, R. C. H., *The Second Bank of the United States* (Chicago, IL: The University of Chicago Press, 1903).

Chambers, W. N., *Old Bullion Benton: Senator from the New West* (Boston, MA: Little Brown, 1956).

Chernow, R., *Alexander Hamilton* (New York: Penguin Books, 2004).

Clark, V. S., *History of Manufacturers in the United States*, 3 vols (New York: McGraw-Hill, 1929).

Cole, A. H., 'Cyclical and Sectional Variations in the Sale of Public Lands, 1816–1860', in V. Carstensen (ed.), *The Public Lands: Studies in the History of the Public Domain* (Madison, WI: University of Wisconsin Press, 1963), pp. 229–52.

Conkin, P. K., *Prophets of Prosperity: America's First Political Economists* (Bloomington, IN: Indiana University Press, 1980).

Coxe, T., *A Statement of the Arts and Manufactures of the United States, for the Year 1810* (Philadelphia, PA: A. Cornman, 1814).

Cremin, L. A., *American Education: The National Experience 1783–1876* (New York: Harper & Row, Publishers, 1980).

Cunningham, N. E. Jr, *The Presidency of James Monroe* (Lawrence: University Press of Kansas, 1996).

Dangerfield, G., *The Awakening of American Nationalism 1815–1828* (New York: Harper & Row, Publishers, 1965).

Dewey, D. R., *Financial History of the United States* (New York: Longmans, Green and Co., 1922).

Dobson, J. M., *Two Centuries of Tariffs: the Background and Emergence of the U.S. Internal Trade Commission* (Washington DC: US Government Printing Office, 1976).

Dodd, W. E., *The Life of Nathaniel Macon* (Raleigh, NC: Edwards & Broughton, Printers and Binders, 1903).

Dunbar, C. F., 'Deposits as Currency', in *Economic Essays* (New York, Macmillan, 1904).

Eblen, J. E., *The First and Second United States Empires: Governors and Territorial Government, 1784–1912* (Pittsburgh: University of Pittsburgh Press, 1968).

Eiselen, M. R., *The Rise of Pennsylvania Protectionism* (New York: Garland Publishing, Inc., 1974).

Ellis, J. J., *His Excellency George Washington* (New York: Vintage Books, 2004).

Ellis, R. E., *The Union at Risk: Jacksonian Democracy, States' Rights, and the Nullification Crisis* (New York: Oxford University Press, 1987).

—, *Aggressive Nationalism: McCulloch v. Maryland and the Foundation of Federal Authority in the Young Republic* (New York: Oxford University Press, 2007).

Emerick, C. F., *The Credit System and the Public Domain* (Nashville, TN: Cumberland Presbyterian Publishing House, 1899).

Feller, D., *The Public Lands in Jacksonian Politics* (Madison, WI: University of Wisconsin Press, 1984).

—, *The Jacksonian Promise: America, 1815–1840* (Baltimore, MD: The Johns Hopkins University Pres, 1995).

Fishlow, A., 'Antebellum Interregional Trade Reconsidered', *American Economic Review*, 54:3 (May, 1964), pp. 352–64.

—, 'Internal Transportation in the Nineteenth and Early Twentieth Centuries', in S. L. Engerman and R. E. Gallman (eds), *The Cambridge Economic History of the United States, Volume II: The Long Nineteenth Century* (Cambridge and New York: Cambridge University Press, 2000), pp. 543–642.

Forbes, R. P., *The Missouri Compromise and Its Aftermath: Slavery and the Meaning of America* (Chapel Hill, NC: The University of North Carolina Press, 2007).

Freehling, W. W. (ed.), *The Nullification Era: A Documentary Record* (New York: Harper & Row, Publishers, 1967).

—, *Prelude to Civil War: The Nullification Controversy in South Carolina, 1816–1836* (New York: Harper Torchbooks, 1968).

—, *The Road to Disunion: Secessionists at Bay, 1776–1854* (New York: Oxford University Press, 1990).

Gallatin, A. 'Memorial of the Committee of the Free Trade Convention, 1831', in F. W. Taussig (ed.), *State Papers and Speeches on the Tariff* (New York: Burt Franklin, 1895), pp. 108–213.

Gates, P. W., *History of Public Land Law Development* (Washington: US Government Printing Office, 1968).

—, 'The Role of the Land Speculator in Western Development', in *The Jeffersonian Dream: Studies in the History of American Land Policy and Development* (Albuquerque, NM: University of New Mexico Press, 1996), pp. 6–22.

Giles, W. B., *Mr. Clay's Speech upon the tariff, or, The 'American system', so called, or, The Anglican System, in Fact Introduced Here, and Perverted in its Most Material bearing upon Society, by the Omission of a System of Corn Laws, for the Protection of Agriculture: Mr. Giles' Speech upon the Resolutions of Inquiry in the House of Delegates of Virginia, in Reply to Mr. Clay's Speech: also, his Speech in Reply to Gen. Taylor's, Accompanied with Sundry Other Interesting Subjects and Original Documents: the Whole Containing a Mass of Highly Useful Information at the Present Interesting Crisis* (Richmond, VA: Thomas W. White, 1827).

Goodrich, C., *Government Promotion of American Canals and Railroads, 1800–189* (New York: Columbia University Press, 1960).

Govan, T. P. *Nichols Biddle: Nationalist and Public Banker, 1786–1844* (Chicago, IL: The University of Chicago Press, 1959).

Hammond, B., *Banks and Politics in America from the Revolution to the Civil War* (Princeton, NJ: Princeton University Press, 1957).

Hammond, J. D., *History of Political Parties in the State of New York*, 3 vols (Albany, NY: C. Van Benthuysen, 1842–48).

Harden, E. J., *The Life of George M. Troup* (Savannah, GA: E. J. Press, 1859).

Hargreaves, M. W. M., *The Presidency of John Quincy Adams* (Lawrence, KS: University Press of Kansas 1985).

Heidler, D. S., and J. T. Heidler, *Indian Removal* (New York: W.W. Norton & Company, 2007).

Heiskell, S. G. (ed.), *Andrew Jackson and Early Tennessee History, Illustrated*, 3 vols (Nashville, TN: Ambrose Printing Company, 1921).

Henkin, D. M., *The Postal Age: The Emergence of Modern Communications in Nineteenth-Century America* (Chicago, IL: University of Chicago Press, 2007).

Hibbard, B. H., *A History of the Public Land Policies* (Madison, WI: University of Wisconsin Press, 1965).

Holdsworth, J. T., and D. R. Dewey, *The First and Second Banks of the United States* (Washington, D. C.: Government Printing Office, 1910).

Holt, M. F., *The Rise and Fall of the American Whig Party* (New York: Oxford University Press, 1999).

Howe, D. W., *The Political Culture of the American Whigs* (Chicago, IL: University of Chicago Press, 1979).

—, 'The Evangelical Movement and Political Culture in the North During the Second Party System', *The Journal of American History*, 77:4 (March 1991), pp. 1216–39.

—, 'Jacksonianism and the Promise of Improvement', *Reviews in American History*, 25 (1997), pp. 58–62.

—, 'Church, State, and Education in the Young American Republic', *Journal of the Early Republic* 22:1 (Spring 2002), pp. 1–24.

—, *What Hath God Wrought: The Transformation of America, 1815–1848* (New York: Oxford University Press, 2007).

Hummel, J. R., 'The Civil War and Reconstruction', in *Government and the American Economy: A New History* (Chicago and London: The University of Chicago Press, 2007), pp. 188–231.

Jackson, A., 'Gen. Jackson on the Tariff', in *Andrew Jackson and Early Tennessee History, Illustrated*, ed. S. G. Heiskell, 3 vols (Nashville, TN: Ambrose Printing Company, 1921), vol. 3, pp. 69–71.

—, 'Jackson's Denunciation of Nullification: the Nullification Proclamation', 10 December 1832, in *Andrew Jackson, Nullification, and the State-Rights Tradition*, ed. C. Sellers (Chicago, IL: Rand McNally & Company, 1963) pp. 7–15.

Jefferson, T., *The Portable Thomas Jefferson*, ed. M. D. Peterson (New York: The Viking Press, 1975).

Johnson, W., *Soul by Soul: Life Inside the Antebellum Slave Market* (Cambridge, MA: Harvard University Press, 1999).

Jourdan, W., T. Stocks and G. R. Gilmer, "Land Policies and the Georgia Law," in *The Removal of the Cherokee Nation: Manifest Destiny or National Dishonor?*, eds. L. Filler and A. Guttmann (Lexington, MA: D. C. Heath and CO., 1962).

Ketcham, R. (ed.), *Selected Writings of James Madison* (Indianapolis, IN: Hackett Publishing Company, inc., 2006).

Knupfer, P., *The Union as It is: Constitutional Unionism and Sectional Compromise, 1787–1861* (Chapel Hill, NC: University of North Carolina Press, 1991).

Kolchin, P., *American Slavery, 1619–1877* (1993; New York: Hill & Wang, 2003).

Larson, J. L., *Internal Improvement: National Public Works and the Promise of Popular Government in the Early United State* (Chapter Hill, NC: The University of North Carolina Pres, 2001).

Leepson, M., *Flag: An American Biography* (New York: St. Martin's Press, 2005).

Licht, W., *Industrializing America: The Nineteenth Century* (Baltimore, MD: The Johns Hopkins University Press, 1995).

Lindstrom, D., *Economic Development in the Philadelphia Region, 1810–1850* (New York: Columbia University Press, 1978).

McCullough, D., *John Adams* (New York: Simon & Schuster, 2001).

McGrane, *The Panic of 1837: Some Financial Problems of the Jacksonian Era* (Chicago, IL: The University of Chicago Press, 1924).

McLaughlin, A. C., *A Constitutional History of the United States* (New York: D. Appleton-Century Company, 1935).

McLoughlin, W. G., *Revivals, Awakenings and Reform* (Chicago, IL: University of Chicago Press, 1980).

Markham, J. W., *Financial History of the United States: From Christopher Columbus to the Robber Barons 1492–1900*, 3 vols (New York: M. E. Sharpe, 2001).

Masur, L. P., *1831: Year of the Eclipse* (New York: Hill and Wang, 2001).

Meacham, J., *American Lion: Andrew Jackson in the White House* (New York: Random House, 2008).

Meyer, D. R., *The Roots of American Industrialization* (Baltimore, MD: The Johns Hopkins University Press, 2003).

Mooney, J., *History, Myths and Sacred Formulas of the Cherokee* (Fairview, NC: Bright Mountain Books, Inc., 1992).

Nelson, J. R. Jr, *Liberty and Property: Political Economic and Policymaking in the New Nation, 1789–1812* (Baltimore, MD: The Johns Hopkins University Press, 1987).

North, D. C., *The Economic Growth of the United States, 1789 to 1860* (New York: W. W. Norton & Company Inc, 1966).

Onuf, P. S., *Statehood and Union: A History of the Northwest Ordinance* (Bloomington, IN: Indiana University Press, 1987).

Pease, J. H., and W. H. Pease, 'Economics and Politics and Charleston's Nullification Crisis', *The Journal of Southern History*, 47:3 (August 1981), pp. 335–62.

Peskin, L. A., *Manufacturing Revolution: The Intellectual Origins of Early American Industry* (Baltimore, MD: The Johns Hopkins University Press, 2003).

Peterson, M. D., *Thomas Jefferson and the New Nation* (New York: Oxford University Press, 1970).

—, *Olive Branch and Sword – The Compromise of 1833* (Baton Rouge, LA: Louisiana State University Press, 1982).

—, *The Great Triumvirate: Webster, Clay, and Calhoun* (New York: Oxford University Press, 1987).

Preyer, N. W., 'Southern Support of the Tariff of 1816 – A Reappraisal', *Journal of Southern History* 25:3 (August 1959), pp. 306–22.

Prucha, F. P., 'Andrew Jackson's Indian Policy: A Reassessment', *The Journal of American History*, 56:3 (December 1969), pp. 527–539.

— (ed.), *Documents of United States Indian Policy* (Lincoln, NE: University of Nebraska Press, 1975).

Raja, M., *Evangelizing the South* (New York: Oxford University Press, 2008).

Ratner, S., *The Tariff in American History* (New York: D. Van Nostrand Company, 1972).

Raymond, D., *The American System* (Baltimore, MD: Lucas & Deaver, 1828).

—, *The Southern Excitement, Against the American System* (Poughkeepsie: Platt & Parsons, 1829).

Remini, R. V., 'Martin Van Buren and the Tariff of Abominations', *American Historical Review*, 63:4 (July 1958), pp. 903–17.

—, *Andrew Jackson and the Bank War* (New York: W. W. Norton & Company, Inc., 1967).

—, *The Life of Andrew Jackson* (New York: Harper & Row, 1988).

—, *Henry Clay: Statesman for the Union* (New York: W. W. Norton & Company, 1991).

—, *Andrew Jackson and His Indian Wars* (New York: Penguin Books, 2001).

Rezneck, S., 'The Social History of an American Depression, 1837–1843', *The American Historical Review* 40 (July 1935), pp. 662–87.

Richardson, H. C., *The Greatest Nation of the Earth: Republican Economic Policies During the Civil War* (Cambridge, MA: Harvard University Press, 1997).

Risjord, N. K., *The Old Republicans: Southern Conservatism in the Age of Jefferson* (New York: Columbia University Press, 1965).

Robbins, R. M., 'Preemption – A Frontier Triumph', *The Mississippi Valley Historical Review* 18:3 (December 1931), pp. 331–49.

Rohrbough, M. J., *The Land Office Business: The Settlement and Administration of American Public Lands, 1789–1837* (New York: Oxford University Press, 1968).

Rousseau, P. L., 'Jacksonian Monetary Policy, Specie Flows, and the Panic of 1837', *The Journal of Economic History* 62:2 (June 2002), pp. 457–88.

Salmons, D., *The Monetary Difficulties of America and Their Probable Effects on British Commerce, Considered* (London: P. Richardson, 1837).

Sato, S., *History of the Land Question in the United States* (Baltimore, MD: The Johns Hopkins University, 1886).

Satz, R. N., *American Indian Policy in the Jacksonian Era* (Norman, OK: University of Oklahoma Press, 2002).

Sellers, C., 'Banking and Politics in Jackson's Tennessee, 1817–1827', *The Mississippi Valley Historical Review*, 41:1 (June, 1954), pp. 61–84.

—, *The Market Revolution: Jacksonian America 1815–1846* (New York: Oxford University Press, 1991).

Shade, W. G., *Banks or No Banks: The Money Issue in Western Politics* (Detroit, MI: Wayne State University Press, 1972).

Shankman, A., *Crucible of American Democracy: the Struggle to Fuse Egalitarianism & Capitalism in Jeffersonian Pennsylvania* (Lawrence, KY: University Press of Kansas, 2004).

Sheriff, C., *The Artificial River: The Erie Canal and the Paradox of Progress 1817–1862* (New York: Hill and Wang, 1996).

Schocket, A. M., *Founding Corporate Power in Early National Philadelphia* (DeKalb, IL: Northern Illinois University Press, 2007).

Smith, A. G. Jr, *Economic Readjustment of an Old Cotton State: South Carolina, 1820–1860* (Columbia, SC: University of South Carolina Press, 1958).

Smith, W. B., *Economic Aspects of the Second Bank of the United States* (Westport, CT: Greenwood Press, 1969).

Stanwood, E., *American Tariff Controversies in the Nineteenth Century* (Boston, MA and New York: Houghton Mifflin Company, 1903).

Sydnor, C. S., *The Development of Southern Sectionalism 1819–1848* (Baton Rouge, LA: Louisiana State University Press, 1948).

Sylla, R., J. B. Legler and J. J. Wallis, 'Banks and State Public Finance in the New Republic: The United States, 1790–1860', *The Journal of Economic History*, 47:2 (June 1987), pp. 391–403.

Taussig, F. W. (ed.), *State Papers and Speeches on the Tariff* (New York: Burt Franklin, 1895).

Taylor, G. R., *The Transportation Revolution, 1815–1860* (New York: Rinehart & Company, 1957).

Temin, P., *The Jacksonian Economy* (New York: W. W. Norton & Company Inc, 1969).

Timberlake, R. H., *The Origins of Central Banking in the United States* (Cambridge, MA: Harvard University Press, 1978).

Thomas, J. L., 'Romantic Reform in America, 1815–1865', *American Quarterly* 17:4 (Winter, 1965).

—, *Monetary Policy in the United States: An Intellectual and Institutional History* (Chicago, IL: The University of Chicago Press, 1993, original publication 1978).

Treat, P. J., *The National Land System, 1785–1820* (New York: E.B. Treat 1910).

Van Atta, J. R., 'Western lands and the Political Economy of Henry Clay's American System, 1819–1832', *Journal of the Early Republic* 21:4 (Winter 2001), pp. 633–65.

—, '"A Lawless Rabble": Henry Clay and the Cultural Politics of Squatters' Rights, 1832–1841', *Journal of the Early Republic* 28:3 (Autumn 2008), pp. 337–78.

Van Deusen, G. G., *The Life of Henry Clay* (Boston, MA: Little, Brown and Company, 1937).

Wallace, A. F. C., *The Long Bitter Trail: Andrew Jackson and the Indians* (New York: Hill and Wang, 1993).

Walters, R. Jr, *Albert Gallatin, Jeffersonian Financier and Diplomat* (New York: Macmillan, 1957).

Walters, R. G., *American Reformers 1815–1860*, revised edn (New York: Hill and Wang, 1997, original publication 1978).

Weiner, A. S., 'John Scott, Thomas Hart Benton, David Barton, and the Presidential Election of 1824', *Missouri Historical Review*, 60:4 (July 1966), pp. 460–94.

Wellington, R. G., *The Political and Sectional Influence of the Public Lands* (Cambridge, MA: Riverside Press, 1914).

Wetterau, J. O., 'The Branches of the First Bank of the United States', *Journal of Economic History*, 2, supp. *The Tasks of Economic History* (December 1942), pp. 66–100.

Wilentz, S., *The Rise of American Democracy: Jefferson to Lincoln* (New York: W. W. Norton & Company, 2005).

Williams, D., *Georgia Gold Rush: Twenty-Niners, Cherokees and Gold Fever* (Columbia, SC: University of South Carolina Press, 1993).

Wilson, M. L., *Space Time and Freedom: The Quest for Nationality and the Irrepressible Conflict 1815–1861* (Westport, CT: Greenwood Press, 1974).

Wiltse, C. M., *John C. Calhoun: Nationalist, 1782–1828* (Indianapolis, IN: Bobbs-Merrill Co., 1944).

—, *John C. Calhoun: Nullifier, 1829–1839* (New York: Russell & Russell, 1968).

Wright, B. F. (ed.), *The Federalist* (Cambridge, MA: The Belknap Press of Harvard University Press, 1966).

Wright, R. E., *The Wealth of Nations Rediscovered: Integration and Expansion in American Financial Market, 1780–1850* (New York: Cambridge University Press, 2002).

Young, J. S., *A Political and Constitutional History of the Cumberland Road* (Chicago, IL: University of Chicago Press, 1904).

Unpublished Dissertations

Barry, S. J., 'Nathaniel Macon: The Prophet of Pure Republicanism, 1758–1837' (PhD dissertation, State University of New York at Buffalo, 1996).

Binkley, R. W. Jr., 'The American System: An Example of American Nineteenth-Century Economic Thinking Its Definition by Its Author Henry Clay' (PhD dissertation, Columbia University, 1949).

Harrison, J. H., 'The Internal Improvement Issue in the Politics of the Union, 1783–1825' (PhD dissertation, University of Virginia, 1954).

Schoene, S. W., 'The Economics of U.S. Public Land Policy Prior to 1860' (Unpublished PhD Dissertation, The University of North Carolina, 1981).

Young, J. S., *A Political and Constitutional Study of the Cumberland Road* (PhD dissertation, University of Chicago, 1903).

INDEX

Abolition, 58–9, 70–1
Adams, Henry Carter, 48
Adams, John, 17, 133
Adams, John Quincy, 1–2, 3, 84–6, 103, 133
   American System, 2, 34, 79, 83
   cultural improvement, 12–13, 80, 82, 9
   internal improvement, 10, 93–6, 96–7, 117–18
   Monroe Doctrine, 79
   presidential elections
      of 1824, 79–80, 109
      of 1828, 83, 104, 131
   protectionism, 8, 104, 130
   views on public lands, 10–11, 88, 89, 91
   Secretary of State, 67, 79, 108–9
   Transcontinental Treaty, 79, 109
   views on John C. Calhoun, 72
   views on Virginia, 122
   see also Corrupt Bargain
agriculture, (specific produce),
   cotton, 4, 21, 58–9, 60, 102–3, 110–14, 121, 130
   flour, 21, 65
   molasses, 73, 104
   rice, 21, 112
   sugarcane, 112
   wheat, 21, 115
   see also artisans/mechanics; manufactures; shipping; slavery; tariff bills
Allison, David, 108
American Civil War, 57, 112, 115, 121, 123, 125, 130, 132, 133
Annals of Congress, 27, 54
Anthony, Susan B., 81

Arkansas Legislature, 89
artisans/mechanics, 8, 19, 20–2, 31, 133
Austin, Benjamin, 49

Baker, Pamela L., 9
Baldwin, Henry, 64, 66
Bank Bill
   of 1816, 52–3
   of 1832, 8–9, 124–5
Bank of the United States, First (1BUS),
   comparisons to 2BUS, 50, 52, 100
   contribution to commerce, manufactures and internal improvement, 7–8
   counterfeiting law, 29
   incorporation, 5–6
   notes, specie, and deposits, 50–1
   re-chartering fights, 29–33
   see also state banks
Bank of the United States, Second (2BUS), 79, 128
   Bank War, 119, 123–6
   Bonus Bill of 1817, 54
   component of the American System, 3, 5, 8, 11, 123
   contribution to commerce, manufactures and internal improvement, 7–8
   incorporation, 33, 50
   loans, 7–8, 60, 98–9, 100, 102, 125
   McCulloch v. *Maryland*, 124
   national currency, 100
   notes, specie and deposits, 51, 97–8, 100–1
   Panic of 1819, 60, 97
   post-War of 1812 economy, 46, 51, 52–3
   post-War of 1812 nationalism, 53
   regional perspectives on, 119

veto of re-charter, 124–5
see also Biddle, Nicholas; Jackson, Andrew; state banks
Barbour, James, 83
Barbour, Phillip P., 4, 5, 55, 64, 66, 69, 70, 73–4
Barlow, Joel, 43
Barton, David, 85–92,
Baxter, Maurice G., 5
Bedinger, George M., 25
Bemis, Samuel Flagg, 4, 12, 82
Benton, Thomas Hart, 10, 11, 37, 84–93, 118, 130, 131
Biddle, Nicholas, 29, 97, 99, 123–5
Bonus Bill of 1817, 52, 53–5, 56, 69, 72
Brooke, Francis, 128
Brooke, John L., 13, 81
Brown, James, 67
Brown, Thomas, 130
burned-over district, 80
Burr, Aaron, 89

Calhoun, John C.,
  nationalist,
    Bank Bill of 1816, 52, 54
    Bonus Bill of 1817, 52, 54, 55, 56
    Internal Improvement, 56–7, 69, 72
    Tariff Bill of 1816, 48–9
  sectionalist,
    anti-protectionism, 102–3, 122
    South Carolina Exposition and Protest, 102
    state loyalties, 129–30
Catterall, Ralph C. H., 99
Chase, Salmon P., 132
Chauteau, Auguste, 85
Chesapeake and Ohio Canal, 69, 82, 97
Cheves, Langdon, 99, 123
Clark, Christopher H., 25
Clark, Victor S., 23
Clark, William, 85
Clay, Henry, 48, 117, 133
  American System, 2–3, 128, 129–30
  Bank of the United States, 30, 32, 52, 124
  cultural improvement, 12, 82–3, 95
  internal improvement, 7, 13, 53, 70–1, 119

land speculation, 37
presidential elections,
  of 1824, 79–80, 84, 104, 109
  of 1828, 11, 83
  of 1832, 11, 83, 124
protectionism, 3–4, 10, 11, 66, 73, 74–5, 92, 103, 122
views on public lands, 10–11, 34, 88–9, 92, 93, 118, 119–20
see also Corrupt Bargain, Maysville Road Veto
Clinton, George, 33
Cobb, Thomas W., 91
colonization of free blacks, 10, 82, 83
Congressional committees, 10, 24, 25, 40, 41, 54, 61, 66
  Committee on Agriculture, 73
  Committee on Manufactures, 8, 47, 64, 66, 73, 102
  Committee on National Currency, 52
  Committee on Public Lands, 42, 63, 85, 86, 89
  Ways and Means Committee, 42
Cooper, Thomas, 4, 103–4, 122
Corrupt Bargain, 79–80, 109
cotton gin, 58
Crawford, William H., 8, 30, 31, 56, 62, 95, 109, 122
The Crisis, 103, 122
Cumberland/National Road, 24, 25, 54, 68–9, 88, 94, 108
  Ohio Enabling Act, 24
  Toll Gate Bill, 60, 68–9
Currie, David P., 5

Dallas, A. J., 33, 46–7, 50, 52, 64
Dallas, George M., 124
de Nemours, Dupont, 43
Delaware and Chesapeake Canal Company, 107
Distribution Bill, 9, 11, 83, 118–21
Duane, William J., 125
Duncan, Joseph, 89

Easton, Rufus, 85
Eaton, John, 111
Edwards, Ninian, 37
Erie Canal, 12, 116

Federalist Papers, 2, 18
Feller, Daniel, 4, 9, 90
Finney, Charles G., 80
Fishlow, Albert, 130
France, 17, 21, 86
French Revolution/Napoleonic Wars, 11, 20–1, 22, 26

Gallatin, Albert,
 American System, 45
 Bank of the United States, 28–30, 32
 cultural improvement, 95
 internal improvement, 23–4, 25, 26–7, 57, 69, 95, 117
 views on public lands, 35–6, 37, 40–2
Garrison, William Lloyd, 81
General Survey Bill of 1824, 7, 57, 69–70, 72–3, 75, 76, 79, 96, 117, 121
Georgia Legislature, 96
Giles, William B., 4, 5, 24–5, 30
Girard, Stephen, 8
Graduation Bill, 10, 84, 86–93, 118, 120, 131
Great Britain, 19, 21, 29, 30, 33, 45, 46, 48, 49, 54, 58, 61, 65, 67, 102, 103, 108, 112, 121
Great Lakes, 116
Grimké, Sarah and Angelina, 81

Hamilton, Alexander, 2, 3, 5–6, 17–19, 29, 34
Hamilton Jr, James, 73
Harrison, William H., 11
Hemphill, Joseph, 69
Hempstead, Edward, 85
Holland, 21
Holt, Michael F., 9
home market, 3, 11–12, 15–16, 18, 22, 47–8, 60, 65–6, 73–5, 80, 103, 105, 121, 130, 132
Homestead Act of 1862, 131
Hopkinson, Joseph, 52
Howe, Daniel Walker, 1, 12–3, 109

immigration, 10–11, 90, 114–15, 120, 127, 133
Indiana General Assembly, 85

Indiana Territorial Legislature, 37
Ingham, Samuel D., 47

Jackson, Andrew,
 American System, 119–21, 129, 131
 Bank of the United States, 60, 123–5
 cultural improvement, 128, 131
 Indian Removal, 109–12
 internal improvement, 5, 72, 107, 116–17
 involvement in land speculation, 37, 108
 Nullification Crisis, 122
 personal character and background, 107–8
 presidential elections,
  of 1824, 79, 84, 104, 107, 109
  of 1828, 11, 83, 104–5, 107, 108, 109, 110
  of 1832, 83, 120
 protectionism, 5, 75, 104, 107
 views on public lands, 85, 127,
 see also Maysville Road Veto; Corrupt Bargain; 2BUS; War of 1812; Native Americans
Jackson, Rachel Donelson, 108
James River Company, 23
Jefferson, Thomas,
 American System, 2, 89, 94–5, 133
 Bank of the United States, 6, 28–9, 60, 76–7,
 cultural improvement, 27–8, 42–3
 Embargo, 43, 45, 46, 140, 141
 internal improvement, 23–4, 26, 27–8, 49, 68–9
 Notes on the State of Virginia, 49, 87
 protectionism, 21–2
 views on public lands, 87
Johnson, James, 60
Johnson, Richard M., 30
Jones, William, 98

King, Rufus, 63

Land Acts,
 of 1796, 35, 36
 of 1800, 36, 40–2, 61
 of 1804, 40–2, 61
 of 1817, 60–1

of 1820, 40, 61–4
credit system, 40, 41, 42, 61–3, 64
Land Offices, 50, 61, 62
Latrobe, Benjamin, 43
Leake, Walter, 63
Library of Congress, 11
Licht, Walter, 130
Lieb, Michael, 25, 30, 31
Lindstrom, Diane, 130–1
Logan, George, 43
Louisiana Legislature, 89
Louisiana Purchase, 59, 86
Lowndes, William, 47, 48, 66
Lucas, Charles, 85
Lucas, John B. C., 85

McClane, Louis, 125
McCoy, William, 66
McCulloch v. Maryland, 6, 124
McDuffie, George, 72, 73
Macon, Nathaniel, 52, 55, 63, 71, 82, 92, 95
Madison, James,
   American System, 94–5, 133
   Bank of the United States, 28, 30, 46, 50
   cultural improvement, 42–3, 46, 76–7
   internal improvement, 23, 27–8, 46, 53, 55–6, 68–9
   'Madisonian Platform', 45–6
   protectionism, 21–2, 45–6, 65
Mallary, Rollin, 102
manufactures, (specific industries),
   copper, 22
   cotton, 22–3, 46–7, 64–6, 73–5
   distilleries, 73–4, 104
   flax, 73, 103
   gunsmiths, 22
   hemp, 66, 69, 73, 74, 75, 103, 104
   iron, 22, 65, 66, 73, 74, 75, 103, 104
   lead, 75
   spinning jenny/looms, 4, 74, 102
   wool, 8, 47, 64, 65–6, 73–5, 102–3, 104, 121
   see also agriculture; artisans/mechanics; shipping; slavery; tariff bills
Marshall, John, 6
Maysville Road Veto, 5, 16–17, 118
Mediterranean Fund, 20
Meigs, Josiah, 62

Meyer, David, 131
millennialism, 80
Mississippi River, 110, 111, 112, 115
Mississippi Valley, 87, 111
Missouri Crisis/Compromise, 45, 57–60, 67, 71, 76
   Missouri Enabling Act, 57, 59
   Tallmadge amendment, pp.57–9
   Thomas Proviso, 59
   see also Tallmadge, James; Thomas, Jessie
Missouri Legislature, 84, 89
Monroe, James, 56, 57, 67, 72,
   American System, 1, 3, 60, 94–5, 133
   Bank of the United States, 123,
   cultural improvement, 76–7
   internal improvement, 68–9,
   Monroe Doctrine, 79
   protectionism, 65, 73,
Morrill, Justin Smith, 132
Morrill Land Grant Act, 133
Morrow, Jeremiah, 25, 42

National Bank Act, 132
nationalism, 2, 13, 24, 25, 27, 45, 47, 48, 50, 53, 55, 57, 67, 70, 74, 75, 79, 102, 105, 109, 121, 129, 133
Native Americans, 108, 109–12, 117, 127, 128, 131
   Creek War, 108
   First Seminole War, 108
   Trail of Tears, 111–12
Nelson, John, 18–19
Nelson, Roger, 25
New Orleans, 4, 28, 108, 114, 115, 116, 127
New York City, 20, 32, 51, 95, 115, 127
Newton Jr, Thomas, 30
Nicholson, Joseph, 40, 41
Niles, Hezekial, 10
   Niles' Weekly Register, 4, 10–11, 61,

Ohio Company, 88
Ohio Enabling Act, 24
Ohio River, 23, 25, 54, 62, 69, 115
Ohio Valley, 116
Otis, Harrison Gray, 63

Pacific Railroad Act, 132–3
Panic of 1819, 8, 57, 60, 62, 65, 67, 97, 121

Pennsylvania Legislature, 23–4, 65, 123
Peskin, Lawrence A., 12
Peterson, Merrill D., 9–10
Philadelphia, 8, 12, 20, 22, 23–4, 31, 33, 65, 123, 125, 127, 131
Philadelphia Gazette, 102
Pickering, Timothy, 52
Pleasants, James, 52
Political Parties,
   Anti-Masonic, 83
   Federalist, 13, 15, 19, 24, 25, 34, 36, 63, 64, 66, 69, 73, 95
   Republican, 15, 23, 24, 30, 35, 40, 47, 63, 64, 132
   Democratic (Jeffersonian)-Republican, 28, 37
   Jacksonian-Democrat, 89, 124, 125
   National Republican, 56, 82, 83, 95, 119, 124, 129
   Old Republican, 65
   Whig, 13, 82, 129
Potomac Company, 16
Potomic River, 23, 25
Pratte, Bernard, 85
pre-emption, 36, 37, 40, 41, 131
Preyer, Norris W., 49

Quitman, John, 81

Raja, Monica, 80
Randolph, Edmund, 6,
Randolph, John, 42, 52–3, 54, 70–1, 130
Raymond, Daniel, 4, 7
Reform Movements/Second Great Awakening, 1, 13, 79–83, 131
regions and states
   New England, 7, 25, 33, 36, 51, 53, 66, 72, 73, 102, 103, 104, 116, 120, 125
   Connecticut, 42, 119
   Maine, 59
   Massachusetts, 4, 31, 42, 73, 101, 119
   Rhode Island, 46, 119
   Vermont, 9, 102
   mid-Atlantic, 7, 66, 72, 75, 104, 120
   Delaware, 30, 119
   Maryland, 24, 25, 30 54, 66, 119
   New Jersey, 22
   New York, 2, 17, 33, 72, 80, 81, 83, 91, 101, 127
   Pennsylvania, 22, 23–4, 25, 31, 35, 54, 65, 66, 83, 91, 103, 123
   Northwest, 64, 72, 75, 92, 104, 112, 113, 114–16
   Illinois, 61, 85, 86, 89, 119, 126
   Indiana, 37, 85, 89, 119, 126
   Kentucky, 5, 22, 32, 42, 74, 80, 116, 119, 128, 129
   Missouri, 45, 57–60, 67, 71, 76, 84, 85, 86, 89, 119, 126
   Ohio, 24, 27, 36, 74, 89, 115, 130
   South Atlantic, 8, 58, 59, 63, 66, 72, 92, 112
   Georgia, 5, 8, 96, 108, 110, 112
   North Carolina, 71, 72, 80, 84, 107, 112
   South Carolina, 4, 8, 32, 72, 96, 102, 103, 107, 109, 121, 122, 123
   Virginia, 4, 5, 17, 23, 25, 32, 42, 54, 68, 72, 76, 80, 95, 112, 122, 128, 130
   Southwest, 8, 58, 59, 60, 63, 64, 66, 72, 80, 92, 108, 109, 112, 127
   Tennessee, 74, 80, 84, 92, 107, 108, 109
   Alabama, 61, 85, 89, 92, 108, 112, 116, 119
   Louisiana, 8, 89, 92, 112, 119
   Mississippi, 61, 92, 112, 119, 126
Remini, Robert V., 4
revivalism, 80–3
Robertson, Thomas Bolling, 52
Rush, Richard, 10, 91, 93, 103,
Russel, William, 85

St Louis Enquirer, 62
Schocket, Andrew M., 12
Scott, John, 84, 85, 86, 88–9
Sellers Jr, Charles, 1
Sheriff, Carol, 12
Sherman, John, 132
shipping, 8, 11, 15, 20, 21, 73, 74, 104, 112
slavery, 1, 7, 8, 9, 57–60, 67, 69, 70–1, 80, 81, 82, 94, 102, 103, 104, 110, 112, 113, 122, 130
Smith, William, 102
Society for Establishing Useful Manufactures (SEUM), 19

South America, 3, 79
South Carolina Legislature, 4, 96, 102, 122
Spain, 3, 21, 54, 79, 86, 108–9
Specie Circular, 127
state banks, 30–3, 50–1, 60, 97–8, 100–2, 123, 125, 127, 132
   Bank of Columbia, 32
   Bank of Kentucky, 32
   Bank of Pennsylvania, 31
   Bank of South Carolina, 32
   Bank of Virginia, 32
   Boston Bank, 31
   Farmers and Mechanics' Bank of Philadelphia, 31
   Manhattan Bank, 32
   pet banks, 125
   Union Bank, 31
Storrs, Henry R., 64
suffrage movement, 80
Symmes, John Cleves, 88

Tallmadge, James, 57–9
Taney, Roger B., 125
Tariff Act/Bill,
   of 1789 (to 1812), 19–21
   of 1816, 46–8, 53, 64–5, 66–7
   of 1820, 64–7, 73
   of 1824, 3, 8, 73–6, 79, 104, 107, 121
   of 1828, 102, 104–5, 121
   of 1832, 3, 8, 121
   of 1833 (Compromise Tariff Bill), 120, 122–3
   of 1861 (Morrill Tariff Act), 132
   see also agriculture; manufactures; shipping
Tennessee Legislature, 109
Territories, 40, 54, 59, 110, 112, 114, 131
   Indiana Territorial Legislature, 37
   Northwest Territory, 24–5, 36
   Ohio Territory, 24, 36
Thirty Years' View, 84

Thomas, Jessie, 59
Thomas, John L., 81
Thornton, William, 43
Tiffen, Edward, 62
Todd, John, 73
Tracy, Uriah, 25
transportation revolution, 1, 27, 56, 114–16, 131
Trimble, David, 60
Tucker, Beverly, 128
Tucker, Henry St. George, 52
Turnbull, Robert J., 103, 122
Tyler, John, 66, 92

US Corps of Engineers, 69
University of Virginia, 76

Van Atta, John R., 9–10, 12,
Van Buren, Martin, 88, 95, 111, 117, 127
Van Deusen, Glyndon G., 4
Van Rensselear, Daniel, 73, 104, 124
Virginia Legislature, 4, 5, 17, 23, 76

Walker, Felix, 66
Walker, John W., 37, 61
War of 1812, 20, 22, 27, 34, 43, 45, 49, 50, 51, 61, 64, 100, 101, 102, 108, 127
   Battle of New Orleans, 108
   Creek War, 108
Washington, George,
   American System, 1, 6, 15–17, 94, 133
   Bank of the United States, 15, 28
   cultural improvement, 15, 43, 76
   internal improvement, 23
   views on public lands, 34
Webster, Daniel, 73, 104, 124
Wellington, Raynor G., 92
Whitney, Eli, 58
Wilentz, Sean, 1
Willard, Emma Hart, 96
Williams, Thomas H., 11, 63
Wilson, Major L., 9–10